REBIRTH
OF THE
SALESMAN:
TALES OF THE SONG
& DANCE 70'S

OTHER DELTA BOOKS OF INTEREST:

CELEBRITY
by James Monaco

MEDIA CULTURE
by James Monaco

SNAP, CRACKLE, AND POPULAR TASTE
by Jeffrey Schrank

STOP THE PRESSES I WANT TO GET OFF!
edited by Richard Pollak

REBIRTH
OF THE
SALESMAN:
TALES OF THE SONG
& DANCE 70'S

RON ROSENBAUM

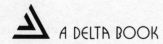 A DELTA BOOK

A DELTA BOOK
Published by
Dell Publishing Co., Inc.
1 Dag Hammarskjold Plaza
New York, New York 10017

Some of the essays in this book first appeared
in the following periodicals:

"Tommy the Traveler" as "Run, Tommy, Run!", "Secrets of the Little
Blue Box," "The Corpse as Big as the Ritz," and "Tales of
the Heartbreak Biz" appeared in *Esquire*.

"Whipple's Last Squeeze," "Death & the Nite Owl," and
"The Four Horsemen of the Nightly News" appeared in *More*.

"Chariots of the Insurance Salesmen" and
"Notes on Con Games" appeared in *New York*.

"Soap Gets in Your Eyes" appeared as "T. V. Commercials" in *New Times*.

"Troy Donahue Was Always Just Like He Is," "The Exaltation of Rabbi
Baal Ha Tov," and "Life in These United States" appeared in
The Village Voice. Reprinted by permission of *The Village Voice*.
Copyright © The Village Voice, Inc., 1971, 1973.

Delta ® TM 755118, Dell Publishing Co., Inc.
Printed in the United States of America
First printing—June 1979

Library of Congress Cataloging in Publication Data

Rosenbaum, Ron.
    Rebirth of the salesman.

    (A Delta book)
    1. United States—Popular culture—Addresses, essays,
lectures. 2. Mass media—Social aspects—United States—
Addresses, essays, lectures. I. Title.
E169.12.R64 1979   301.16'0973   79-955
ISBN 0-440-57226-6

FOR DAN WOLF AND HAROLD HAYES.
INSPIRED EDITORS.
AND, FOR CAROLINE.

Among the many others who have helped me out along the way with encouragement, advice, and inspiration I'd like to thank in particular Craig Karpel, Mary Nichols, Alan Weitz, Lee Eisenberg, Richard Pollak, Tom Forcade, Rebecca Wright Fox, Ed Fancher, Don Ericson, Dick Bell, Nat Hentoff, Jim Monaco, Martha Kinney, Mike Drosnin, Joe Flaherty, Carol Realini, John Larsen, Cindy Degener, Kathryn Paulsen, Richard Horowitz, Claudia Cohen, Meyer Vishner, and my sister Ruth Rosenbaum.

CONTENTS

REBIRTH
OF THE
SALESMAN:
TALES OF THE SONG
& DANCE 70'S

INTRODUCTION

I covered the seventies, that Oakland of decades. Of Oakland, of course, it was said, "There's no *there* there"; of the seventies it may come to be held, "There was no *when* then."

The flight from the seventies began before the decade did. The week I started work for *The Village Voice* in the final days of the sixties, a story on the revival of the fifties was featured on the first page. A year or so later, after I'd begun writing for *Esquire*, one of the assistant editors up there confided to me that although they'd scored a coup by being the first magazine to do a "Forties Revival" issue, they feared they were running out of decades to revive. Fortunately for the magazine business there were bits and pieces of other periods to patch together until a decent interval had passed and it became permissible in the second half of the seventies to begin reviving the sixties.

In some ways the seventies have been an amiable Johnny Carson kind of decade, allowing other decades to step in and guest host a year or two. This has caused some to wonder whether the seventies ever "went on" at all, whether they had an independent existence or were merely a sequel to the sixties or a "pre-quel" to the eighties.

The Name That Decade game can get pretty silly, but certain entries have been illuminating. Tom Wolfe's 1975 coinage "The Me Decade" is still the best to date, but on closer inspection the obsessive pursuit of self-fulfillment he says characterizes the seventies is not much different from the self-centered pursuit of "the happiness explosion" Wolfe once said (in his introduction to *The Pump House Gang*) was the essence of the sixties. What I'm saying is that by Wolfe's definitions the sixties could qualify as the real "Me Decade," which would make the seventies merely "Me II."

Was there a seventies? Did the decade have an identity of its own? Did any characteristically seventies figure emerge to represent the spirit of the seventies?

When I began selecting stories to include in this collection, I had only a vague notion of what they had to do with the decade until I recalled an intuition I'd had when I was in the middle of writing about a strange undercover agent known as Tommy the Traveler.

In the winter of 1971 I was driving back from a place called Geneva, New York, trying to figure out how to tell the tangled tales of Tommy's treacheries I'd picked up from the people he'd betrayed. Tommy had been a traveling salesman for a veterinary-drug firm who spiced up his sales trips by posing as a rabid bomb-happy revolutionary in order to spy on student radicals at the colleges along his route.

Tommy had managed to sell the eager young revolutionaries a story that he was an exiled Crown Prince of Thailand who had converted to "Maoist Leninism," as he called it. He brought round samples of gunpowder bombs he would teach them to make out of pimple-remedy bottles; he prompted schemes to fire bomb R.O.T.C. centers in order to "really put the campus on the map." In the aftermath—when he'd finally succeeded in seducing some of his closest friends into setting off a fire bomb, when he'd betrayed them to the police and then had finally blown his cover by leading a drug raid on the rest of his "friends"—I'd spent some time with the people who had been closest to Tommy, the friends most completely fooled by his fake identity. I was trying to figure out how they had allowed themselves to be taken in by a fellow who seemed, in retrospect, like such an outlandish fraud. Why had they bought his story?

Part of the answer, of course, lay in the confusions peculiar to the revolutionary romanticism still reigning in the early seventies, when a passionate pose and the proper political "line" was enough proof of revolutionary authenticity to preclude much probing into past personal history.

But driving back from Geneva along Tommy's sales route, it struck me that Tommy's triumph was less a political phenomenon than an old-fashioned American traveling-salesman story.

Tommy had promoted his identity (radical), his brand name (S.D.S.), and the authenticity of his pitch with the same combination of subtle skill and blunt persistence that are the essence of the traveling salesman's art.

Indeed, the story of Tommy's seduction and betrayal of the radical innocents followed the classic pattern of traveling-salesman stories from the French *fabliaux* that predated Chaucer to the dirty jokes about farmers' daughters told at American Legion smokers. The smooth-talking traveling slicker insinuates himself into the confidence of the client, the bed of the farmer's daughter, the plans of the plotter with the skill of his patter; takes their money, their virtue, their secrets; leaves them wondering the morning after "Who was that masked man?"

And so in order to put the Byzantine intrigues and identity shifts in the Tommy Traveler tale in a more familiar perspective, I began telling it by noting, "This is a traveling-salesman story."

As I read over the stories in this collection, I realized that most of them were, on one level or another, traveling-salesman stories.

There is, for instance, the itinerant producer of TV telethons (in "Tales of the Heartbreak Biz"), who in a gesture characteristic of the seventies salesman uses the peace-and-love rhetoric of the sixties to sell scams of the seventies. Promoting an ill-fated twenty-two-hour-long telethon for Easter Seals—he's calling it "a Woodstock-style festival of love"—he talks about how it's going to be a "sincere," "honest" telethon, yet he can't resist describing his intricate strategy for manipulating the tote board to hype the heartache of the final hours.

There is the ecstatic autograph-hunting Hasidic rabbi at Nixon's Inaugural Ball, who travels around doing a song and dance for drinks and for his dream of a face-to-face meeting with the Chairman of the Republican National Committee. There is David Whiting, the strange go-getting Gatsby-like PR man for actress Sarah Miles who traveled the world to promote her to stardom and himself to her heart, but who ended up dead on the bathroom floor of her motel room with a mysterious star-shaped wound on the back of his head.

There is Joe Karbo, a pioneer of the marathon pitch for vegetable choppers and freezer plans on early local TV, born again in the seventies as a success guru who makes his fortune selling "The Lazy Man's Way to Riches," a scheme for using the meditative techniques of the East to accumulate the cash of the West.

And there is "Inspector" Pat Doyle, the veteran police reporter for the New York *Daily News*, "The Man Who's Seen 18,000 Murders," as he likes to call himself, a man who has transformed himself into a promotion man for the incredible variety and grotesqueries of Death itself.

In my experience of the seventies, Arthur Miller's report of the death of the salesman three decades ago was altogether pre-

mature. In fact the traveling salesman may be the most characteristic figure of the seventies. In his most recent cosmic guise his
wares are no longer pots, pans, pewter, and snake oil, but identities,
ideologies, images, and idols: spiritual snake oils. In this Decade
of the Salesman we discover the Great American Salesman never
really died, he was born again.

Why now? What about the seventies has made the decade
the special province of the salesman and self-promoter? I found
it instructive to look back not only to our sixties, but to the 1860's,
to look at what has been called the original "Birth of the Great
American Salesman" to help understand his rebirth in our time.

Harvard cultural historian Daniel Boorstin traces that first
birth to the post-Civil War insurance-sales frenzy that swept the
reunited continent. Boorstin spotlights a fanatical insurance-
empire builder named Henry Hyde who built the Equitable Life
Assurance Company from birth to billions by using what he called
"religious principles" to promote insurance policies.

Hyde treated his corps of salesmen like an army of apostles,
held regular revivalistic sales conventions to whip them into fresh
missionary fervor, convinced them they were not merely selling
policies, they were saving souls.

And thus, says Boorstin, "The Great American Salesman was
born: The aspiring American salesman would henceforth trace
his lineage not to peddlers, charlatans or showmen, to the hawkers
of patent medicine, but to the great preachers and reformers and
philanthropists, the benefactors of mankind . . . In the early
decades of the twentieth century Bruce Barton, founder of a great
advertising agency, would praise Jesus as the world's greatest
salesman."

It's not hard to see how such quintessential born-again salesmen
of the seventies as Jimmy Carter and Werner Erhard (ex-traveling
salesman guru of est, born originally as Jack Rosenberg) fit into
that tradition with their talents for fusing religious zeal and sales
appeal to promote redemption and themselves. Nor is it hard to
see how the historical circumstances of each century's sixties and
seventies created the preconditions for the success of such evan-
gelical salesmen as our Dr. Leary and their Mr. Hyde.

The insurance-sales boom followed upon the decade of civil
strife, war, assassination, big booms, and bigger panics. Henry
Hyde and his fellow policy promoters thrived by exploiting an
untapped demand for invisible commodities: assurance, peace of
mind, faith.

Following a similarly disorienting decade, the archetypal salesman of our seventies also deals in invisible commodities. Traveling

sales gurus offer not merely insurance for the physical life, but insurance for the life of the soul—*eternal* life insurance, internal bliss, authenticity, sincerity, truth, The Answer.

Just as that century-old birth of the Great American Salesman followed upon the completion of continental expansion, so the consciousness expansion in the sixties opened up new internal territories for the salesmen of the seventies to exploit.

What might seem puzzling at first is that we find these semi-scoundrels so lovable. But there is something in that tension between the religious and the selfish, the piety and the pitch that appeals to Americans, a reflection no doubt of the dual motives that fueled the expansion of the country, that gives the name Manifest Destiny to massive land grabs and calls supermarket premium stores "Redemption Centers."

What is the attraction of these pitchmen that persists regardless of decade? I found when rereading these stories that the characters I couldn't resist were the PR men, admen, promoters, and self-promoters of all types. There is in their tone of voice some special intensity, some grandiose inventiveness, an exuberant insincerity that delights by perpetually travestying itself.

The real source of the appeal of the pitchman—something Arthur Miller misses entirely in *Death of a Salesman*—is the energy and artistry (okay, con artistry at times) of the salesman's song and dance. Nowhere in *Death of a Salesman* do we hear a hint of the *life* of a salesman: his patter, his pitch. We only hear Willy Loman at home muttering wistful depressed thoughts about lost dreams; we never hear him, even in the exuberant flashbacks, out on the road traveling his territory, doing his song and dance. When Willy talks about making an impression, it is only a *visual* impression—his smile. We never hear the central mode of the salesman's existence—his selling voice and the highly charged oral love poetry he fashions from it.

In the ninth grade I had a terrifying geometry teacher. When he caught a student trying to bullshit his way through the answer to a question, Mr. G. would thunder out: "I want an *answer*, sir. Don't give me a song and dance." We value the seventies salesman not because we think he has The Answer, but precisely because we enjoy his song and dance for the artistry of its prevarications which are—like literature—not so much lies as delightful evasions of the stern geometries that increasingly rule civilized life.

Boorstin acknowledges that advertising is "our most vital national literature"—no small statement—but in calling it a literature (he appears to confine that tribute to printed ads) he excludes perhaps the most vital and dramatic element of that literature—

the scripted and unscripted seduction dramas that make up the intimacies of buyer and seller. (For a mock serious theory of the sexual dynamics behind the sales, see Napoleon Hill's discussion of the "secret of sex transmutation" in "Chariots of the Insurance Salesmen.") Whether it is the one-to-one intimacy of the buyer and seller in a hotel room or the mass medicine show of the TV commercial, whether it's a PR man selling his client to a reporter, a promoter plugging an event, a self-promoter himself, the confidence man taking you into his confidence, we tend to admire the intrinsic artistry, the sheer imaginative inventiveness of the webs they weave. However aware we are that they practice to deceive, we are almost seduced into becoming their coconspirators.

Among American writers Poe was quick to recognize the fellow artist in the con artist. In a long essay on the traveling con men of mid-nineteenth-century New York City called "Diddling, Considered as an Art," Poe proclaimed that the con artist or diddler "knows plot, knows dramatic construction . . ." In the seventies *The Sting* raised the con man to lovable-hero status, and it's no accident Robert Redford went on from there to play a reporter, a kind of licensed con man, in *All the President's Men.* But in *The Confidence Man* Melville takes a darker view of the effect of con artistry. His mysterious traveler, called only "The Cosmopolitan," is a shape shifter on a ship of fools—he takes on eight different disguises during a steamboat trip down a short stretch of the Mississippi. Melville does not deny the artistic virtuosity of his mysterious traveler, but there is something more demonic to the performance. Is he Hermes Trismegistus, trickster god of the underworld and, in addition, muse of the rhetoric of salesmanship, wonders one commentator? Is he the devil himself tempting men into complicity in the ultimate sale—of the soul?

Melville's Confidence Man is something of an exception in being a shape shifter. The more characteristic American figure is the *place* shifter. The traveling quality is important in the appeal of the traveling salesman. The place shifter is constantly moving, looking for new and innocent places in which to practice his art, rather than new artifices for the same old faces. The place shifter is a more romantic notion; he appeals to the American pioneering sensibility, the outward quest for new territory that requires physical mobility, rather than the upward quest in the European novel for higher social status that requires imposture and disguise.

The appeal of the place-shifting traveling-salesman story may also have something to do with the appeal of the Western hero, who wanders into town out of nowhere, stirs things up, separates the sheep from the goats (even if the salesman fleeces rather than protects the innocent lambs), and disappears into nowhere leaving everyone wondering about his identity (and their own) in his wake. Such was certainly the case with Tommy the Traveler and star-struck promoter David Whiting, who modeled himself on the most romantic of all American self-promotion figures—Jay Gatsby.

Needless to say all of this has been post facto analysis. When I was doing these stories I was mainly aware of the appeal of these salesman figures as "characters." Something in their tone of voice, the bullying self-confidence that allowed them to seize and tell a story themselves.

What I *did* begin to realize in the process of doing these stories was that I was becoming something of a traveling salesman myself. After a couple years of apprenticeship, both Dan Wolf at *The Voice* and Harold Hayes at *Esquire* had enough confidence in me to let me wander around city and country following my instincts to stories that appealed to me. It took me about forty states, but it was not the number of states that turned me into a traveling salesman, rather the song and dance that a reporter learns to do for the people he interviews.

To get people to talk to you, particularly people who are not public figures, who don't have anything to gain from talking to you, you have to win their confidence. They want to know who you are, why you're doing the story, what your angle is, why they should trust you with their privacy. After you speak to thirty people about the same story, this process of winning confidence inevitably becomes your pitch—you've seen which ways of presenting yourself and your mission work best with this particular constellation of people. Subtle adjustments are made in the way you identify yourself. You learn to tell the story of your story; anecdotes are picked up from earlier interviewees and trotted out; personal reminiscences and past stories are offered up, all in the effort to sell the notion that you, the reporter, are no ordinary traveling salesman but a merchant of truth, understanding, and empathy—in exchange for which commodities the innocent interviewees are asked to pay with pieces of their privacy. If you're good at it, people fall for it. And they always tell more than they need to, more than what's good for them, leaving them open to feelings of betrayal.

I learned about the fine line between reporting and betrayal with something of a shock when I was in the midst of traveling through the invisible empire of the phone phreaks (see "Secrets of the Little Blue Box"). Close to the center of that network of electronic con artists who had succeeded in turning the entire empire of the phone company into their toy kingdom was a subnetwork of blind electronic geniuses who had pioneered phone-phreak free-call techniques. And at the center of *that* network was Joe Engressia, a young blind kid who was living alone in a Memphis rooming house when I came to visit him. I did my song and dance, he did his. I brought him gossip from the West Coast phone phreaks and took him to dinner at his favorite restaurant, a Holiday Inn overlooking the Mississippi River, where he told me about his personal troubles and asked me to describe the lights on the river he'd never seen. He responded with a dazzling demonstration of his phone-phreak virtuosity, including illegal free calls he bounced off satellites to Moscow and Australia and charged to some obscure toll-free 800 number. Two weeks after I left town, phone company security people broke into Joe's room, tore it apart, and arrested him. Joe somehow got the word that his arrest had been the work of a phone-company undercover agent "posing as a reporter for *Esquire*." In other words, me. Joe was quoted as bitterly regretting having "trusted" the reporter-imposter. At first I was outraged at the idea that he could be so wrong about me, I thought that in some way we had become friends that evening. But then I realized that in essence there wasn't anything I did that evening a good undercover agent wouldn't have done—make friends, elicit empathy, solicit illegal acts. Just like Tommy the Traveler.

It is unfortunate that many people still have too much faith in reporters. Reporters themselves don't. Both the book and movie of *All the President's Men* reflected awareness that the reporter is as much con man as saint, conning trust and information out of people, performing psychological break-ins on people's privacy not necessarily redeemed by the illegality of the Watergate break-in they were investigating. Like all traveling men, writers—traveling talesmen—have mixed motives. They want to tell the truth, the whole truth and nothing but, with sympathy and justice for all, but they also want to tell a good story that will entertain readers. I hope I have achieved some success in the latter department without doing too much violence to the former. End of song and dance.

TOMMY THE TRAVELER

Tommy the Traveler was no ordinary undercover agent. The thing that originally attracted me to his story was a report that Tommy was one of the few agents ever to foil the "acid test." In the sixties veteran radicals would subject suspected informers to marathon LSD encounter ordeals in the belief that acid was a kind of truth serum that would force an informer to strip the mask from his false pose.

But in the finest tradition of the seventies salesman, Tommy was said to have swallowed the drug, maintained his pose, and convinced the skeptics to swallow his story. The "acid test" as a security measure did not survive the seventies.

The undercover agent is a self-promoter of a special sort: The self he promotes is no mere expansion of his own identity, no mere "advertisement for himself." Instead he peddles an entire novel about a fictional character he plays. Tommy the Traveler was a romantic novelist with grand ambitions: he peopled his fiction with exiled Oriental royalty, idealistic young maidens, a dark and handsome traveling stranger with a secret identity. He plotted a climax that would be explosive and revealing. His only problem was selling that finale—a fire-bombing—to the confederates he would betray.

Rereading this story I was struck by how frantic and feverish was Tommy's final search for somebody, anybody, to set off one of his bombs so that the entire complex edifice of his undercover life would find justification. He was a salesman caught in the throes of a frustrating closing. He would not take no for an answer.

Is the feverish extraversion of the salesman a sign of some kind of inner hollowness? Certainly Tommy was happiest *living in his fictions. After the explosion, the riot, and the aftermath subsided back in 1971, he moved from one small-town police job to another. Newspapers ceased to take note of his passage from place to place. Recently one of his victims heard a rumor that he had been shot dead. She found herself unable to trace the story—or Tommy—anywhere. She had a feeling he may well be back under cover again.*

This is a traveling-salesman story. It's about a salesman for horse and cattle remedies who called himself a Crown Prince of Thailand, who infiltrated S.D.S. activity at a dozen New York State colleges along his route, who encouraged two nineteen-year-olds to bomb an R.O.T.C. building and had them jailed for it, and whose presence finally precipitated the only college riot in America to result in the indictment of the college itself. The traveling salesman was born Momluang Singkata Thomas Tongyai N'Ayaudhya, but most students called him Tommy Traveler.

For almost two years Tommy held a semiofficial job as "regional traveler" for the loosely organized S.D.S. chapters of western New York State. As regional traveler Tommy was a combination errand boy, evangelist, and courier, and like most attentive couriers he soon came to know more about what was going on in his region than almost anyone in the several rather isolated campuses on his route.

In all his months as S.D.S. traveler Tommy never attended college at any of the campuses he visited and never posed as a student. In fact, Tommy took pride in telling students that he was a "professional" traveler. He never concealed his salesman job from students, and frequently used the brand-new blue Mustang Mach 1 supplied by his company—a veterinary-drug firm—to chauffeur S.D.S. leaders to and from conferences and movement actions. It was not unusual for Tommy to participate in an S.D.S. Regional Steering Committee meeting at the University of Rochester and then drive the region's leadership to a good Chinese restaurant nearby and announce that he was putting all of Column A and all of Column B on his company's expense account.

And Tommy never tried to *look* like a student radical or a "movement person." His black hair was cut short, and he kept it neat and slicked down; his sideburns were short and trim. He dressed almost invariably in a three-piece tweed suit, accentuated for movement occasions by a discreet white lapel button bearing the small letters "s.d.s."

Tommy knew that short-haired people in suits who talk conspicuously about killing pigs and who ask questions about "Movement" actions arouse suspicions. So one of the first topics Tommy would bring up to S.D.S. leaders he met for the first time was his image.

"You're looking at this suit and tie and you're thinking, 'Hey, this guy looks like a pig,' right?" he'd challenge them.

"Most of us did think he was a pig at first. He was all kill-pigs and up-against-the-wall, you know. Then he'd tell us that his whole straight act, suit and car, you know, was just a cover for his movement work. He told us he used this traveling-salesman job so he could rip off the company for transportation and expenses for his S.D.S. traveling. He made a big thing of how he was really putting something over on the company." (Karl Baker, Rochester S.D.S.)

Tommy's most effective disguise was his lack of disguise. He had a talent for taking his contacts into his confidence, unveiling one "cover" after another for them, never giving them a chance to look for the one he wouldn't reveal.

He'd start with his name. To most students Tommy introduced himself first as "Thom Thomas," doubling up on the one American element of his five-part Thai name. Then, often while at the wheel of his blue Mustang on a long drive between upstate campuses, Tommy would turn to his passengers and reveal to them his entire name, even passing his wallet around for them to see it for themselves on his I.D. cards.

More unveiling followed. Although he looked "American" on the surface, Tommy admitted he was actually half Thai, a cousin of the royal family of Thailand, he told some, a full Crown Prince of Thailand, he told others.

The story continued, with some variations, like this: his father, a figure in the Thai royal family, had been exiled from Thailand because of a factional dispute within the family and had married an American. Tommy's dream was to return to Thailand one day under his royal Thai name, obtain a high position in the royal Thai government, and then, using the cover of this privileged position, lead a revolution against his own corrupt family. He used the name "Thom Thomas" for his S.D.S. work because he didn't want the royal Thai embassy to link his real name to radical activities and prevent his return to Thailand when the time was ripe. So far he had maintained his cover: his uncle was Thailand's Minister of the Interior and when Tommy met him on one of the uncle's official visits to Washington, there had been not the slightest suspicion. Tommy was certain he could get that high post in the Thai establishment when he returned and could work as an agent for Thai students and guerrilla revolutionaries. He would destroy the corrupt royal government from within: the Vietcong had men just like him high in the Saigon government, he said.

Tommy usually made it a point to conclude his story by telling his American revolutionary confidants that he considered himself neither American nor even Thai-American. He was, he told them, "a Third World person."

With a few, a very few of his closest friends in the movement (the ones who sensed something else beneath his shuffling of covers), Tommy would unveil everything in a final attempt to cover it all up. Wearing his three-piece tweed without the "s.d.s." button, Tommy would walk up behind his friend in a bar or on campus, spin him around by the shoulder, hold open his jacket with one hand to reveal a badge of some sort, and say, "I'm Thom Thomas of the Federal Bureau of Investigation. I know who you are and you'll have to come with me." After the laughter—mostly Tommy's—that followed, Tommy would tell his victim: "Nice piece of guerrilla theatre, huh."

Tommy's father, Singkata Tongyai, brought Tommy up to think of himself as an American, an unhyphenated American, and certainly not an oppressed Third World American. Singkata was a Thai, as was his father, but Singkata's mother was Russian, a Czarist exile, according to one story Tommy told, who witnessed savagery and murder during the Revolution and escaped to Thailand. Perhaps from her influence Singkata became almost religiously anti-Communist. In any case, Singkata, a distant relative of the large Thai ruling family, left Thailand around the outbreak of the Second World War and came to America to study criminology and chemical engineering at Michigan State.

Singkata seems to have been something of an undercover agent himself. Before the war ended he had come to love America enough to join the U. S. Army and return to Indochina as an American Army Intelligence officer. After the war ended Singkata continued to make regular trips back to Thailand on "family business" and there is evidence that he may have done work for the C.I.A. An American relative told an investigator attached to the Scranton Commission that shortly before one of these trips in the early fifties, Singkata took the relative to a meeting in Philadelphia and introduced him to men who identified themselves as Central Intelligence Agency personnel. They told him Singkata was working for the Agency on his trips to Thailand, and asked the relative to serve as an emergency route of communication between Singkata and the C.I.A.—which meant merely turning over to the Agency some letters Singkata might address to him from Thailand. (Although the emergency route was never used, the relative was convinced that Singkata was a C.I.A. informant.)

Singkata married an American girl, and Tommy was born an American citizen at an Army camp in 1944. After the war, Singkata moved his family to Bucks County, Pennsylvania, where his wife's family, the Thomases, had lived for generations. Singkata was a firearms enthusiast and a hunter, and Tommy grew up in a home filled with guns and devotion to America.

Tommy never looked Oriental, or even half Oriental, as a child. Most of the kids he played cowboys and Indians with accepted him as just as American as any cowboy, and saw nothing peculiar about asking him to play Indian occasionally. But a cousin remembers that Tommy was particularly fond of playing *cowboy* in cowboys and Indians. "I think he believed in it more than most kids." (Garry Thomas)

There is a strange and saddening story from Tommy's childhood which hints that his Thai-American background may have caused him pain. When she was eight years old and Tommy was twelve, Tommy's youngest sister, the one closest to him, ran out of a Sunday-school bus into the street and was struck and killed by an oncoming car. Tommy's cousin recalls that the driver of the car, in disclaiming his own responsibility, was heard around town making remarks about the child's "wildness" and lack of control. There were some implications that her mixed parentage, something "foreign" in her blood, or something in her family's "lack of discipline" was responsible for her strange "lack of control."

The youngest sister was the family's favorite, and the Tongyai family underwent an emotional upheaval after her death. Tommy's mother was reported almost insane with grief over the tragedy and the ugly stories that followed it. Tommy's father agreed to convert to Christianity and attend her church.

A cousin recalls, "There was something like a religious revival in the family, as if they almost secretly believed these things and were trying to wipe out the feeling that maybe the un-Christian side of the family was responsible for the little girl's death or wildness or whatever it was that might have caused her death."

Tommy grew up to trade his cowboy pistol for his father's hunting rifles, but he never lost interest in his dream of cowboy life. Shortly after graduating from high school in Doylestown, Pennsylvania, he went out West to try to become a rodeo rider.

Arriving in New Mexico in September, 1962, Tommy enrolled in a college which featured rodeo courses. But all of a sudden, out there in the West, Tommy's "un-American" half began under-mining his most American of dreams: the other aspiring cowboys at his rodeo college began treating him as if he were a half-breed, a Mexican-American. While back East Tommy had been a darkly handsome American boy, out West, on the last frontier, people looked at his slim five-feet six-inch stature, jet-black hair, and dark complexion and called him "Mex." Apparently he suffered some harassment from the other cowboy-students who thought that only one-hundred-percent Americans were fit to play cowboy in a rodeo show.

According to his cousin, Tommy began getting into fights, mostly with Mexican-Americans who, Tommy claimed, were harassing him with threats and knives. Full of resentment at hav-ing to prove he was not a Mexican-American, but more painfully aware of his own secret hyphenation, and full of anger at the *real* Mexican-Americans, Tommy dropped out of rodeo school in December, 1962. However, that very winter, at age nineteen, Tommy found a job with a traveling rodeo that covered a circuit from New Mexico north to the Dakotas. After the last of the real cowboys left the range to become extras in Hollywood cowboy films, the rodeo circuit was the last place an American could be a cowboy with a straight face, the last place the cowboy could do his stuff—tame savage beasts, the way they had tamed savages and beasts in the good old days. For six months Tommy traveled the circuit, riding broncos and steers and having the time of his life, according to his later stories. Then something happened. It's not clear if Tommy had a bad fall or got into another fight over his "Mexican-American" identity, but Tommy's rodeo life was cut short and he returned East in mid-1963 and the next year became a traveling salesman, a lesser—but no less American—dream.

In fact, in becoming a traveling salesman Tommy was following a tradition on the American side of his family. His mother's father and brother had been traveling men along the roads of northern Pennsylvania, the elder Thomas peddling Sipe paints, the younger selling lumber. When Tommy took his first traveling-salesman job he told his mother's family he was happy to carry on the Thomas tradition.

His first assignment was selling dog food for Kraft in Phila-delphia, but after taking some courses in veterinary medicine at a community college, Tommy was able to move up from dog food to selling veterinary drugs. His love for horses and cows may have made the shift from rodeo rider to purveyor of horse serums and flea powders that much easier for him.

In August, 1967, Tommy's employer, the Schering Corporation, asked him to shift his route north and take on territory in the western New York Finger Lakes region. Tommy, married and father of a three-year-old boy by this time, moved his family to Penn Yan, New York, the site of Keuka College, a small Baptist-founded women's school. That fall Tommy's wife Lynn enrolled for some courses at Keuka, and one evening she and Tommy attended a meeting of the Keuka peace group. That evening—Tommy's first contact with the student movement—turned out to be rather traumatic for both him and the movement.

Keuka College was not notorious for its radicalism in those days. When Columbia exploded in April, 1968, the biggest issue at Keuka was whether curfew for the girls should be extended past eleven P.M. on weekdays and past one A.M. on weekends. The ten or fifteen girls, mostly freshmen and sophomores, who showed up irregularly for the irregular meetings of the Keuka peace group were hardly the equivalent of the Mad Dogs, the Crazies, and the Motherfuckers to whom the F.B.I. paid the respect of assigning infiltrators. Keuka peace-group girls were "radical" back then only in the sense that they might support a treaty banning underground nuclear tests *if* it provided for proper inspection by neutral parties. So it is unlikely that Tommy attended his first meeting of the Keuka peace group representing any agency but himself.

The night Tommy attended, the peace-group girls had invited a genuine radical, Douglas Dowd, an antiwar Cornell professor, to speak to them. Dowd attacked the war, attacked the spread of American presence throughout Southeast Asia, and in passing made some remarks about Thailand, which was beginning to experience guerrilla warfare in its northern province. His remarks implied that the Thai government was a puppet with Americans pulling the strings.

Suddenly Tommy was on his feet raising questions.

"How do *you* know anything about what's going on there? . . . What about all the murders the Communists are committing against innocent people? . . . Why do you only call *Americans* the killers?"

A heated argument broke out, with most of the audience attacking Tommy, bombarding him with examples of American atrocities ("Don't you read *The New York Times*?"), and telling Tommy, "It's their country, why don't we let them fight it out themselves, it's a civil war."

Tommy was having difficulty holding his own. "Why are the Communists always right and Americans always wrong?" he repeated.

All at once Tommy's wife Lynn was standing up shouting back

at Tommy's attackers. "Why won't you listen to him! He doesn't have to read *The New York Times*! He's from the royal family of Thailand. He knows what it's like over there. You won't even listen to him!" She broke into tears and ran from the room. Tommy followed after her and didn't return that night.

Students were, therefore, surprised when Tommy began to show up regularly at peace-group meetings from that point on, even the small meetings with no speakers, attended by just six or seven Keuka girls. More surprisingly, at most of the meetings that fall and winter, Tommy sat quietly. The occasional question he asked was not hostile; he sounded instead interested, or puzzled, by the left-wing critique of the war.

In addition, Tommy began to show up frequently at the R&M Restaurant and the Wagner Motor Inn in downtown Penn Yan, the bars where Keuka girls went to drink before curfew. He started hanging out in the bars with some of the girls he met at the peace-group meetings. They talked a lot that fall and winter over beers, about politics and personal things, and Tommy began confiding to some of the girls the story of his mysterious background.

Tommy cut a strange, half-glamorous, half-comic figure among the teenage Keuka girls he adopted. Although most Keuka girls didn't take Tommy too seriously—he was "too weird" to be an ordinary liar, but "too weird" to be believed either—a few believed in him, and Tommy grew very close to one girl in particular.

Tommy met Diane, an eighteen-year-old freshman, at one of the peace-group meetings and they became close friends over beers at the R&M Restaurant. Later Tommy confided to another Keuka girl that Diane reminded him of his youngest sister, or the way she would have looked if she had not been killed at eight. Tommy told them the story of his little sister's death and confessed that he blamed himself for it. He was on that Sunday-school bus the day she ran out in front of that car, he told them. He could have reached out and restrained her, but she broke loose. He had never forgiven himself for that moment.

Tommy said that he shot his own dog because it bit Diane. Tommy always had huge dogs around his house, the better, he said, to protect his wife and children while he was away traveling his sales route. This one was an African razorback hound, a lean muscular breed produced, Tommy told people, by mating dogs with wild jackals or hyenas. One day, after Diane, Melanie Wallace, and Tommy came out of a bar in town, Tommy opened the door of his car and the dog jumped out, leaped at Diane, and nicked her hand, frightening her immensely. Some days later, Tommy said, he took his dog outside and killed it. Tommy claimed that for weeks after he killed the dog he could hear its ghost return to his house at night, whimpering and pawing at his door, asking to be allowed back in again. He loved the dog, Tommy said, but he never got up to let it in.

("Tommy was always telling us he was in touch with strange powers back then," Sally Gilmour once said, "things like a ghost in his wife's family home in Pennsylvania. I usually didn't believe Tommy's stories, but he looked so, you know, *moved*, talking about his sister, Diane, and the dog, that I couldn't dismiss it.")

Tommy and Diane maintained their brother-sisterly friendship throughout that winter. In the spring he suddenly began asking her to introduce him to people she knew who had S.D.S. connections, and started letting people know he was a radical.

"Tommy began coming to meetings about curfews with us and started telling us the way to handle it was to take over the Dean's office and occupy the President's house. He said it seriously. We couldn't believe it. I mean it was curfews. He told us we had to do something that will attract national attention and get national coverage. 'Something big like at Columbia,' he was always saying." (Melanie Wallace)

"There were only about ten of us, but he was always talking about getting national coverage. It was weird." (Alison Fisher)

And in the R&M Restaurant and the Wagner Motor Inn, Tommy began talking long and loudly about his hatred for the Establishment, the war, and capitalism. He began using Marxist terms although at first he displayed some inexperience in handling them: he would earnestly drop phrases like "socialist-Marxism" and "Mao-Leninism" into his heated political conversations, much to the puzzlement of the Keuka girls.

When Diane introduced him to some of her friends with S.D.S. contacts, Tommy began to pump them for information and literature. One girl, Melanie Wallace, touched by Tommy's moody resentments and coltish enthusiasms, told him he'd like reading about Prince Myshkin and once left her copy of *The Idiot* in his car. (Three years later Tommy had not returned it, and Melanie had been indicted, on Tommy's testimony, on riot charges.) Other girls loaned him S.D.S. periodicals and books on Marxism. He began asking them to introduce him to "real" S.D.S. people, but they don't remember any such meeting taking place at Keuka that spring.

In the summer of 1968 Tommy moved his family from Penn Yan to Geneva, New York, about twenty miles northeast. By the

time Tommy showed up at Keuka again—early the following fall—
there had been quite a change. Tommy arrived with a carload of
S.D.S. and Resistance people from Rochester, a trunkful of S.D.S.
literature, spoke the latest movement catchphrases, and acted as
if the S.D.S. people were all old friends. He told the girls at Keuka
he was a regional traveler for S.D.S. chapters in the Finger Lakes
region, and the S.D.S. people seemed to accept him as that. The
Keuka girls couldn't believe it.

At a family reunion in Pennsylvania over the Christmas holidays
in 1967, Tommy had told a cousin that he was thinking of infiltrating the student movement—he mentioned the McCarthy-for-
President movement in particular—in order to expose the leaders
as Communists and Communist sympathizers. If Tommy's father
sympathized with this, he may well have introduced Tommy to
some of his former contacts in Army Intelligence and other government agencies. (Army Intelligence began its extensive civilian-
surveillance operations in the spring of 1968.)
    The F.B.I. had maintained a strong presence in western New
York ever since World War II when many Trotskyites and Communists moved to Buffalo to take jobs in defense plants and to try
to organize heavy industry. There is a large F.B.I. field office in
Buffalo which is reported to have about one hundred agents. And
the F.B.I. people in Buffalo could not help noticing the sudden
emergence of strong S.D.S. chapters, along with other radical anti-
draft and antiwar groups, at the University of Buffalo, Rochester
University, Cornell, and Syracuse, during the winter and spring of
1967–68. With Columbia and Chicago blowing up, it is quite
likely that the F.B.I. in Buffalo, like F.B.I. offices around the
country, had already begun doing something about infiltrating the
student movement when Tommy arrived on the scene.
    In addition, there are reports that the Bureau occasionally made
it a practice to help place informants on various matters in
traveling-salesman jobs. Such jobs offered informants a legitimate
cover for showing up in any town in the region at regular inter-
vals; there was no need to establish a cover residence and a private
life in any one place.
    Tommy, however, did not begin to venture off the Keuka cam-
pus and show up conspicuously at S.D.S. functions until June,
1968. The months from Christmas to June at Keuka *may* have
been spent in training under an investigative agency and estab-
lishing a solid identity as a radical before moving on, but it is also
possible that until June, and even for months after he moved to

Geneva, Tommy was acting completely on his own. He may have plunged under cover with no one on the surface to report back to.

Fitzgerald saw to it that Dick Diver, ex-expatriate, touched bottom and disappeared in, of all places, Geneva, New York. Geneva is one of those towns in New York State whose pioneer founders preferred taking classical and European names—Rome, Carthage, Athens, Troy, Albion, Waterloo—rather than accepting the descriptive Indian name for their settlement. Geneva grew to become a nineteenth-century manufacturing town, and still has that crumbling red-brick atmosphere. The current population of 17,000 contains large Irish and Italian working-class groups. Hobart College has been in Geneva since 1822 when it was established to teach missionaries, convert Indians to Christianity, and civilize young men. (William Smith, a coordinate girls' school, joined Hobart in 1908.) In 1968 Geneva was just beginning to discover that under the guise of "college students" Hobart was sheltering Communists, drug pushers, and hippies—the very elements of savagery Geneva had always tried to eradicate.

Tommy moved to Geneva ostensibly because it was closer to the center of his network of veterinarian customers. By this time he did more than just take orders for drugs—he was a detail man, entrusted with the task of distributing his company's literature, the "details" on new drugs, and explaining their advantages to the vets. He began to stop regularly in Buffalo, Syracuse, Rochester, and Ithaca, presumably because he was assigned a new set of customers by his company. But Tommy wasted no time in developing a network of S.D.S. chapters to supplement his veterinarian network.

First stop on his S.D.S. route was the office of Glad Day Press, a movement printing shop just off the Cornell campus. Glad Day Press printed *Notes from the Green Piano*, an underground paper distributed sporadically to other schools in the region, and created posters, pamphlets, leaflets, and broadsides for S.D.S. and other arms of the movement.

Bill Siebert of Glad Day Press remembers seeing Tommy at the June, 1968, National S.D.S. Conference at East Lansing, Michigan, but not meeting him until later that summer. Tommy appeared at the Glad Day Press office and introduced himself as an S.D.S. organizer from Keuka where his wife was a student. Tommy began spending considerable time among S.D.S. people in Ithaca: "He was there at meetings and dances, always hanging out with leadership people, laughing loudly and acting like a traveling salesman." (Bill Siebert)

Tommy began taking certain people into his confidence—nearly everyone in Cornell's S.D.S. leadership as it turned out—and telling them his entire Third-World-revolutionary-posing-as-traveling-salesman story.

"He told me that if the Thai government found out about his S.D.S. activity he would be deported to Thailand and probably not live too long there. Back at that time these were enough credentials for me." (Bill Siebert)

Cornell's S.D.S. leadership, particularly Chip Marshall and Joe Kelley, along with Jeffrey Dowd, had been "traveling" the schools of the region that spring and planned on calling a conference of S.D.S. chapters to get them together as a region when schools reopened in the fall. Shortly after schools were in session in September, Tommy appeared at the Glad Day Press office, and offered to drive some literature up to Hobart and Keuka since they were "on his way." Nobody trusted Tommy enough for them to reveal any movement *secrets* to him, but the literature—pamphlets, underground papers—was all in public domain, and there was no one else around to get it distributed. So it was loaded into Tommy's car. When Tommy returned from completion of his first errand he offered to drop literature off at the other colleges along his route. It happened to be a time when Tommy and his route were particularly handy to S.D.S. people because they wanted to keep all schools in the region, including the smaller out-of-the-way campuses, informed of plans for the regional organizing conference in November. These schools always seemed to be "on the way" for Tommy and his company car. So, in addition to delivering literature, Tommy delivered the latest word on the conference. And to students at the smaller schools to whom he delivered the word, Tommy seemed to be an official courier from S.D.S. leadership, perhaps a leader himself.

But back at Cornell, Tommy was still treated as an overeager messenger boy. He kept offering rides to S.D.S. people, particularly Chip and Joe. He drove them up to Geneva that fall for the first meeting of the newly formed radical alliance on the Hobart campus, the Hobart Student Movement.

Not all of Tommy's riders trusted their driver.

"Sometimes," Siebert recalls, "we'd get calls from people we knew who told us they just got a ride with this guy Tommy and they were sure he was a pig. Then Tommy would call us up and tell us to be careful of the guy he just gave a ride to because he was sure *he* was a pig. We assumed it was just a case of mutual paranoia. And Chip or Joe would say Tommy's okay. . . . Chip sort of looked on him as a little kid. He'd send Tommy places he thought he couldn't do any harm, and Tommy would go to places Chip and Joe wouldn't bother to go. There just wasn't anyone else who could get the papers distributed regularly the way he did."

Tommy drove a car full of Keuka girls to Rochester in November, 1968, for the regional organizing conference he had helped prepare. By that time he had already become a familiar figure to many of those attending, and at the last session of that conference Tommy's salesmanship was rewarded.

"They were asking for people to do some traveling for the regions, and nobody from Cornell or the Finger Lakes area volunteered. Chip and Joe were too busy with more important stuff, so Tommy said he'd do it and everyone said okay. Everyone thought he was a friend of someone else." (Alison Fisher)

On the drive back to Keuka from the conference, Tommy was in a very good mood. So elated was he with his success and the way things were going with the revolution that he opened his glove compartment, took out his pistol, and displayed it and loaded it for the girls, explaining that it wouldn't be long before the time for shooting pigs arrived.

At first, Tommy's travels were little more than advance work for the recognized heavies of S.D.S. He was their detail man. He might go to a small campus, seek out a student political group interested in S.D.S., distribute copies of *Notes from the Green Piano* and other literature, and tell the group he could bring some real S.D.S. leaders down from Cornell to speak at the college if the group could sponsor them. Then he'd return to Ithaca and tell leaders like Chip Marshall and Joe Kelley that the students at, say, Auburn Community College really wanted to hear them speak—did they think they could find time, did they need a ride? Or he'd tell students at Keuka interested in learning draft counseling that he could bring down some very good people from Rochester Resistance to teach them. And after he explained the demand for draft-counseling trainers at Keuka to the Resistance people, with perhaps a provocative comment or two about the attractions of Keuka girls, he'd drive them the forty miles to Penn Yan.

Tommy was always eager to chauffeur movement celebrities around. There was the time Mark Rudd came to Ithaca to talk to S.D.S. at Cornell. Tommy stayed close to Rudd throughout his visit, and offered him a ride to the Syracuse airport when the visit ended. Rudd had seen enough of Tommy to decline the ride, but shortly after Rudd arrived at the airport Tommy appeared in the waiting room and tried to make conversation. As soon as Rudd arrived in New York City that night, he called the Cornell leadership to warn them about Tommy. Tommy later explained to Jeffrey Dowd that he was at the airport merely to meet a couple of stewardesses he knew.

Tommy introduced himself to a girl at Auburn as "S.D.S. regional traveler from Buffalo." He introduced himself to S.D.S. people at the University of Buffalo as "S.D.S. traveler out of Ithaca." Some people at Cornell remember him as S.D.S. traveler "for the Finger Lakes region." It was hard for anyone to contradict any of these statements. S.D.S. chapters and S.D.S. people in western New York were never quite sure if they were one big region or several overlapping regions, or whether there ever was anything as formalized as a "region" at all. In fact, Tommy's courier service became the closest thing there was to a regional organization. He kept S.D.S. informed of itself. And for the hundreds of non-S.D.S. students at small out-of-the-way teachers' colleges or communities with no S.D.S. chapters, Tommy's appearance to speak or show films was all they saw of S.D.S. that year.

"I remember he had this big thing about regional conferences. I mean, his whole thing was to try and call these regional conferences all the time," a Buffalo activist recalls. "I mean, we'd get to these conferences and they'd usually be terrible and we'd look at each other and say, 'He called it.' . . . 'I thought you called it.' . . . 'No, I didn't call it.' . . . 'I thought he called it.' I got the feeling that Tommy would go to Rochester and say 'Buffalo wants one,' then he'd go to Buffalo and say 'Rochester wants one,' and there we'd be at this regional conference."

Tommy treated these regional conferences as if they were parties and he was the host. (He did, in fact, as steering-committee member, help plan them and set the date, and as traveler he distributed invitations.) He liked to move around at the conference, meeting and greeting, making introductions, playing one-of-the-boys with the top leadership, name-dropping to the lesser members, watching the flow of interaction around him with an almost proprietary air.

By the time of the big S.D.S. conference at Albany State in January, 1969, Tommy had already become known to S.D.S. people from schools all over the state as "Tommy Traveler," although others at the conference knew him as Thom Thomas, some as Tom Travis, and a few as Tom Tongyai.

"Tommy never felt bad about using two or three names," recalls Mark Smeraldi, who saw Tommy at the Albany get-together. "He'd always act like you were in his confidence and he was shucking the other guy. He'd tell me, 'Well, *these* guys here think I'm Tommy Thomas,' but I was in on the real truth."

But that Albany State conference had a surprise to offer which spoiled the whole party for Tommy. The surprise was "The Name Game." People from New York City's Bread and Puppet Theater called everyone together for a session of theater and encounter games. Tommy played too. After some preliminary touching and feeling exercises, the rules for "The Name Game" were announced.

"The first thing was you'd take off your shoes and lie down on the floor and roll around and every time you bumped into somebody—there were a lot of people there—you'd repeat your names to each other. Then you'd sit yourself opposite somebody and you'd repeat your name at them over and over, and they'd do it at you until the names have absolutely no meaning to you or them. . . ." (Mark Smeraldi)

With so many people shouting their names, Smeraldi didn't hear which one of his names Tommy shouted into his partner's face.

"Anyway, there was a lot of chicks there and like the last thing was everyone piled into this huge heap, you know, and breathed in unison—it was kind of a rush actually."

Not for Tommy. "He was very freaked out by the whole thing," Smeraldi continues. "He came up to me after the body pile and told me, 'Hey man, I got ahold of a nice girl in there.' That's how he handled it. And the name thing really got him uptight. He told me the whole thing was bullshit and had nothing to do with the revolution."

Despite all he knew about S.D.S. and the revolution in general, Tommy found it hard to get close to individual revolutionaries. With men, particularly those he knew were leaders, Tommy played aspiring second-banana tough guy. He was Michael Pollard—they were Bonnie and Clyde. Tommy seldom talked about anything but politics, which meant, for Tommy, talking about guns and pigs.

Tommy's few attempts at small talk or personal conversation with some men in S.D.S. usually began with sex: he had a kind of traveling salesman's repertory of stories about girls he had waiting for him in cities and on campuses along his route. Tommy would tell people in Rochester about how he "shacked up with two stewardesses every time he got to Syracuse . . . he'd even show us those little airline bottles of gin and Scotch like it was proof." He'd pass around photographs of his "stewardesses" to Cornell people. He'd tell Hobart students about girls he picked up on his trips to Keuka.

With the women in the movement Tommy found it more difficult to know how to act.

"At first he had a hard time understanding what he called 'free love.' He used to tell us that all these girls would try to ball him all the time, but he refused because he didn't believe in 'free love.' " (Melanie Wallace)

That was back in 1968. Later Tommy seems to have become reconciled to the concept. He began to tell girls in bars in Penn Yan and Geneva the old traveling-salesman line, that his wife didn't really understand him—didn't share his radical politics—and resented his traveling for S.D.S.

"He was always trying to get laid," one of his traveling companions recalls. "And he had some of the *worst* lines. We'd go into a bar on a campus with some chicks and Tommy would go into a whole rap about how many of his heavy movement friends had been worked over by the pigs and how one of these days he was gonna lose control and take a pig out, and these chicks would be looking at him wide-eyed, oh my hero, you know—it was incredible." (Mark Smeraldi)

"I thought he was quite good-looking, quite a package in fact, but I was turned right off when he mentioned his wife . . . and his line was pure 1950's, 1956 to be exact; I'm sure he never made it anyplace but the backseat of his car." (A Geneva girl)

"I never saw him going around with a girl on anything but S.D.S. business, but he was always talking about how he'd pick a girl up for a night and forget about her—like that made him one of the boys." (Smeraldi)

But Tommy never even tried to pretend he was one of the boys as far as drugs went. In fact, almost everyone who knew Tommy recalls him repeatedly denouncing all drugs, including marijuana, as counterrevolutionary. Tommy didn't like dealing with people when they were high—they seemed less likely to take his plans seriously and they giggled too much at his rhetoric. Tommy was almost a fanatic on the subject, convinced that people who take drugs lose control of themselves. "You freak out your mind and you can't take action against the pigs," he'd tell people. "And worst of all," he'd add, "if the pigs can't bust you for politics they'll bust you for drugs."

It took no less an authority than Jerry Rubin to persuade Tommy to take his first puffs on a joint.

"A group of us were in this room with Tommy and there were some people smoking marijuana," a Hobart student recalls. "Tommy never smoked and he said it was very counterrevolutionary, but somebody burst out and said, 'Bullshit! Jerry Rubin says it has to be a *stoned* revolution.' And just like that, sort of on that authority, Tommy took a couple of tokes, nervously but like it was his duty because of what Jerry Rubin said."

Tommy was slightly more permissive when it came to veterinary drugs. Two Keuka girls claim that he offered certain pills for horses and cows which he said would cause an abortion if they ever needed one. "He told us he once got a girl in Syracuse pregnant and that these pills worked. He said if they worked on horses they ought to work on us." (Sally Gilmour)

Tommy never had much in common with the people he was infiltrating. But he never pretended to. He only had, or thought he had, two things in common with them: a cowboys vs. Indians view of revolutionary struggle, and a devotion to guns and violence as the only solution. Tommy assumed that radicals hated pigs in exactly the same way he knew pigs hated radicals, so very little internal emotional adjustment was required, only a transposition of names, for him to act just like his image of a radical.

S.D.S. people at the University of Buffalo remember Tommy as the crazy who told them he wanted to organize a gun-toting "regional terrorist committee" to retaliate against right-wingers.

"He told us he wanted to get the heaviest people from each city together to go places where right-wingers or jocks were harassing movement people. He said we had to teach them a lesson."

Tommy told the Buffalo people that he got the idea for the "terror squad" when he was doing some organizing down in Mansfield State College in northern Pennsylvania and some jocks attacked him.

"He told us he was always in danger of his life in the small college towns he visited," a Buffalo radical says. "He mentioned Fredonia, Corning, and Elmira. He said the only thing the right-wingers understood was guns, so the terror squad would have to be armed. He went into this fantasy trip about all of us waiting in a room for some right-wingers who were on their way to beat us up. 'We'd be waiting with three shotguns,' he'd say. 'You're here, you're here, and I'm here.' He'd be pointing to places around the room. 'We could blow 'em all to pieces with just three shotguns.' "

"Tommy told me he wanted to get revenge on these jocks who beat him up down in Pennsylvania by ambushing them with Mace so he could see them fall down on their knees crying." (Mark Smeraldi)

Several University of Buffalo people recall Tommy taking them into his confidence—"Don't let anyone else know about this . . . it's too heavy"—and detailing an even more elaborate cowboys and Indians scheme: "The Olean Assault Force."

Olean is a town of 19,000 located on an empty stretch of Route 17 not far from Cuba, New York, and Bolivar, New York. Over a confidential cup of coffee Tommy explained the Olean Assault Force to a Buffalo activist this way:

" 'Things are getting heavy around the nation,' Tommy said. 'The right wing is attacking the left wing. We can't let them get away with it, we gotta show 'em we're tough. So we're getting together assault forces all over the state and you can join the Olean division.' Tommy said we'd live in the hills around Olean for about six weeks of training, while he'd investigate me to make sure I could be trusted; then he said, we'll ask you to do your first job, which might be investigating someone else in the movement to see if they could be trusted, or casing a place to be blown up. Eventually we'd go to the Adirondacks and live there and make raids, like around Lake George we'd take over the tourist traffic, from there we'd expand and eventually control New England.

"He was always trying to get us interested in retaliating against some local right-winger. He would get really excited about his Olean plan. . . . I mean he was the kind of guy who would threaten to wipe out the whole University of Buffalo chapter of Hare Krishna because they couldn't see the importance of regional security."

After a while Tommy became known to people at the University of Buffalo as Maxwell Smart or as Captain Peachfuzz.

At Hobart, Clarence Youngs, a black student, remembers Tommy first approaching him in 1969 about the time of the black students' armed protest at Cornell, and "telling me that the blacks on campus weren't together because we hadn't taken over any buildings and hadn't burned anything down and that just sitting around was letting the Administration make fools of us.

"In March of 1969," Youngs remembers, "right after Easter vacation, he told me he could show us how to use explosives and that anytime we needed guns or dynamite he could get it for us . . . and about that time he drove me and Mark Smeraldi out to a field to shoot off his M-1 with him."

At the University of Rochester S.D.S. people remember Tommy because "all he'd ever talk about was killing pigs, putting pigs up against the wall, and guns." In the fall of 1969 while attending a regional S.D.S. steering-committee meeting at Rochester, Tommy approached Karl Baker, a Rochester S.D.S. organizer, and, according to Baker, "offered to get me some black powder for making explosives and 'anything else' I needed. He said he could get Army surplus guns cheaply and talked about which guns were better for what jobs."

Students at Auburn Community College and at Hobart remember Tommy appearing before them just prior to the November 15, 1969, Moratorium in Washington. Tommy advised them that the Moratorium itself was "liberal bullshit," but that the Weathermen were going to march on the South Vietnamese Embassy near Du-Pont Circle and burn it down or blow it up. Tommy counseled people going to Washington to stick with the Weathermen "because that's where all the good violence will be."

On the night of November 14, 1969, when Weathermen gathered at DuPont Circle two blocks from the Saigon Embassy, people from Hobart and Buffalo reported seeing Tommy, wearing a crash helmet, dark glasses, and carrying an N.L.F. flag, in the front ranks of the march on the Embassy. The next evening Jeffrey Dowd recalls coming upon Tommy, flag and all, on Constitution Avenue after the first big gassing at the Justice Department. Back at Hobart, Tommy gathered together a few students and gave them a little illustrated chalk-talk about the best tactics to use in the kind of street fighting that followed the DuPont Circle and Justice Department actions.

"He was literally drawing these football diagrams with X's and O's for the cops and protesters. He would show us end runs around police lines, but he said the best tactic was for six or seven of us to get one cop in a corner and kick the shit out of him."

In the fall of 1969 Tommy knocked on the door of Rafael Martinez, a thirty-six-year-old radical, a friend of the Berrigan brothers, who was enrolled as a senior at Hobart. Introducing himself as a regional traveler from the S.D.S., Tommy told Rafael "he had heard a lot about me. He said he'd heard that I was a real revolutionary, not like the other bullshit liberals and rich kids posing as radicals at Hobart. He said it was time for something really revolutionary to happen and told me he could provide me with weapons and bombs. He told me, 'We could really create a heavy scene at Hobart.' He said we could blow up Coxe Hall or the R.O.T.C. office. . . . 'I'll provide the materials,' he said."

Rafael told Tommy that he was a nonviolent person and didn't want to blow up buildings. "He told me you can't accomplish anything with nonviolence—that's an Establishment trick to maintain the status quo.

"He told me that he knew I was a friend of Dan Berrigan and that he admired Berrigan because he was a real revolutionary, but told me, 'I'd like him to change and get him to do more violence. He'll get a good following that way.'

"Think it over," Rafael remembers Tommy saying as he left. "I'll come back and I'll see you around campus. If you want I can get hand grenades, materials for bombs, anything you want, to give to the kids."

"The kids" at Hobart and William Smith remember Tommy railing against nonviolence over and over again.

"The first time I saw Tommy he was in Bruce Davis's room trying to recruit people for this goon-squad mission to protect S.D.S. chapters. . . . We got into this discussion of tactics and nonviolence. Tommy became extremely irate, just started beating his hand into his fist, jumping around the room, at first arguing against nonviolence, but eventually he became so inarticulate, so excited, that all he could do was beat his hand into his fist and jump around the room . . . his eyes were wild and he really even looked like he couldn't control himself. . . . My initial impression was wow, what's the matter with him. I remember thinking if he's a radical I suppose that's okay, it doesn't really matter how he got that way, but it seemed strange." (Chris Wardell)

And stranger still, Melanie Wallace, who knew Tommy well, swears this story is true: she was sitting in Tommy's car alongside Tommy's young son. "Tommy told me he was teaching his kid how to call policemen pigs. 'Watch this,' he said, and he turns to the kid and says, 'Say pig.' And the kid said, 'Pig,' and Tommy said, 'How about that.' "

"Tommy talked about killing pigs the way guys in Vietnam talk about killing gooks." (Bruce Davis)

For most of 1969, Tommy's talk of violence and killing pigs was sporadic, he made no concerted effort to get anyone to blow up something with him or with his explosives—or else he just couldn't find anyone to agree to it. But he tested almost every S.D.S. and radical leader he took into his confidence.

Only occasionally would Tommy's obsession with killing pigs, blowing up and burning down buildings, bring him under real suspicion. In the fall of 1969 Tommy made one of his few appearances on the University of Buffalo campuses and was heard talking loudly about "blowing up Precinct 6"—the campus-area precinct. One Buffalo radical reportedly walked up to Tommy and told him, "You're a pig, man, and if you're not off the campus in fifteen minutes you're dead." Tommy met the deadline.

Tommy usually continued to respond to such accusations by telling everyone he knew at the school, and often people at other stops along his route, that his accuser was himself a pig. After Rafael Martinez refused a second offer from Tommy and began voicing suspicions that Tommy was a provocateur, Tommy began going around to some of the other radicals at Hobart and confiding to them his suspicion that Rafael was a pig. But no one took either Rafael's or Tommy's charges too seriously: "I guess most of us thought Tommy was just too screwed up to even be a pig." (Bruce Davis)

It's hard to believe, in retrospect, that more people didn't suspect Tommy, but S.D.S. and the Movement were changing then: the leadership was putting on combat boots and leather jackets, the talk was of trashing and "heavy actions," and next to the pigs the worst enemy was "liberal bullshit." "Revolution has come/ Time to pick up the gun"; "Seize the time" and "Either-Or" were the slogans. The original Weathermen statement advised radicals to give up the ideal of remaking America in their own image, abandon hope for a successful *American* revolution, and to consider themselves agents of the Third World Revolution, operating behind enemy lines.

In addition, S.D.S. and the Movement had been drawing a new kind of recruit as it spread from Ivy schools to state colleges—the kid who had been wearing leather jackets and combat boots all his life, rather than the kid who learned to imitate Che from reading *Evergreen Review*; people who were just fed up, pissed off, and didn't fit anywhere else but the Movement; crazies; people who smoked dope and gobbled acid without turning into flower children; people who came to radicalism without being liberal intellectuals first.

And Tommy always had a secret appeal for student radicals who *had* been liberal intellectuals first, and who were still aware of how much their readiness to act was sicklied over with the pale cast of thought. Tommy was Fortinbras in the field to their Hamlet. You're Either part of the problem Or part of the solution. Either-Or. Tommy was always around with his grenade, carried like a forbidden fruit in his hand, offering the means for a quick leap over the hyphen from Either to Or.

It wasn't until April of 1970, after many offers, that Tommy finally made his sale. Big changes had taken place in Tommy's network in the six months before that April. His S.D.S. network had crumbled beneath him, he had been fired by his drug-company employer, hired by the county sheriff as an undercover narcotics agent, and may have been dropped for mysterious reasons by the F.B.I. or whatever intelligence agency he worked for.

A factional dispute split his S.D.S. region in the spring of 1969, and Tommy seems to have used his courier's network to circulate an "open letter" from some Rochester S.D.S. people critical of Chip's and Joe's leadership to other schools on his route. When

Chip and Joe left Cornell in the fall of 1969 Tommy spread the word along his route that Chip and Joe had run off with funds. With Chip and Joe gone, Tommy was the region's only regular traveler. In fact, "by that time Tommy was probably the only regional traveler left in America," according to a Buffalo activist.

Apparently aware that traveling as an S.D.S. regional traveler made him rather conspicuous in the absence of an S.D.S. region, Tommy tried offering his network to a new radical client in the fall of 1969. He began showing up at the Buffalo office of Newsreel, the radical documentary filmmakers near the University of Buffalo campus. Tommy knew some of the Newsreel people from S.D.S. activities and told them he'd like to take some films around to campuses in his region, places like Plattsburgh, Keuka, Hobart, and the community colleges Newsreel hadn't reached before, and use the films as organizing tools.

"He always wanted someone from Newsreel to travel with him to these campuses to show the films—to give him legitimacy, I guess. He was always pressing real hard about going down to Hobart—'Nothing's going on there now,' he'd say; 'we can get something heavy going.'" And of course Tommy rushed to assure the Newsreel people that despite his straight appearance, he was a Third World person, not a pig.

The Newsreel people never really trusted Tommy, but lacking a network of their own to reach the smaller upstate campuses, they finally began giving Tommy some films to take around and show— even if he was a pig, he was spreading the word—and Tommy had himself a Newsreel network to supplement his fading S.D.S. route. He began introducing himself to new people as a representative of Buffalo Newsreel.

By mid-1969 Tommy had left the Schering Corporation and had begun traveling for the J. A. Webster Company, another veterinary-drug firm. But in December, 1969, something went wrong and Tommy was abruptly fired by J. A. Webster.

The way Tommy told the story to his student friends, he was being persecuted by the F.B.I. There was a long-distance call, Tommy said, from his boss at Webster. He was asked to drive up to company headquarters in Wakefield, near Boston, immediately for a "special sales conference." When he walked into the company offices for the conference, he found no conference at all, just his boss, who asked Tommy to hand over the keys to the company car, and told him he was finished traveling, finished at Webster. Tommy told his student friends he was sure the F.B.I. was behind it.

There may be some truth to that. Neither Tommy nor the F.B.I. will admit that there was anything going on between them. But according to Ontario County Sheriff Ray O. Morrow, who hired Tommy as an undercover narcotics agent, Tommy came "highly recommended" from a higher government agency. "If I were to tell you just one word you'd know what I was talking about," Morrow has said. After Tommy's violent surfacing at Hobart on June 5, 1970, he is said to have applied for a drug-control job in Bucks County and to have used as a reference Geneva's resident F.B.I. agent Jerome O'Hanlon. Tommy's close friend, Detective Simon of the Geneva Police Department, explains Tommy's refusal to talk to the press by saying, "There are other agencies involved here, but he can't talk about them. You can't defend yourself when you're doing undercover work for higher agencies." And according to a report of a Special Grand Jury which investigated the events at Hobart:

". . . Tongyai testified at length concerning the contact he had with a governmental agency and his interest in furnishing such agency with information of subversive activities. During this period of time, Tongyai was a sales representative for a large drug corporation in a territory covering western New York State. This position facilitated his ability to travel about western New York State and to establish and maintain relationships with various persons on college campuses in this area."

The Grand Jury report never identifies the "government agency" and has sealed the details of Tommy's testimony about his relationship to that agency.

Did the F.B.I. get Tommy's boss to fire him from J. A. Webster because his activities were proving embarrassing to the Bureau? Was the F.B.I. itself Tommy's boss? Was he fired for not producing enough, or was he dropped because he was in danger of exposure as an agent? Or did Webster fire him merely because he wasn't selling enough veterinary drugs while peddling his S.D.S. line? It's impossible to be sure.

Whatever went on in the shadowy background behind Tommy's traveling route, a change came over him in late 1969 and early 1970, about the time of the firing. He was no longer the wide-ranging traveler. He settled down in Geneva for some hard selling, door-to-door in fact, at Hobart College.

His task was not easy, for something strange had happened within the Hobart community that year. The campus was swept by a wave of sensitivity-training sessions: a series of seventy-two-hour, one-room, one-weekend marathons, an experience shared in groups by almost all Hobart students. "People were all suddenly on an internal trip, and Tommy's politics were so external, so unreal, you know, all rhetoric and empty inside, that no one could take him around. It wasn't that we thought he was a pig, but a lot of us had seen inside each other and knew what was inside, while with Tommy you got the idea he had only one dimension to show." (Bruce Davis)

Although disappointed, even embittered, by the way Hobart's "internal trip" had shut him out, Tommy persisted. In the fall of 1969 he appeared on campus just as school opened, and proceeded to stuff leaflets advertising the Weatherman "Days of Rage" action ("We are going to Chicago to kick ass") into the orientation kit distributed to all Hobart's freshmen. Later that fall he went around trying to recruit volunteers for the new Venceremos Brigade. He asked Sally Gilmour to set up a women's liberation group at William Smith, Hobart's coordinate college, "to radicalize the chicks there." He asked John Kitagawa, a Japanese student, to join with him in forming an Asian-American group of "Third World radicals." He told a meeting of two hundred Hobart students that Weatherman was going down to Washington to blow up the South Vietnamese Embassy "whether they like it or not," and of course told them about the X's and the O's when he came back. While sitting around in Slattery's bar in downtown Geneva, Tommy tried to convince a group of nurses from the local nursing school to go out on strike from their hospital jobs and demand abolition of curfews at the nursing school.

But Tommy had bigger things in mind for Hobart. Late in 1969 it was announced that the area's hawkish Congressman Samuel Stratton was to speak at Hobart on January 15, 1970. Students began planning a protest for Stratton's visit.

"He came up to my room for just the second time that fall," Rafael Martinez remembers. "He told me, 'Stratton's coming, Stratton's a pig,' and that we could capitalize on this and 'create a heavy scene.' He told me he could get people from Cornell, Rochester, and Syracuse to come down and help, 'if the action was heavy enough.' He told me, 'We have the equipment to lock up Stratton inside Albright auditorium with the people inside. I've got a heavy chain that could be used to lock the doors.' He wanted to keep Stratton locked in for a couple of days. He said we could even kidnap him, get him out while the other people are still locked in the auditorium. 'Think what this will create, this will be the first time a congressman has been kept captive. This will give us national and international publicity.' "

When Rafael declined, Tommy approached a group of students planning a protest at Stratton's speech and detailed his imprisonment idea. Tommy had other suggestions for them, including rolling his defused grenade down the aisle toward Stratton while he was speaking, as a "piece of guerrilla theater." He even tossed out to them the idea of kidnapping the congressman.

When the protest group rejected Tommy's ideas, Tommy was enraged. He called their attitude "liberal bullshit." He said Hobart students were a bunch of rich kids who would never stop talking and act. He concluded in disgust that "Hobart isn't worth getting arrested at."

The first time Tommy actually displayed a bomb to Hobart students had been back in February, 1969, when he drove Clarence Youngs and Mark Smeraldi to a snowy field outside Geneva to practice firing Tommy's M-1 rifle.

"He told us when the revolution came to the school and it was time for seizing buildings we would have to know how to use guns."

The three of them practiced shooting the ancient M-1 at icicles, with Tommy hitting "maybe one in five," according to Smeraldi.

"The gun was no good, you could fire it fast, but it was the most unsound thing I've ever had the misfortunate of getting hold of."

Perhaps dismayed by his gun's inadequacy Tommy brought a surprise out of the trunk of his car: a green Phisohex-soap squeeze-bottle topped with a stiff red fuse and filled, Tommy said, with black powder.

"He'd put this big bottle down in the snow and light it, then we'd truck off to see what happened. Nothing happened. The fuse went out but Tommy was kind of like nervous and jittery wandering around. I don't know. I still figured he was in S.D.S.—to be that much of an asshole he had to be." (Smeraldi)

Perhaps because of this embarrassingly inauspicious debut Tommy didn't talk much about bombs or bombing until the fall of 1969 when he entered his Black Powder Period.

Tommy began asking Smeraldi to join him in blowing up a U.S. Army recruiting trailer parked in a lot in downtown Geneva, using Tommy's Phisohex bomb.

Mark declined but, he says, "In order to get Tommy out of our hair for a while," he agreed to accompany Tommy on a late-night expedition to paste a "Fuck the Army" poster on the trailer. It wasn't actually a bombing but Tommy was excited by the idea.

"Every time I've ever done anything like this with Tommy, he was alway uptight. He was really paranoid. It wasn't even illegal putting up that poster, but as we're walking down toward the parking lot he was very nervous, really speeding his ass off, he was like hiding behind cars—a car would come into the parking lot and Tommy would crouch down and hide.

"He really got such an adrenaline rush after we did it, he started talking about it as if we'd bombed it, it was really odd, he'd say, 'Boy, would it be great to be sittin' in Slattery's just drinking and hear it go B O O M.' "

Late in the fall of 1969 Tommy invited a black student at Hobart, Kenneth Gilbert, to his house, and offered to teach him how to use guns. He is reported also to have offered to show Gilbert how to use black powder or supply him with black-powder bombs.

In late January, 1970, on the eve of a speech by Dave Dellinger of the Chicago 8, Tommy approached Bruce Davis and Peter Keenan of Hobart, and told them that someone should bomb a building or set off a bomb in the quadrangle to let Dellinger know "something's really happening here." He offered to supply bombs, but got no takers.

In March, 1970, Tommy entered Peter Keenan's room. He had grown a moustache and his sideburns were longer. He was carrying a Phisohex bottle with a fuse stuck in it. Tommy said it was filled with gunpowder and asked Keenan, and Bruce Davis who was also present, if they wanted to "take some action" on the anti-R.O.T.C. issue then building on campus. Peter Keenan recalls that not much more than ten days passed before Tommy approached him again, and asked him again about taking action on R.O.T.C. "He told me that after it was over he could get me out of the country because he knew the underground."

About that time Tommy entered Bruce Davis's room while Davis was alone, carrying a fused Phisohex bottle in one hand and a smoking fuse in the other.

"It was just after that West Eleventh Street explosion, and I freaked and told him to get out," Davis recalls.

In April, 1970, during Hobart's official academic moratorium, Tommy approached Clarence Youngs and asked him if he'd like to explode some dynamite at a school-wide meeting in Bristol gym. The meeting had been called to discuss nothing more inflammatory than curriculum changes, but Tommy told Clarence the students "had to show the faculty they were serious about things."

According to Clarence, Tommy offered to bring some small charges of dynamite to place under the stands at a few spots in the gym.

"He said that would be enough to shake everybody up, and that it wouldn't kill too many people."

When Clarence asked Tommy why he didn't do all the bombing he wanted himself, Tommy replied, "It's your school, I'm not a student here, so it's not my job to do things for you, you've got to do it yourself."

Meanwhile Keuka College, Tommy's old haunt, was having its first real demonstration ever that April—a sit-in to demand a black-studies program—and Tommy was on the scene.

"He walks into the sit-in, wearing this safari jacket and holding his hand out; there was a piece of cloth wrapped around it and he said he had cut it earlier pulling out the pin of a grenade." (Lisa Feinberg)

After this dramatic entrance Tommy proceeded to "borrow" a projector from the college and show two Newsreel films, and to explain that he had come to Keuka to show the girls the proper technique for running a demonstration.

"When we wanted to know what he meant, he told us the only proper way to get things done would be to blow the campus into the lake, to start with the President's house and the Administration Building." (Buffy Roche)

Two students said Tommy walked around, saying the only way to do things was to blow things up. He had a line he'd repeat about the revolution and violence—"just a line as if his mind wasn't there," reminding one of them of a Fuller brush salesman. (Lisa Feinberg, Jane Van Fleet)

Finally the sit-in leaders asked Tommy to leave and stop disrupting their protest. Tommy stood and argued with them. "He encouraged us to blow up Hegeman Hall and said he'd give us the matches." The Keuka girls laughed at him. But Tommy hung around the sit-in for the next twenty-four hours "mostly playing cards and trying to pick us up," one girl recalls. His favorite card game was two-handed "War."

At one point during the Keuka sit-in Tommy met Clarence Youngs, who was visiting from Hobart, and asked him if he wanted to help the Keuka girls by blowing up the President's house for them. Tommy told Clarence he could be back with dynamite and powder in ten minutes if he was interested. Clarence wasn't.

But it wasn't long after these disappointments that Tommy's moment arrived at Hobart. Hobart's first big student protest began its two-week run on April 16, when forty students occupied the lobby of Sherrill Hall outside the locked offices of Hobart's Air Force R.O.T.C. program. The sit-in demanded an immediate end to the R.O.T.C. program which then involved twelve students. After only four and one-half hours, when the Hobart Administration promised to bring the question before an emergency faculty meeting to be held that week, the first sit-in was called off.

Tommy was very busy during the next two weeks. First he visited Mark Smeraldi and, according to Smeraldi, said he thought it would be a good idea to set off a bomb during the emergency faculty meeting. "Tommy said it would be a good thing to raise the level of tension around here." Smeraldi turned him down.

"But he came down to the room later and he was talking about this and that type of bomb—he wanted to burn some gunpowder and mix it with some shit to see if it would make a better bomb— he was a pretty haphazard scientist—anyway, my roommate had a Triumph bike and there was some chainlube in a spray can in the room, so Tommy said, 'Hey, let's mix it up and see if it flashes higher.' He had it in an ashtray and I told him to take it out in the hall. So he did it in the hallway. There was gunpowder and chainlube and alcohol, he was mixing a lot of stuff, the whole place smelled of sulfur. After that he thought it was a pretty funny deal so he took out this flare gun he had and shot off a few flares." (Smeraldi)

Later, Tommy finally persuaded Smeraldi to go with him to set off one of his Phisohex bombs on campus to raise the level of tension: "He just wanted some huge tremendous explosion so everyone would be uptight and more radical or something. I don't know how his mind works.

"We went out walking—this is another case where he's scared shit too—he's got another smaller Phisohex bottle, and we must have walked two miles looking for the right place. He kept saying this place wasn't cool and that place wasn't cool—too many people here, you know . . . so we finally did it out in the empty lot between Sherrill and Superdorm, we used a cigarette fuse and we were sitting up in the dorm in the window and two cats walked out to this car about five feet away and there's this huge flash, a lot of smoke and absolutely no noise. These poor guys who were going out to their cars must have been pretty wrecked at the time because they were saying to each other, 'I didn't do that, did you do that?' "

About this time, apparently dissatisfied with the performance of the Phisohex bomb, Tommy approached John Gilmour, Sally's brother and one of his closest friends. According to Gilmour, Tommy asked him if he knew anything about explosives, and told him he would get him explosives if he would make them into a bomb for Tommy. Gilmour asked Tommy what kind of bomb he wanted. "Plastic," said Tommy. Gilmour didn't continue the conversation.

On the evening of April 18 Tommy approached Kathy Venturino, a secretary in the R.O.T.C. office. Apparently because some students had told him she was sympathetic to the sit-in, Tommy treated her as if she were an undercover agent for "his," that is the students', side. He asked her where the R.O.T.C. files were located and asked her if he could borrow the keys to the R.O.T.C. office one night. He told Kathy he wanted to remove the files so they could be "messed up" because the sit-in hadn't accomplished anything.

"He told me, 'If you give me the keys I'll give you anything you want.' I asked what that meant. He said, 'I've got a hundred dollars.' When I said no he kept asking me questions—he asked me if I knew anyone on campus who knew how to make bombs, he said he had the materials for them and he could get guns too." (Kathy Venturino)

Meanwhile the Hobart faculty, meeting in emergency session, approved a compromise which called for phasing out R.O.T.C. by June, 1971. The compromise split the student body. The more radical group, demanding a more immediate end to R.O.T.C., began a second sit-in on the ground floor of Sherrill Hall. Tommy showed up for this second, more radical sit-in remarkably well-equipped. He brought with him three walkie-talkies, several Newsreel films, and an N.L.F. flag which he proceeded to hang up inside the windows of the lobby. The flag, Tommy explained, "would get everyone pissed off and the only way to get people to do things is to get them pissed off." As for the walkie-talkies, Tommy explained that in the event another building or two—such as the Administration Building—were to be seized, it would be a good idea for the leaders in all buildings to be in communication. He even led expeditions out to "reconnoiter" the quad and test out his walkie-talkie network.

Tommy told people he looked forward to naming the liberated buildings after Che, Malcolm X, Huey Newton, and other heroes of the Third World. But he soon became impatient with the slow place of the second sit-in, which lasted four days. "He was going around from group to group really excited and speeded up, telling us that we ought to break the door down, get in, and rip the place up." (Ilan Awerbuch)

Finally some of the radicals and the leadership of the sit-in (including Clarence Youngs and Rafael Martinez) became so fed up with Tommy, his walkie-talkies, and his constant talk of violence they decided he had to be expelled from the sit-in (the moderate Hobart Student Association had already voted to bar Tommy from the campus). Over Tommy's shouted protests the students at the sit-in voted to kick him out.

"This isn't a revolutionary action. This is counterrevolutionary," Tommy declared as he left.

Shortly thereafter Tommy encountered another rejection. He

asked Sally Gilmour if she wanted to help him bomb the R.O.T.C. office. When she declined Tommy told her bitterly, "Okay. Forget it. You're just like the rest of them," and walked off.

But when the second sit-in came to an end on April 24 without succeeding in speeding up the compromise plan for gradual phase out of R.O.T.C., there were still enough students left unsatisfied to give Tommy one last chance.

The fire-bombing was first proposed two days later, Sunday night, April 26, at a meeting in Greg Shepperd's room in Sherrill Hall. With the exception of the three-room R.O.T.C. office on the ground floor, Sherrill was a dormitory for freshmen, and Shepperd's room was just one floor above the office to be fire-bombed. Present at the meeting were five freshmen and Tommy. Four of the freshmen were surprised to see Tommy there, since they hardly knew him personally, hadn't spoken to him during the sit-in, and hadn't known he was going to be present that night. Friday, when the sit-in broke up inconclusively, the sit-in people agreed they should all break up into small groups over the next weekend and talk over what had been accomplished and what hadn't—a legacy perhaps of Hobart's encounter-group phase. The five freshmen—Ilan Awerbuch, Gary Bennett, Gilbert Dillon, Neil Himelein, and Greg Shepperd—all personal friends, decided informally to get together Sunday night. Tommy arrived with Gary Bennett.

The Sunday-night meeting began with a discussion of how the freshmen might continue to harass the R.O.T.C. office to pressure it to leave the campus sooner than June, 1971.

"We went in there and our suggestions were things like continual phone calling of the office, tying up the lines, forcing them to take them off the hook or something. Then Tommy started talking about how we should take the files. He said we could break a window and slip in. He said he'd get a station wagon and bring it around and we could dump them in the back and throw them in the lake, or else take them into a field and burn them." (Neil Himelein)

Not all the freshmen wanted to go that far. "We were talking about doing something symbolic to show that the issue wasn't dead, but then Tommy got into black powder and fire-bombing." (Ilan Awerbuch)

The conversation leaped from taking the files out and burning them to burning them *in* the office.

"I think the talk was about fire bombs, but I really can't remember who brought it up first, but I remember he was, Tom was, the first one to mention black powder." (Neil Himelein)

Suddenly in the middle of this discussion Tommy took out a

long coil of fuse, cut a foot of it off, and stuck a lighted cigarette on one end of it.

"He just kept talking while the cigarette burned down to the fuse. Every once in a while he'd look at it and give us this sly smile. I think it was then he said, 'Let's make this thing a one-shot deal,' and he told us if we wanted to use black powder he could get us some." (Gilbert Dillon)

The cigarette touched off the fuse which flared and sputtered in Tommy's hand. "He told us it was a clever device for a time fuse and if we wanted to set off a bomb with a time fuse it would give us time to get away. . . . And then he opened the windows and aired out the room because there was quite a bit of smoke from the fuse."

Greg Shepperd told Tommy black powder was crazy: Sherrill was primarily a dormitory, their friends would be sleeping in it, and any kind of explosion could bring it down.

The talk returned to gasoline bombs for a while. There was discussion of whether using gasoline bombs they could start a small enough fire to be extinguished easily after the files were burned.

"Tommy finally asked us if we'd prefer gasoline bombs or black powder."

The freshmen weren't ready to make that kind of Either-Or choice, but neither were they able to tell Tommy to drop the whole subject.

"Tommy said he'd take Gary out to the fields Monday and they'd set off home devices and test things out, and let us know afterward. We wouldn't commit ourselves to anything definite. I guess we sort of said, 'If you want to go out and do that, we can't stop you.' We just agreed to meet again Tuesday and talk again." (Ilan Awerbuch)

"There was an empty Clorox bottle in the room and they asked if they could use it for the gasoline tomorrow." (Neil Himelein)

The way Tommy tells the story of the Sunday-night meeting, however, is that he was there to try to *prevent* violence. In his testimony to the Special Grand Jury investigating the incident, Tommy admits that he proposed black-powder bombing to the students. But he insists that this was only a "technique" to divert them from fire-bombing. According to Tommy's story, the freshmen at the Sunday-night meeting were talking about fire-bombing from the outset, and he first tried to divert them by suggesting that they steal the R.O.T.C. files and dump them in the lake. But Tommy says the freshmen rejected this as "Mickey Mouse" and continued to talk about fire-bombing. In order to avoid losing his status as one of the boys, Tommy escalated his "diversionary" proposals: "So I told them, you know, 'Rather than fire-bomb,' I said, 'how about black powder?' Black powder was something you could always throw at somebody because if you get them waiting for something and it never comes it dies out."

That is, Tommy told the Grand Jury, he wanted to persuade the freshmen to plan on using black powder, because while gasoline was very accessible, they would have to depend on him to get black powder—he had an explosives permit and they didn't—and he could delay them until they lost interest in bombing.

When the Grand Jury questioned Tommy about whether this tactic of fighting fire bombs with black powder was a good way to reduce the possibility of violence, Tommy spoke of past success with the tactic:

". . . I have used this to divert bombings in the past, the same technique. . . . People could get hurt. I just—a normal thing I think anybody . . . in this room [the Grand Jury chamber] would do the same thing if they had the opportunity and ability to divert a bombing, you know."

On the Monday night after the Sunday meeting Ilan ran into Tommy by chance at the Keuka College snack bar. Tommy told him excitedly about experiments he and Gary had conducted that afternoon, setting off black-powder and gasoline bombs in the clay fields west of Keuka.

"He told me the R.O.T.C. building was gonna 'blow sky high,' " Ilan remembers.

Ilan had been under the impression that the bomb-testing was supposed to come up with a less devastating device. He began thinking about dropping the whole project. So did Gil Dillon. Neil Himelein decided not to show up at the Tuesday meeting because of a scheduling conflict and because he really didn't want to be involved: the group had talked about scheduling whatever action they took for Friday night, May 1, when most people would be out of the dorm attending a spring weekend rock concert. Since his girl friend was coming to visit him spring weekend, Neil decided to drop out entirely.

The final meeting before the fire-bombing took place in secrecy late Tuesday night at Odell Pond, behind the William Smith campus. The four freshmen met Tommy in front of the log-cabin shelter on the edge of the pond. "Where's the tall kid?" Tommy snapped at them. They told him about Neil's decision.

"Now this is no time to drop out," Tommy told the others.

"He didn't say it like a warning. It was more like we were letting him down when he needed us, it kind of put us on the spot, made us feel bad about thinking of dropping out." (Ilan Awerbuch)

Then Tommy and Gary described the results of their bomb-testing the day before: "They said they had set them off by firing Tommy's M-1 rifle. Gary told us that one black-powder explosion had showered both of them with rocks and dirt and they had tried some Molotovs and one almost blew up in his hand." (Gilbert Dillon)

Tommy conceded they could do some more testing Wednesday and meet again Thursday night, but he insisted that they get everything straight, including a timetable, meeting places, and plan of approach, then and there at Odell Pond. He talked in commando terms about attacking the R.O.T.C. office with squadrons from the front and rear, and the necessity for synchronizing watches.

When his freshmen protégés asked why a timetable was so urgent Tommy told them he was planning to leave for New Haven for the big Panther demonstration on May Day weekend and he just wouldn't be able to be around for the actual fire-bombing.

"But he said he wanted to get everything straight, make sure everything was taken care of before he left, so like he wouldn't have to worry about us screwing it up or letting him down when he was gone." (Ilan Awerbuch)

Tommy didn't get his synchronized timetable that night, and two of the four freshmen dropped out of the entire scheme as soon as the Odell Pond meeting broke up. But the other two didn't let Tommy down this time.

At four A.M. Friday morning three Molotov cocktails smashed through the windows of the R.O.T.C. office in Sherrill Hall. Only one of the three worked. As soon as they had thrown the bottles Gary and Greg ran around inside Sherrill to pull the four fire alarms in the building. Three of them wouldn't work. (It was discovered later that their fuses were missing.) Students put out the fire with extinguishers before the fire department arrived, and there were no injuries.

Three hours later Geneva police picked up Gary and Greg in their rooms and took them to the station. The detectives who questioned them that morning boasted openly that they knew every detail of the plan, every meeting, everyone else who attended, and what went on. The only thing that surprised them, said the detectives, was the *day* of the bombing. They told the two suspects that if they had done it Friday night as they originally planned, "we'd have been waiting there for you."

Later the detectives brought in Mr. Jerome O'Hanlon and introduced the F.B.I. man to Gary and Greg. They were told and were advised to cooperate with the Geneva police unless they wanted the Bureau to step in.

That weekend Tommy appeared, out of the blue, at a big dance at tiny Canandaigua Community College twenty miles from Geneva. Scott Chiverton and his wife (friends of both Tommy and Gary Bennett) were surprised to see that Tommy had shaved off the moustache and the sideburns. He was in a talkative mood that night, although he was not completely pleased with the way the fire-bombing had come off:

"He told us Bennett was stupid because he bombed the R.O.T.C. building a day early and didn't give Tommy enough time to get out of Geneva, and that Bennett was also stupid because he used the wrong kind of bottle. He used wine bottles and Tommy was highly perturbed about that. He said that he told them to use milk bottles because they break easier. Then I asked him about the fuses missing from the fire-alarm boxes. He wasn't saying anything about that, but he left me with the impression he had something to do with it but he didn't want to stick his neck out and tell me." (Scott Chiverton)

Greg Shepperd and Gary Bennett, both twenty years old as this is being written, are serving six- and eight-month terms, respectively, in the Ontario County jail, after pleading guilty to reduced charges. The judge in their case refused to allow youthful-offender pleas because he "wanted everything out in the open."

As for Tommy's role in the fire-bombing, the Special State Grand Jury called by Governor Rockefeller to investigate the Hobart blowup heard sworn testimony from almost everyone named here about Tommy's activities on the Hobart campus.

The Grand Jury did not indict Tommy for anything. However, on the basis of sealed testimony by Tommy, County Sheriff Ray O. Morrow, and presumably F.B.I. agent Jerome O'Hanlon, the Grand Jury issued the following criticism of Tommy:

"On or about April 25, 1970, Deputy Tongyai learned in the course of his duties as a Deputy Sheriff that certain persons were conspiring to commit the crime of arson first degree in the City of Geneva, New York. Deputy Tongyai did not report his knowledge of this conspiracy to his superior, Sheriff Ray O. Morrow, but reported the same to a member of another investigative body whose action to avert the proposed arson was unsuccessful. This Grand Jury finds that the failure of Deputy Tongyai to report his knowledge directly and immediately to his superior law officer constitutes neglect in office."

Both former F.B.I. agent O'Hanlon and the F.B.I. itself have refused to make any comment about Tommy's relationship to the F.B.I.

On the morning of the fire-bombing arrests, Hobart student Rafael Martinez saw Tommy in the parking lot of the Geneva police station, which gave him reason to suspect Tommy had something to do with the arrests. Rafael told other students what he saw and suspected, and when Tommy next ventured on campus, May 6, he began getting hostile reactions.

He saw Sally Gilmour, whom he considered his friend, and asked her, "Why don't the kids want me here?"

"Because you're a pig."

"What do you mean? How do you know that? Me a pig?" Tommy laughed incredulously.

"I told him that Rafael had seen him at the police station that morning," Sally recalls, "and Tommy said he wasn't there for the police station but to go across the street to Jones's restaurant for coffee."

In the middle of his talk with Sally, Tommy suddenly spotted Rafael and began shouting at him:

"You're calling *me* a pig, Rafael, ask the students. They know *you're* the pig, you liar." There were more words and Tommy finally lost control, lunged at Rafael, swinging his fist and yelling, "Watch your ass, I'll kill you, you pig," managing to hit a Hobart dean who had tried to step between them. Rafael then went to the police and swore out a warrant against "John Doe a/k/a Thom Thomas" for harassment, and Tommy chose not to set foot on Hobart territory again until June 5.

This blowup with Rafael put Tommy's job as an undercover narcotics agent for the county in peril. County Sheriff Ray Morrow had hired Tommy in March when Morrow was under great pressure from Geneva townspeople to take some action on the drug scene at Hobart before the students left for the summer, and Tommy's mission—for which he was given the code name "Maxwell Smart" and paid $2.17 per hour—was to get evidence for search warrants and big-dealer arrests. Tommy must have seemed like the perfect agent for Morrow; he didn't have to establish a cover or contacts of his own, he already had a network of drug-using friends he could deliver to the sheriff. But for those next two months Tommy was too busy dabbling in black powder to pay much attention to drugs for the sheriff. After the fire-bombing and the incident with Rafael, Tommy's access to Hobart was cut off, and the sheriff—under more anti-Hobart pressure than ever—may have advised Tommy to come up with something soon, or both their jobs would be in danger.

So one night in May, Tommy leaned over to two Geneva girls he was drinking with in a Seneca Street bar filled with Hobart students, announced that he wanted to score some dope, and enlisted their help. The two Geneva girls scouted the bar and came upon a Hobart student they knew and asked him if he knew any dope connections. As the bartender tells the story: "This Hobart dude, Vinnie, wasn't a dealer and didn't even know the dealers on campus—it would take him three hours to score an ounce himself—but he's short of cash and wants to do some *drinking* that night. Tommy bought him some drinks and he scouts up a nickel bag and says he wants $5 for it to drink with." (David Wethey)

The girls served as his intermediaries, and Tommy had the goods on a big Hobart dope dealer for Sheriff Morrow.

At one A.M. the morning of June 5, Tommy led a squadron of sheriff's men to Vinnie's room in Rees Hall, marched through the door, and told him—one salesman to another—"Vinnie, you know that dope you sold me? It was shitty stuff, man." Vinnie was then arrested and taken away.

The other room busted on Tommy's information was the room frequented by his friend Mark Smeraldi. Smeraldi and his roommates had moved elsewhere on the floor so that this room could be converted to a common living room called "the open room."

"The open room was the kind of thing where you just left dope out on the table for anyone, you just came in and smoked whatever was there, we were all friends, so it didn't matter." (Mark Smeraldi)

By the time Tommy, with Detective Bill Simon, returned to the patrol car in the parking lot outside Rees Hall, a large crowd of his Hobart friends had gathered in the area. After Tommy and Simon got in the car, the students surrounded it. In time there was a crowd of three hundred students, and it was rough inside the car. There were faces pressed against all the windows, shouting "PIG," "PIG," at Tommy, who was in the front seat. Students on the hood pounded fists at the faces behind the windshield, students banged and stamped on the roof just over their heads. Once when Simon, in the driver's seat, opened his window to negotiate with the crowd which was demanding the release of the five students arrested that night, someone came up to his window and spit across Simon at Tommy. Tommy lunged violently across Simon toward the window, but Simon restrained him. Eventually Simon decided to try to continue negotiating elsewhere, rolled up his window tight, got out, and locked the door behind him, leaving Tommy alone in a glass cage.

Tommy was alone inside the locked patrol car for two hours. The pounding at his face continued. New arrivals pushed their way through the crowd and around to Tommy's side of the car chanting PIG and KILL THE PIG—Tommy's very own lines—in his face. Tommy tried to face straight forward and look as if he saw right through the faces pressed against the windshield. But suddenly a powerful flashlight beam glared into his eyes from the windshield, blinding him. Tommy turned away but the beam followed his eyes back and forth, tormenting him as the pounding and chanting picked up.

Finally Tommy responded. With elaborate deliberate gestures he held open the left lapel of his suit jacket with one hand, revealing the large pistol he carried beneath the tweed. Rafael Martinez remembers seeing Tommy take the gun in his hand and then return it to its conspicuous concealment inside his jacket.

At that point, several students, including Rafael and Bruce Davis, began urging the crowd to stay calm and not press too close to Tommy's gun. The remaining time spent waiting for a settlement to be negotiated was more a vigil than a riot. Students chatted with policemen in the other cars of the raiding party, and the cops left the doors and windows of their cars open and walked around unhindered. But Tommy kept his doors locked, windows shut, and stared straight ahead for the duration. Occasionally he would take a notebook out and make a show of writing down names.

Sheriff Morrow's reputation in Geneva suffered from the "deal" that was made between students and police that night. Geneva police in full riot gear were on the scene ready to wade into the crowd of students and free Tommy and the other trapped officers. But all sides feared stumbling into another Kent State, and a deal was negotiated—by Rafael Martinez and Tim Taylor for the students, by the Dean and President for the College, and by Sheriff Morrow, the Assistant Chief County Detective Anthony L. Cecere, the Geneva Police Chief, and Detective Simon for the drug raiders.

According to the written agreement, all students arrested that night were to be given amnesty, the evidence collected in the room searches was to be destroyed, and no further prosecution attempted. The final student demand was that Tommy himself must be placed under arrest on the spot as the John Doe in Rafael's John Doe warrant. In return, the students permitted Tommy to leave his glass cage, enter a functioning patrol car, and drive off untouched.

Jubilant Hobart students skipped hand in hand in the wake of the departing patrol car singing, "Good-bye Tommy," and hopefully waving him out of their lives. At first it did appear to be a splendid victory: the only arrest produced by Tommy's spectacular surfacing was his own.

Six days later the Geneva police—humiliated and vilified for permitting students to run wild and dictate orders and laws to them—arrested six students and one faculty member on riot and obstruction charges. Six months later the Special and Extraordinary Grand Jury called by the Governor indicted six students and one faculty member on riot, coercion, and criminal facilitation charges; three students on drug charges; and one college, Hobart, on charges of coercion.

Among the students indicted by the Extraordinary Grand Jury are some of Tommy's closest associates from his traveling days: Melanie Wallace who left *The Idiot* in his car back in early 1968 when the young exiled prince was just becoming "radicalized"; Clarence Youngs who turned down several bombing offers from Tommy and finally drove him off when Tommy tossed his favorite hand grenade at Melanie Wallace; Gilbert Dillon who witnessed Tommy's seduction of Gary Bennett and Greg Shepperd into the bombing scheme; Rafael Martinez, the radical pacifist who suspected Tommy but failed to convince the Hobart students (Rafael, after all, was over thirty and not as easily trusted); and Bruce Davis, one of Tommy's original contacts at Hobart, who thought that Tommy's "external trip" was just too one-dimensional, "too screwed up" to be a conscious disguise.

Tommy's traveling in recent months has been limited to trips from Jones's restaurant (now called Perry's) around the corner to the police station, down the street to Pinky's Restaurant, a hard-hat place, and over to Hessney's Family Shoe Store. The Geneva police night shift gets off at eight A.M., so when Tommy enters Perry's restaurant he's sure of finding a couple of the night-shift guys having home fries and eggs in the back booth, relaxing until the kids get sent off to school and they can go home to sleep. By nine o'clock when the night-shift guys are yawning and stretching out of the booth, a couple of the department's detectives will wander into Perry's to join Tommy in the back booth for coffee, setting their squawk boxes down beside them to keep in touch. They may not stay long but by nine thirty Detective Bill Simon has opened up his real-estate office and has left his secretary in charge while he goes around the corner to have a coffee or two with Tommy at Perry's.

As for Mr. Hessney, owner of the shoe store, he is a big admirer of Tommy's. When Tommy was arraigned last August on a charge of defrauding the state by collecting unemployment compensation while also collecting a salary from the sheriff, Mr. Hessney and a few of his friends raised the $1,000 bail in a matter of minutes, just in time to save Tommy—who happened to be genuinely unemployed at the time and couldn't raise it himself—from jail.

Mr. Hessney is one of the many people in Geneva who look upon Tommy as a local Nathan Hale, or at least as a Benedict Arnold for the right side. Before he stopped talking to the press, Tommy would occasionally deliver lines about the number of Communists he had discovered on the Hobart faculty and about the threat to America posed by Hobart College students. Such lines pleased some Geneva citizens whose names were listed in an ad for an anti-Hobart demonstration at Hobart's Commencement that June, pleased veterans' organizations and service clubs in Geneva. Tommy began to get dozens of fan letters in the Geneva *Times*. One of them read:

". . . Tommy, a most polite, gracious, respectable young man, hunts, fishes, golfs, and skis with the many friends he has made among several of the very best young family men in our city. Dinner parties house to house, birthday parties for all their children, home movies made and shown, and other good wholesome recreations highlight some of his family life. . . .

THANK YOU, GOD, FOR TOMMY, and please don't lose the pattern."

Last winter there was even talk—and not just idle talk in Pinky's —of running Tommy against Sheriff Morrow when he comes up for reelection.

For a time last fall Tommy drove his two-tone Cougar convertible twenty miles over to Canandaigua where he had enrolled as a student of police science in the Community College of the Finger Lakes. Every Wednesday from one to three thirty Tommy attended two courses, Penal Law and Law of Evidence, taught by Mr. Jerome O'Hanlon, the man who was once Geneva's F.B.I. agent. A fellow student of Tommy's describes O'Hanlon's courses as "an attempt to explain how the good guys become good and how the bad guys went bad." A local newspaper highlighted Tommy's achievement in police science last winter by running his photo with an announcement that his grades were B+ and B.

The only thing that shadows Tom Tongyai's happiness now is his recent plea of guilty to the charge of collecting unemployment checks while working undercover for the sheriff. The plea may prejudice his chances of getting the police job he dreams of for the future. "My first love is for police work," he said when he left the courtroom after being sentenced to one year's probation, "but

if anyone needs a good clerk or a good salesman now, I'm available." Meanwhile Tommy drinks coffee at Perry's with off-duty
detectives and listens in to the police network over their squawk
boxes. Or he crosses the street to the police station and listens
to the big radio inside the station house itself, when he's not in
the way.

TROY DONAHUE WAS ALWAYS JUST LIKE HE IS

Chaucer's oily, wheedling Pardoner, that prototype of the traveling salesman in English literature, specialized in selling redemption and holy relics. If the fourteenth century is the "distant mirror" of our time as Barbara Tuchman suggests, it is not surprising that the seventies' salesman should also specialize in filling some common craving for those two commodities.

In this story we encounter two promoters trotting around a holy relic of the fifties to promote a Charles Manson movie they claim will offer purgative redemption from the sins of the sixties, and make them a big bundle in the seventies. They graciously offered me the opportunity to buy some stock in their production company and get in on the ground floor, a bribe that was fairly easy to resist since their movie was heading rapidly from ground floor to subbasement both aesthetically and financially.

After the story was published I received three interesting reactions. A porno-film producer called me to say that his *Charles Manson movie was real and "sincere," and that he was planning a "relevant treatment of other sixties things," such as a soon-to-be-released epic he was calling* Vietnam: War and Sex.

Then a representative of the Mel Lyman family called. The Lyman family was a group of East Coast urban communes who believed that their leader Mel, a former jug-band player, was God, and who were said to indulge in authoritarian internal practices with disquieting resemblances to Manson family life. I had dinner with them. They said they were glad I recognized that neither Troy Donahue nor Charles

*Manson was in the image of God. Then they forced me to
listen to their God's new jug-band record before they allowed
me to leave.*

*Finally, I got a call from the press agent who is a chief
character in the story, the one who offered me the hot stock
tip. Apparently unperturbed by his portrait in the story, he
told me he had another hot story for me: "a talented young
actress who would do anything to get her name in print, and
I mean anything." When I declined the privilege he tried to
sell me the stock again.*

Why interview Troy Donahue anyway?

"Believe me, you won't believe Troy when you see him," the
press agent tells me. "He's a bearded hippie! And believe me, *he
is fantastic in this picture.* He plays Charles Manson! Actually we
can't call him Charles Manson because of the legal thing, but it's
the Charles Manson story. Troy is this sex- and drug-crazed Jesus-
type cult leader of a hippie commune who kills a pregnant actress
and her Hollywood friends. You see the parallel? This is going to
be a very big picture. I have a feeling this is going to be bigger
than *Love Story.*"

And if that's not enough, the press agent offers another entice-
ment. "Listen we'll take you to lunch with Troy at the Top of the
Sixes. You'll like the Top of the Sixes. They have steaks and sea-
food. Do you like steak?" The press agent sets a date for the Top
of the Sixes and promises to send me Troy's "bio." He tells me I
will recognize him, the agent, "because I wear wild shirts and wide
ties. But I guarantee you won't recognize Troy."

From the *Biography of Troy Donahue* received special delivery the
next day: "Troy Donahue returns to the screen as Moon, the
passion-possessed leader of a vengeful hippie cult . . . in this
poignant, moving drama which is inspired by the awesome series
of events surrounding the Sharon Tate murder case and other
related wanton killings of this decade."

Enclosed with the bio is a newspaper story headlined "Troy
Donahue Now Bearded Hippie." The story features before and
after photos of Troy, showing him as sunny angelic Sandy Win-
field II of Warner Brothers' *Surfside 6* and then as sullen demonic
"Moon." A note from the press agent attached to the story states:
"This Associated Press story on the 'new' Troy Donahue appeared
not only in the Sunday *New Jersey Bergen Record* but in countless
other major Sunday newspapers in the nation."

* * *

Troy is dressed in white. White sneakers, white Levis, white T-shirt, white Levi jacket. A silver crucifix and some other trinkets hang from a chain around his neck. Troy is a large man and his white clothes look a little too small for him, as if he doesn't want to admit he has put on weight. He looks like those one-time slim and healthy California surfers who grow older, grow paunchy—and maybe a little punchy too—and turn into bikers or dopers or both. There are gray hairs scattered through Troy's blond beard, and tiny red crinkles of visible veins on his cheeks. Troy is thirty-five.

I'll never forget Troy's first words to me, when he stepped over his motorcycle helmet to greet me at his table at the Top of the Sixes. This is a literal transcription: "Hey brother. Dig the scene. Dig the scene. Wow man. Dig the scene."

If I had any doubts left that Troy was in fact a bearded hippie, he set them at rest when he twisted the conventional handshake I had offered into an interesting version of the Movement "power" grip, and concluded the greeting by saying, "Yeah. Dig the scene." Just us hippies together.

Well, there were two others waiting at Troy's table in addition to us hippies. There was the press agent, in a wild shirt and a wide tie, and Bob Roberts, the producer of *Sweet Savior*, Troy's Charles Manson movie.

"Don't sit next to them," Troy told me. "Sit over here next to me so we can really rap."

When I am seated and turn to Troy, I find we are looking into each other's eyes. The heavy gaze continues in silence until Troy breaks it off, and nods slowly. "Yeah. Right," he says with finality.

We begin to talk about Charles Manson. "I knew the dude," Troy tells me. "I used to play volleyball with him on the beach at L.A. years ago. He had short hair back then, but even then he was very big with the chicks."

"What was his secret?" I asked.

"It was his cock," says Troy.

"His cock?"

"His cock."

Before I could ask Troy for more details the press agent interrupts: "Of course the film is not completely about Charles Manson. We have Troy there at the scene to commit the murder himself while Manson didn't do it himself. We rented a whole mansion in Teaneck, New Jersey, for the murder scene. The script was written by a Pulitzer prize winner, although under a pseudonym. Troy's performance is going to shock people. I think it's an Oscar performance although the Academy would never have the guts to give it to him."

Troy talks about his role: "It was a bad scene, man," says Troy to me. "It was real. You know, but it was dirty. I felt dirty, man, evil. But it had to be done. But it's real. Death is real. Wow. Down there just a few blocks away they killed, what's his name, Joe Columbo. That's heavy. It's funny. Sitting here and talking when it's so real out there. Last night I'm with this black girl in a bar. Beautiful girl, and I'm sitting next to her just wanting to get my cock into her, and she turns to me and says, 'You know the guy who killed Columbo is black. You know what that means.' That's heavy man. That's real."

"I would make a prediction right now," producer Bob Roberts declares in the silence that follows. "I would predict there would be more murders. This Manson thing will be just the beginning. This movie is not about an isolated incident, it's about what's to come. And there *will* be more murders."

The press agent looks over at me nervously, then back at the producer: "Bob, maybe you shouldn't predict murders. Maybe you should change that to tragedies." He turns to me. "Say that Bob feels that this is a movie about a tragedy which may not, let's see, which may not be the last of its kind."

"But I think there will be *murders* too," says Bob a little disconsolately. "I'm willing to be quoted as predicting murders."

"I just don't think it's a good idea," says the press agent.

"Shut up! You don't know anything," Troy tells the press agent.

"That's nice," the press agent says with some dignity. There is an embarrassed silence at the table.

"Oh hey man, I'm just kidding. Here." Troy reaches for the press agent's hand, takes it into a firm "power" grip, looks him in the eye. "Brothers. Right?" The press agent nods dubiously.

Troy gets back on the subject of Charles Manson and begins explaining how Manson either was or wasn't just like Hitler. "So I said to David Frost, I said, 'Did Hitler do it? I mean did he? He didn't. Man, Hitler didn't do it. You know what I mean?' And Frost looks at me and says, 'He didn't do it?' And I said, 'No man, he didn't do it, did he?' It blew Frost's mind. All he could say was, 'He *didn't* do it?' "

Troy looks at me. "But the thing is he really *did* do it. Can you dig it? He *did* do it."

"Do what?" I asked.

"I think it's more than Hitler," said the producer before Troy can respond. "It's not just Hitler. It's the beautiful people."

"Right on," says Troy softly.

"The beautiful people," repeats the producer. "I don't want people to get the idea this is an antihippie movie, because it really portrays the degeneracy and depravity of the beautiful people as well as the hippies. That whole Hollywood scene."

"That's right man," says Troy. "I know that scene. I've been there. It's these people man. It's a thrill to cruise the Strip and pick up some groovy looking hippies and take them home and play with them. Play with them. You know what I mean. Games, dig it. People playing with people. That's what they were all into. I was there when it happened."

"You were *there?*"

"I wasn't there in person, but I was *there*. You dig it. I was there. We were all there."

"I'll tell you one thing," says the press agent, breaking in on Troy's reverie. "This movie is going to polarize. I mean that. It's going to polarize this country. That's why it's going to be so big. I would not be surprised if it isn't bigger than *Love Story* and one reason will be because of this polarization."

Troy is still there. "I was there. You were there. We were all there," he tells us. "I was sitting just a few yards down in the canyon when it happened. I could feel it happen. It was like a warning."

I asked Troy if it was hard on him personally trying to play Charles Manson on screen. "No man. I'm just an actor."

"Wait till you see his performance. It's an Oscar winner," said the press agent.

But how had he been able to get into the Manson part? Had he done acid? "I took acid man. I took acid and I met the Man. I met the *Man*. And the Man said cool it."

"Cool it?"

"Cool it. That's what he said. I was with these doctors, and . . . now you know some people take two hundred fifty, three hundred fifty mikes and play around and think they did acid. But I did acid. I was with these doctors in Miami and I was standing by this metal railing watching the ocean and all of a sudden there was a thunderstorm, man, like the end of the world. And lightning, man. So I'm holding on and this lightning hits the railing, comes right along to me and right through me. I should have been fried, man. Then I knew. Cool it. That's what the Man was saying. Cool it."

"Troy's still big with the women though," the producer interjects. "I don't know how he does it. Have you got that set up with the girl in the hotel, Troy, this afternoon? You do, don't you? I don't know how he keeps going."

Troy points to his crotch and grins. "The day I stop going here is the day I stop going. Going to see [a black singer] tonight. Wow."

The press agent takes out some glossy pictures. There is Troy in shoulder length hair, parted blond beard, and black leather jacket leaning familiarly on the shoulder of a stout pregnant woman.

"She plays the Sharon Tate type," the press agent explains. "And the amazing thing is she was really pregnant during the shooting. Isn't that something?"

He takes out another glossy and there's Troy in a shot from one of his Warner Brothers-Connie Stevens movies, a blond wave in his neatly parted hair, wearing a neat sweater and sportshirt. "And here's Troy before. You could use these as before and after pictures."

"Yeah, but that's bullshit," says Troy. "That 'before and after' thing is bullshit. I was always the way I am now. See that picture of me with my hands in my pockets, looking so clean-cut? You know what I've got in my pocket? You know what?"

I shake my head no.

Troy gives me a sly look, puts two fingers up to his mouth, and takes an imaginary drag on an imaginary joint. "You know what I'm talking about now? That's right," he says with satisfaction.

Our conversation is interrupted by three elderly ladies who have come over from a nearby table to ask for Troy's autograph.

"I can't believe it. The women still recognize him everywhere," the press agent says.

Troy flirts graciously with the ladies who say they want the autographs for their nieces and granddaughters. When they leave to return to their table, Troy turns to me. "Crazy. Aren't they great. Wow. Look at those heavy legs." He smacks his lips. "Wouldn't you like to mow their lawns?"

"Troy, you have a two thirty appointment at that hotel, don't you? I don't believe this guy and his women."

Troy wants to finish explaining how there was never any before and after. "I was always like this, man. All I want in life is maybe three drinks and like half a joint"—he takes another drag from his imaginary joint—"and then I hop on my bike and I'm off. That's the real Troy Donahue, you know. It's because I'm spontaneous. Spontaneous, man. I'm so spontaneous I could cry. Sometimes I go to movies and just cry. Listen, have you got any more questions? Anything else you want to know?"

"What about that crucifix you're wearing around your neck," I ask him. "How much does it mean to you?"

"Listen man, I'm not into any cults or anything. I don't believe in cults. Look, it's not just the crucifix. That's for my Man, but

I've also got this Hebrew letter here, it's a Hebrew symbol. I don't know what it stands for but it's good to have. Then I've got this little Buddha figure here and, dig this, he's got one ear missing which is very heavy. You know what that means, don't you? Then this thing here, this is just a piece of junk to remind me of the junk in the world."

Troy gets up to leave. He picks up his motorcycle helmet and takes out of it a shiny white package which had been stuffed inside. "You want to see junk. Look at this. Somebody up at the Warner Brothers promo office laid this on me."

He hands me a package which turns out to be a white T-shirt with three bright red roses emblazoned on the front. Superimposed over the roses in large jolly letters is the word "JUNK." Below that are the words "Dusty and Sweets McGee," the title of Warner Brother's newly released junkie movie.

"You can have that if you want," Troy tells me.

I thank Troy but decline.

"Well, I'm off on my cycle now, man. Wish I had one of these" —he takes a final drag on his imaginary joint. "Listen, are you really gonna write this up? You really are. Wow. You know if you do, you know that before and after shit—it's been done before man. It's not me. I was always just like I am, man."

"Troy is a fantastic guy, isn't he?" says the press agent after Troy leaves.

"Troy is a fantastic guy to work with," says the producer. "I was amazed. He was on time for everything; he's signed for two more pictures with me. In the next one he's playing a Weatherman leader in a picture called *The Weathermen.* Then in '72 there's another big one called *The Lucifer Cell.* It's about a Chinese Communist invasion of the U.S. that succeeds. Troy is an underground resistance fighter."

"The whole thing's going to be very big. This picture. Listen," says the press agent, "one thing you might want to mention in your story is that the company that's distributing this picture is a publicly owned company. It's traded over the counter. That's kind of interesting, you know, you might want to work that into the story when you mention that Trans-World Attractions Corporation is producing and distributing Troy's movie. You know. That it's publicly owned. Something like that. I'll tell you it's only selling for maybe a buck a share now, right Bob? But when this picture is released. . . . Of course it wouldn't be ethical for me to tell you to buy. . . ."

"But I could tell him, couldn't I?" chuckled the producer.

* * *

A young sweet-faced girl wearing a black robe and a large silver crucifix stops me on the sidewalk outside 666 Fifth Avenue (see Revelations 13:18 about that). In a spacey voice the girl asks if I would like to help the work of a group called The Process, the Church of the Final Judgment. The girl hands me a slip of paper on which the address of the Church of the Final Judgment has been typed. The slip is decorated with the head of Jesus and the horned head of the devil. The girl explains: "We believe each of us has both Christ *and* Satan within us. We believe that we must acknowledge that Satan is in us. Then we can begin to love Satan the way Christ loves, and Satan will be transformed."

The girl, who says she is an acolyte of the Church of the Final Judgment, points to a passage in a booklet explaining "The Process": "Through Love Christ and Satan have destroyed their enmity and have come together for the End; Christ to Judge, Satan to Execute the Judgment." The explanation of The Process continues later with an interesting universal law: "Anything we give, whether positive or negative, will be returned to us in full measure."

I accept the pamphlet from the girl and buy a more detailed book about The Process from her. As she is digging around in her tote bag for change, I notice a familiar shiny white package sticking out. I ask her about it. "Oh, some guy came along a little while ago and gave it to me. I didn't really want it, but he didn't stop to ask whether I did or not."

The girl takes it out. It is Troy's "Junk" T-shirt. She is young enough and sweet-looking enough to have been one of the girls in my junior high school who mooned over Troy a decade ago.

"Did you know that was Troy Donahue who gave it to you?" I asked.

"I don't know. It was just this tall guy with a bike helmet who looked like he was in a hurry. Who is Troy Donahue? Look, would you like it? I really have no need for it."

I have the "Junk" T-shirt now.

TALES OF THE HEARTBREAK BIZ

For some reason hard-sell sales pitches for charitable causes often arouse even more skepticism than those for simple commercial products. One of the shapes assumed by Melville's shadowy Confidence Man is that of the solicitor for the "Seminole Widow and Orphan Asylum." When a fellow passenger questions the existence of this alleged charitable institution, the solicitor merely avers that the institution was "but recently founded."

By doing so little to combat skepticism, that Confidence Man challenges the passengers to prove the strength of their charity and faith over mere rational skepticism.

Most of the admen for disease charities in this story cheerfully confess to being con men, manipulators of mass instincts, and good at it. Their openness about their methods raises a different question about charity: how far should we encourage charities to con us into being good? Are we genuinely good if we're tricked into giving? Does it matter to the beneficiaries of charities how their illnesses are merchandised?

What surprised me in rereading this story was the incredible detail the admen were willing to go into about the concepts and technique of their charity campaigns.

Never before or since had I gotten that much cooperation from admen. Of course, as admen with hearts of gold, there was a desire to impress me with their charitable virtue, but in equal measure there was a sheer delight in showing off their artistic virtuosity. Most of the admen I've encountered are brilliant craftsmen, if not artists, who are frequently discouraged by big-paying clients from disclosing to reporters

the complex process of calculation that goes into the creation
of every single slogan. But most admen do disease work for
free; they don't lose anything if a charity fires them, so they
can dissect the details of their disease campaigns with all the
professional pride they are forced to suppress when they
discuss detergents.

The admen who have taken over the Kidney Foundation account
have a problem. "We joke about it in the agency, we say the
kidney-disease account is a pisser. But kidney disease is not
glamorous," Herb Fried tells me. "It's not like heart disease, you
know, beautiful, THE HEART," Herb says with a gesture. "And
it's not even like cancer which is—*you* know . . . Kidney disease
is—you know, you think of *urinating*."

The problem is that kidney disease just "doesn't have the quote
glamour unquote of these other diseases," Herb adds with a hint
of scorn for glamour diseases.

But that's not the only problem.

There's a minor organ-donor problem, according to Herb's
partner on the Kidney account, Sy Davis. "We've got people,
they're waiting for people to die to get transplants, and we get
most of our organ donations from automobile accidents—"

"Motorcycle accidents especially," says Herb.

"Anyway," says Sy, "because of the fuel crisis there have been
fewer accidents and therefore less donors."

A bigger problem: Herb and his partner Sy of the Davis Fried
Krieger agency are trying to launch a brand-new kidney-disease
campaign and they've run into some trouble over their key sixty-
second TV commercial. They've filmed a sweaty simulated boxing
match, featuring a fighter in dark trunks delivering a crippling
"kidney punch" to a game young heavyweight who spends most
of the remaining fifty seconds collapsing in agony, writhing on the
canvas, lunging desperately for the ropes and—with the last of his
strength—trying to pull himself up again.

"We're running into some flak with that one," Sy tells me, "flak
from one major network."

He and Herb and J. Hamlin Day of the Kidney Foundation are
reluctant to talk about the flak. But it seems that certain TV-con-
nected censors are concerned that the commercial will teach young
kids the crippling value of a kidney punch, thereby increasing the
incidence of kidney damage in street scuffles.

Flak, too, from boxing organizations, who call the ruthless

detailing of the fighter's kidney-damage collapse unfair to the image of the sport.

Sy is concerned. "Some people don't understand that the idea of this commercial is to be symbolical. . . . When people think of kidney they think of peeing. That's why we had to take this symbolic approach," he says.

Time is running out. It is mid-March, and March is Kidney Month. February was Heart and April will be Cancer. The Advertising Council *Public Service Advertising Bulletin* coordinates a horrorscope of months for organs and organisms so that door-to-door campaigns don't get jammed up. Of course there are more organs and organisms than there are months. Some diseases only get weeks. It was a big step up for Kidney Disease when it was officially given March. But it's already the third week in March and the brand-new "symbolical" kidney commercial has yet to get full network approval. On April 1, TV program directors who choose the public-service ads will start concentrating on Cancer. When a disease's own particular month comes to an end it faces stiff competition from every other disease in the book for the remaining scraps of donated and unsold time, none of it prime.

This is not the first time a kidney-disease campaign has run into controversy. In fact, it was the key slogan of an earlier kidney-disease campaign that first aroused my curiosity about the whole complex business of advertising for diseases.

KIDNEY DISEASE, went that slogan, IT'S NOT JUST ANOTHER CHARITY. IT'S THE FOURTH MAJOR CAUSE OF DEATH IN THE COUNTRY.

There's an implication there, I thought when I first saw that slogan on a subway ad panel two years ago, an implication in those four words NOT JUST ANOTHER CHARITY.

Are some diseases "just other charities"? Which ones? Are some worthy causes more worthy than other worthy causes? Are some getting more than their fair share?

The subway panel ad seemed to back up the implication. A dramatic bar chart of the top twenty charities showed Cancer and Heart were Numbers One and Two, with more than $40,000,000 apiece in 1970. Down near the bottom line was Kidney Disease, Number Nineteen, with only $2,600,000. Far above Kidney on the chart was Muscular Dystrophy, which doesn't kill nearly the number of people as THE FOURTH MAJOR CAUSE OF DEATH IN THE COUNTRY. Also far ahead of Kidney were such charities as Planned Parenthood, Retarded Children, and Nursing Care, none of which are MAJOR CAUSES OF DEATH.

The Kidney Foundation comes off as a scrappy underdog in the ad, boldly challenging the deadwood on the money chart for a place up there with the big killers. There was an Avis-like quality about the ad, I thought.

A visit with Paul Margulies and Michael Ulick, the copywriter/art director team at Wells Rich Greene that created the NOT JUST ANOTHER CHARITY slogan.

I ask them how they came up with that particular line.

"We knew we had an image problem with kidney disease," copywriter Margulies tells me. "It's not romantic, it doesn't have recognition like heart and cancer. . . . In fact, one of the first lines we thought of went something like, 'When we say kidney, is the first thing that comes into your mind a swimming pool?' "

After deciding against the "swimming pool" approach, Margulies and Ulick spent hours sitting around trying out other slogans.

"Each time we looked at a line we said, well, it's okay, but it makes Kidney sound like every other charity," Margulies tells me.

Then, the moment of discovery: "Michael finally said, 'Goddamnit, *it's not just another charity*.' And we knew that had to be part of the line."

I ask them if the other part of the line, the part about Kidney Disease being the Number Four killer but only Number Nineteen in donations, was a play on the Avis theme, the underdog going against the goliaths.

"Well, I guess there is an underdog appeal to it," says Margulies. "But Avis never occurred to me until now. No. If anything, the line is a play on 'not just another pretty face.' "

It was not until after he'd come up with the slogan that Ulick discovered it wasn't just another disease. "The amazing thing is, it wasn't till the middle of the campaign I realized that it was a kidney disease my father died of. . . ."

"You see, Ron, there are twenty-six kinds of kidney disease, a lot with different names, and eleven are fatal," Margulies says.

"You know, Paul, I never fully agreed with you on saying 'Major Cause of Death,' " Ulick tells Margulies. "I wanted to make it stronger. I wanted to say 'Fourth Largest *Killer*.' I sort of like 'killer.' "

"Yes, Michael, but saying 'Fourth Largest *Killer*' made it sound like a plague," Margulies replies. "And when you say 'killer' you think of automobile accidents, things like that. I admit 'Major Cause of Death' may sound a little grand, but sometimes in pomposity there is strength."

They revive another old argument: whether to say FOURTH

MAJOR CAUSE OF DEATH *IN AMERICA* or *IN THE COUNTRY*.

IN THE COUNTRY beat out IN AMERICA because "when I hear 'in America' I see a picture of a flag and when I hear 'Country' it's neutral, it's just geography," Margulies explains. "We didn't want overtones of patriotism. We were appealing not to Americans but to human beings."

The trouble started halfway through the campaign. It didn't come from the JUST ANOTHER CHARITY slogan so much as from the TV commercials to which the slogan was a punch line.

Margulies and Ulick take me into a screening room at Wells Rich Greene and show me a reel of two years of kidney-disease TV commercials.

The first three had been done by the agency before Margulies and Ulick took on the Kidney account. The first three had not set the charity world on fire.

Number one shows door after door slamming shut in the faces of actors representing Kidney Fund volunteers, each door slam accompanied by a patently insincere, barely civil "I-gave-at-the-office" type excuse.

The conception was brilliant: rob the potential door slammer of his defenses by picturing him as a rude, heartless swine; make the Kidney Foundation fund raiser *himself* a kind of victim—the heartbreak of slamming doors—make the potential door slammer give money in order to avoid inflicting further damage to the door-slammed psyche of the volunteer.

"Too negative," Margulies sighed. "We thought it was good but the people out in the local Kidney Foundation affiliates didn't like the negative image."

Kidney commercial number two shows a loud-voiced fast-talking huckster type manipulating a hand puppet, proffering crackling handfuls of cellophane-wrapped candy, and in general being abrasive. The spot concludes with the obnoxious guy suddenly talking straight to our hearts and revealing that kidney disease is so serious and kidney patients need money so badly that "if we have to sell candy to save lives we'll do it." Don't make us degrade ourselves, the spot said. Don't make us degrade *you*. But we will. The threat of more and more abrasive, bad-taste commercials was the muscle behind the pitch.

Some of the local Kidney affiliates were not pleased with this image either. It was a clever Madison Avenue *parody* of a hard sell, but it was such a good parody that it sounded just like another hard sell to some people.

Kidney commercial number three is pure upbeat stuff. A hearty middle-aged salt, looking fresh from grabbing all the gusto he could get in a Schlitz commercial, stands on the bow of what looks like a tugboat and talks about the perfectly normal life he's had since his kidney-transplant operation. The pitch is for organ donations.

"They liked that one," Margulies said, "but we had some problems because you can only use actors to represent victims under certain conditions and . . . But look, the next three are the ones Michael and I did."

The first is also an organ-donor commercial, but it's not sunny and upbeat. It's a classic of the heartbreak genre.

Open upon a cemetery in the rain. A grainy shot of a man trudging past rain-streaked headstones, holding a black umbrella above him, and clutching a bouquet of flowers protectively to his chest.

In shaken tones the voice-over explains how one year ago he was close to death because of kidney failure, how a young girl who died in an automobile accident provided him with the kidney that saved his life.

He stops at a plain unadorned grave marker. He kneels and carefully places the bouquet upon it, gets up, and turns to us.

"This is *her* grave," he says, and trudges away.

It works. My chest aches and my tear ducts throb, but somehow it feels good and I'm ready to sign an organ-donor card on the spot. Not till much later did I realize the clever strategy of this ad. I'm welling up with tears of gratitude for my own generosity. As viewer, and potential organ donor, I am like the dead girl, but unlike the dead girl I get to see the rewards of organ donation before I die. I get to see that organ donors are almost *guaranteed* devotion and love after death—a kind of immortality not limited to their kidneys. So watching the gravestone commercial becomes something like receiving a posthumous award before one dies. I was sold. The next time I saw an organ-donor card I signed it. (It happened to be in Sy and Herb's office. I had Sy and Herb sign the card as my two witnesses.)

"That was something. That really worked," I told Margulies and Ulick in the Wells Rich Greene screening room.

"Never saw the light of day," says Margulies dejectedly.

He launches into an attack on the "double standard" of restrictions placed on advertisers by the F.C.C., the F.T.C., Nader's Raiders, and all the other enemies of advertising.

"They pulled that double-standard shit on us with our cemetery spot," he says. "Too morbid, they said. A lot of stations wouldn't run it, some of the Kidney Foundation local affiliates wouldn't take it."

(There was also some problem with the spot because, traditionally, organ recipients are discouraged from finding out who gave them their organs.)

"And what about that color number they pulled on us?" says Ulick bitterly. "We purposely shot it in black and white. We wanted to have a period-film look like *The Last Picture Show* . . . we even shot it at sixteen, blew it up to thirty-five to get it grainy, to make it more real, and you know the reaction we got?"

"What?" I said.

"They refused to run it. They said the film was bad. They thought the quality was substandard. What can you do?"

"How about the Charlton Heston thing?" says Margulies.

"Show him the 'Empty Chair' spot first," says Ulick.

The Empty Chair spot shows a sound stage set up for filming, with an empty chair in the middle of the set. For sixty seconds workmen are shown progressively dismantling the set, carting off the props, finally folding up the empty chair itself. The voice-over explains that Kidney Disease tried to find a celebrity to sit in that chair and do a celebrity pitch for them, but couldn't find one. A clever twist on the old celebrity pitch, and once again that Avis approach.

"We liked that one because it was in keeping with the underdog image," Margulies says.

But not long after the Empty Chair commercial was completed, the Kidney Foundation signed Charlton Heston to do a celebrity-type commercial for Kidney Disease and the Empty Chair commercial had to go.

"We felt sabotaged," Margulies tells me. "We thought it deserved to be shown. We just hated to see it die."

The whole kidney-campaign experience has left Margulies a bit wounded.

"I feel a lot of pain," he tells me. "We put a lot of energy into coming up with the right kind of campaign, but it's selling the idea after you've killed yourself to come up with it . . ." he sighs.

Thirty blocks downtown, J. Hamlin Day, the public-relations director of the Kidney Foundation, refuses to comment about the ill-starred Margulies-Ulick campaign. Mr. Day is a slow-moving, slow-speaking, pipe-smoking gentleman who only recently changed from Heart to Kidney work. I have the feeling it is the first time he has ever said "No comment," and he seems to savor the words. So much so, he then says, "But off the record . . ." and details some of the reasons the NOT JUST ANOTHER CHARITY campaign was "controversial."

He suggests a "difference in philosophy" has led the Kidney Foundation to switch to the Herb Fried/Sy Davis team and proudly he describes the new kidney-punch campaign they've devised together.

Sy and Herb are more forthcoming about the "difference in philosophy."

"We believe in showing a disease at its worst," Sy tells me. According to Sy, the trouble with the previous kidney campaign was "they had been showing people who had been cured."

Sy cites the tugboat-captain commercial.

Herb cites another commercial, one that I did not recall seeing on the reel at the Wells Rich Greene screening room: "There were problems . . . using a transplant patient—" says Herb.

"Yeah, and that was the girl who died in fact," says Sy.

"There was a commercial of a girl who was supposed to be cured and she died after they made it?" I ask.

"I don't think we should talk about that," says J. Hamlin Day.

A visit with the heartbreak kids. Their names are Alan Kupchick and Enid Futterman.

I first ran across the Kupchick-Futterman combination when I was tracing the creators of the original award-winning Retinitis Pigmentosa campaign. (ONE HUNDRED THOUSAND CHILDREN ARE GOING BLIND FROM A DISEASE YOU NEVER HEARD OF.)

Then I discovered that Alan and Enid were also the creative team for Traffic Death (specifically for "problem-drinker-caused" traffic death). The two of them had become overnight sensations in the heartbreak business with a traffic-death song called *Janie*.

"Janie" sings a McKuenesque rhapsody about her wishes and dreams. "I want to write a novel that will bring the world to tears" is one wish. "I want to see Venice" is one dream. After we hear Janie finish her song, we learn she never made it to Venice.

A solemn voice-over tells us, "Janie died on an endless road in America . . . killed by a lonely man who was drunk out of his mind."

Janie was the first traffic-death song to become a big radio hit. Radio stations have played *Janie*, 350,000 times over a six-month period last year. ("And that's just counting the top hundred markets," a Grey Advertising executive tells me.)

The TV commercials that followed—picturing a gauzily romantic Janie running on the beach, and a smiling Janie fondling her first child in a lacy hammock—got about 6,300 minutes of prime-time exposure in six months, and a prime-time minute is the big prize in the public-service advertising business. And even in an industry glutted with awards, the Janie campaign—song and TV commercial—earned Enid and Alan more than two dozen plaques and citations.

And now Enid and Alan have been asked to take on one of the toughest heartbreak chores in the business: promoting the adoption of "hard to place"—meaning nonwhite/white and handicapped/older than three years—orphans. Enid and Alan only handle two product accounts these days: Kool-Aid and No Nonsense Panty Hose.

Enid returned my call first. I asked her if she'd be talking to Alan so that I could interview them together.

"Yes, I think I'll be talking to Alan," Enid told me. "He's my husband."

A bomb scare at 777 Third Avenue. Most of the employees of Grey Advertising, which occupies eleven floors, are hurrying out of the elevators and there are police in the lobby when I arrive for my appointment with Alan and Enid.

"We've had bomb scares before," the receptionist on the tenth floor tells me. She says the informal policy now is that only non-executive personnel absolutely *have* to leave during the bomb scare. Executives can "exercise an option" to stay and work.

Alan and Enid are executives these days and they are staying. They have just been moved up to the tenth floor from the ninth, and one of the reasons they've been moved up is the stacks of plaques piled on the windowsills of Alan's newly painted corner office—most of them are awards for their Janie antideath commercial.

Enid tells Alan she has some misgivings about staying in the building during the bomb scare.

"What difference does it make?" says Alan.

"What do you *mean* what difference does it make?" says Enid.

There *does* seem to be an incongruity for these crusaders against accidental death to take a bomb threat so lightly. They tell their secretary Iva she can go. She does. But Alan says he's got a client coming in from White Plains for an important conference.

"He comes all the way in from White Plains and what am I gonna say to him? I got a bomb scare here?" Alan says, showing a little irritation.

Enid is not convinced. She is a fanatic about safety. She won't *enter* a car that isn't fully equipped with seat belts. She's "positively *insane* about the matter," she says. She hints to Alan she'd like to leave with Iva the secretary.

"Enid," says Alan. "I got a thing now, I got a thing at three thirty. I got a thing at four o'clock—"

"You might not have anything if you're not careful," says Enid. Nevertheless she agrees to stay.

Enid and Alan no longer have the Retinitis Pigmentosa account. They seem somewhat upset about it. Alan and Enid had presided over the birth of a brand-new charity for a no-name disease. Their campaign, done for free, on their own time, had gained Retinitis Pigmentosa enough money, recognition, and credibility to get off the ground and start getting first-rate research done. It's not easy to make that happen in the charity world.

But last year the charity they'd helped create out of nothing switched to another agency.

"We would have liked to have been asked," Alan says. "The first we knew about it was when a close friend of ours at another agency called and said, 'Guess what! I'm doing the Retinitis Pigmentosa account.'

"There was a lot of misunderstanding about how this thing proceeded, and a lot of what they're doing now is coming out of what we did, our tone of voice. . . . But we have no hard feelings," Alan insists. "We were glad to get them moving."

Alan and Enid tell me about their big break with the Traffic Death campaign. There is a touch of *A Star Is Born* to the story.

"The agency was in trouble with the Traffic Death account," Alan says. The client, the U.S. Government Highway Safety Administration, was growing impatient. "They were just potchkying around with different solutions," Alan says.

Then the big break: "So they gave us a crack at it. We took one weekend and did the whole highway-safety campaign and—"

"That was the weekend Alan fell down the elevator shaft," Enid says. "Almost killed himself."

"So we did that," Alan says, glossing over the elevator mishap, "and after we did that we had a relation with the people in Washington who are influential in handing out that business, so I guess, you know, one success built on another."

They are not naive about the reasons for their rise within the agency.

"When they pitch new business here," Alan says, "and a client sees that stuff on the reel and says, 'That's terrific,' you say to a client: 'If you give us your business we'll give you the people who did that ad.' So it's a selling tactic."

Alan leaves for his Kool-Aid account meeting.

Enid gives me a copy of her album of death songs. She's written a dozen death ballads. The Highway Safety Administration has packaged several of them in a bizarre album called *Songs of the Road*, which intersperses Enid's death odes with jovial numbers like *King of the Road* and *Feelin' Groovy*.

The actual deadly crash is always offstage in Enid's songs and commercials. No screeching tires, shattering glass, and wailing ambulance sirens, none of the familiar fixtures of Traffic Death ads of the past.

The government ordered her to keep death offstage, Enid says. Certain British studies of viewer reactions to films of dismembered bodies and other remains of actual car crashes have convinced the Highway Safety Administration that threatening people with death to get them to drive safely may be counterproductive.

"Whether or not this is true, the government believes it and we're just not permitted to portray death in a deathlike way," Enid says.

They found that out when they tried to kill Janie in two alternate endings of the TV commercial.

"The first was just very, very slow motion—so slow it was beautiful—of a car blowing up, tires flying, horrible but . . ."

Then they tried a graveyard scene. "A girl who you thought was Janie at first, walking into a graveyard, and you think it's her, but then she puts the flowers on the grave and the grave says 'Janie.' "

But the government objected to both alternates and, like the kidney donor's gravestone, Janie's gravestone never saw the light of day.

"I'll explain to you how we finally killed her," says Enid of Janie.

"There's all this lovely footage and she's lying in the hammock with her husband and her baby and the baby's all cute and wonderful and the last line Janie sings is, 'I want to dance/I want to love/I want to breathe.' On the word 'breathe,' " Enid says, "the camera freezes on the faces of Janie and her baby, the picture turns black and white, the camera draws back, and we see it's a black-framed photograph on the wall of an empty hallway." The final shot moves further down the end of the hallway to an empty bedroom, and there is a glimpse of an empty bed.

"It's a pretty empty-looking brass bed, of course," Enid says. "And you have the memories of all the things they were doing on the bed. . . ."

* * *

Alan returns from his Kool-Aid meeting.

It was a Kool-Aid commercial which gave birth to the key slogan of their next heartbreak campaign, the "hard-to-place" orphans campaign, Enid tells me.

They were making a Kool-Aid commercial at an orphanage in Mexico. They spent several days there, costuming the orphans, throwing them a party, giving them gifts, serving them Kool-Aid, and filming the whole thing to illustrate Kool-Aid's appeal to children of all nations.

"It was a beautiful experience for me," Enid says. "I felt it was not just another Kool-Aid commercial. Something *else* happened. . . ."

One thing that happened was that Alan and Enid ended up sponsoring twin ten-year-old girls in a kind of absentee foster-parent arrangement with the orphanage.

Months after the Kool-Aid experience, when Alan and Enid were racking their brains to come up with the perfect slogan for the "hard-to-place" adoption campaign, Enid remembered something Alan had said during the Kool-Aid orphanage experience.

"When we sponsored the twins," Enid recalls, "Alan was playing around and I remembered him saying, 'I've just given birth to ten-year-old twins.' "

The final, precisely crafted slogan that arose out of that playful remark is: HAVE A CHILD. IT'S AS BEAUTIFUL AS HAVING A BABY.

The following day, leafing through early scrap-paper drafts in her Adoption Campaign file, Enid comes upon several earlier versions of the same slogan, each of which was just not right for one or more reasons of policy and nuance:

—We Just Had a 10 Year Old Boy.

—Hard to Place and Easy to Love.

—Having a Child Is Not Like Having a Baby. You Get Twice as Much Love as You Give.

—It's Not the Only Way You Can Have a Child. It's the Special Way.

—Don't Have a Baby. Have a Child.

—Nothing Is as Good as Having a Baby. Nothing Is as Good as Having a Child.

—It's as Natural as Having a Natural Child.

—Nothing Is the Same as Adopting a Baby. Nothing Is the Same as Adopting a Child.

—Don't Have a Child. Save One.

—Let a Child Adopt You.

—Adopting a Child Is Just as Beautiful as Having a Baby.

—Adopting a Child Is as Beautiful as Having a Baby.
—Having a Child Is Just as Beautiful as Having a Baby.

The scary thing about this campaign, Enid concedes, is that its results are so measurable. The New York State Committee on Adoption has exactly 2,149 children, some handicapped, some emotionally disturbed, the hardest of the hard-core hard-to-place children, each of them growing harder to place the older he grows. At some time in the future, after the HAVE A CHILD campaign has run awhile, someone somewhere will be able to count how many of those 2,149 are still waiting to be had.

"Yes, I guess it is frightening," Enid says. "It's so easy to measure."

I asked Enid if immersing herself in all this heartbreak work has begun to intrude on her life.

This adoption campaign may be getting to her, she says. "Adopting a child has always been a fantasy of mine. I mean I have trouble with the whole idea of being a mother because on the one hand I'm thirty and I think, 'If I'm gonna have a real one it's gonna have to be soon,' and it's getting real frightening to me," she says. "I mean I have a real conflict. . . . On the one hand I desperately want it and on the other hand I'm terrified and I don't want it at all, and I have all these conflicting dreams and it's really a difficult thing in my life."

Enid has written a new song, *Lullaby for My Brand New Child*, sung by a young mother who has a "hard-to-place" child, but she keeps winning awards for her young-mother death song.

Her husband comes down the hall whistling and strides into Enid's office. "Guess what," he says to Enid. "Just heard from the coast, a telegram from California up in Jim's office. You won that I.B.A. show last night," he tells his wife.

"Really?" Enid says. "Which one?"

"For *Janie*," says Alan. "Won the highest. You got it. The award is on the way."

Adam Hanft and Don Slater have just come back from scouting locations for the new Retinitis Pigmentosa TV commercials. They've settled on the Empire State Building, but it wasn't their first choice.

Retinitis Pigmentosa is an incurable, irreversible degeneration of the retina which leads gradually to tunnel vision and often to blindness. Transmitted genetically, it can leap generations and blind without warning the children of parents with perfect vision.

Adam and Don (who are both vice-presidents for creative

services at the Rosenfeld Sirowitz and Lawson agency) want to do an ad that will capture the heartbreak of a child's last few weeks of sight.

"We're gonna show a father taking his kid up to the Empire State Building, like for the last time," Don says.

"So the kid can see as much as he can before . . .?" I ask.

"The whole world," Adam says, "the vastness of it all."

Don's first choice for location had been the Museum of Natural History.

"The father showing the kid the dinosaurs?" I ask.

"Yes," says Don. "*I wanted that visual.* Boy, I wish we could— but we lost it," he says sorrowfully.

The Museum, he explains, wanted the agency to pay a "prohibitive" amount of money for security and custodial services during a dinosaur filming.

"Disgusting," Don mutters. (Don is known in the trade for his frank-talking abortion-referral ad campaign for Zero Population Growth. Sample slogans: WHEN WAS THE LAST TIME YOU HAD YOUR PERIOD? and THE ALTERNATIVE TO A WIRE COAT HANGER IS 212 — ——. Adam at twenty-three is spoken of with awe around his agency as "the youngest vice-president in the business." Both he and Don have done anti-heroin-program award winners. Adam has also done seals—not Easter Seals, but the endangered species up north.)

The first thing that Adam and Don did when they took on the Retinitis Pigmentosa account was to trim down the name. "Retinitis Pigmentosa" had to go, at least in the headlines. They changed it to "RP," although Retinitis Pigmentosa is still spelled out in the body of the print-ad copy.

"We want to get everything down to 'RP' soon," Adam tells me. "Just to cut it *down*. It's just outrageous. 'Retinitis Pigmentosa' is one of the most outrageous things to try to get anybody to remember. So we sign all our new ads *RP* Foundation . . . so then we have RP. Everybody can remember RP."

Even reduced to RP, selling Retinitis Pigmentosa commercials in what Adam calls "the brute world of television" is no easy job.

"When you talk about hemophilia and RP, you're talking about things that affect a fraction of the population," Adam says. "That's why Mental Health for years said something like mental illness touches nine out of every ten. . . . You don't have that with RP. You have to be competitive, you have to be exciting, you have to separate yourself from everyone else's commercial. Otherwise you end up with your spot running after *Dialing for Dollars. Celebrity Bowling.*"

"That's the name of the game," says Don. "Separate yourself from everyone else."

"What a telethon is—and anyone who tells you different is a fool —is a twenty- or twenty-two-hour-long commercial," Myles Harmon tells me.

Myles Harmon is a free-lance producer of telethons. He's produced other events, but lately he's been specializing in telethons.

Myles hit it big last year, taking over the New York segment of the Second Annual Easter Seal Telethon, and almost doubling the tote-board income of the First Annual. This evening at New York Easter Seal headquarters Myles is working late plotting his strategy for the twenty-two-hour Third Annual, coming up in four nights.

"I went up a hundred percent last year and I hope to be able to bring it up a hundred and fifty percent above last year, this year," Myles says.

Myles tells me some of the techniques of telethon orchestration he uses to wring money and drama from his twenty-two-hour commercial.

"Everybody has a different formula for putting money on a tote board," Myles tells me. "The basis for every telethon is not the phone pledges, much as you need them. You've got to have your nut made ahead of time. You've got to have your advance gift pool."

With his "advance gift pool" (a five-figure sum provided ahead of the telethon by the charity's local affiliates) Myles can exercise some control over the tempo and momentum of his telethon. "When I want increases or changes on the tote board," Myles says, he will use that advance gift pool to "goose the total . . . for dramatic value."

"It's just good dramatic programming," he says. "If I have an important guest coming on I'll do it while he's on because it adds dramatic impact."

Myles outlines the hour-by-hour strategy that's worked for him in telethons past.

"What I try to do is make a substantial increase in the tote board before people go to bed and then I'll keep a steady flow into the tote board throughout the middle of the night so that when people wake up in the morning they'll see there's been a substantial change."

Myles recalls that "at seven thirty in the morning last year I put in a whopper and then another substantial one at ten."

Those morning hours are the slowest hours of any telethon. Up until dawn his momentum is sustained by "telethon freaks," an audience whose peculiar obsession "I haven't quite figured out yet," Myles says.

But from eight to ten A.M. it's hard to find people to man the "Celebrity Phone Panel" and the "V.I.P. Phone Panel," and guests to come on and entertain.

Myles takes out his work sheets for eight A.M. "All I have are the Bic Banana and Mr. Burger King," he says, slightly ruefully. "But then, I've got the circus coming in at eleven."

From there on in until the end at nine P.M. Sunday night, the only thing worrying Myles is that his momentum might diminish when the local station interrupts his telethon to switch away to an exhibition baseball game.

"I'll build that pool during that time because we have to maintain that momentum even though we're off the air. It's a very dangerous thing to drop momentum."

If the ball game doesn't halt his momentum, Myles maintains, the final hours of a telethon are beyond his orchestral control. "The thing takes on a life of its own," he says, recalling last year's windup with wonder. "There are points in the production when it suddenly becomes a living thing. You virtually have no control of it. It just starts to roll like a massive pliable ball and it gathers speed and it carries a lot of good things with it."

And this year Myles hopes to produce more than just another telethon. Yes, he wants to register a hundred and fifty percent jump over last year's hundred percent jump (that would mean more than $800,000 on the New York tote board). But he also wants to leave his mark on the institution of the telethon itself, "to thrust the telethon away from the old images of telethons, from the Jerry Lewis and Cerebral Palsy telethons, away from that appearance of age."

He's calling his twenty-two-hour New York segment "A Festival of Love." He's staging a rock concert from two A.M. till eight the next morning. He's aiming at a younger generation of donors.

And he's going to cut down on tear jerking.

"There will be no hard pitches," he says. "Unless they come from the heart," he adds.

There's always a chance that some well-meaning guest will come up with a spontaneous "hard pitch" from the heart, but it will have to be spontaneous because Myles controls what pitches are printed up for the TelePrompTers and he's only printing "educational and informational ones," he says.

"And this is a hard rule of mine," Myles says. "We don't use children. We don't parade them as some telethons do."

Myles has had "some resistance" to his telethon philosophy, he concedes, but he's hoping the final tote-board figure will vindicate him.

It's seven P.M. Sunday night. The ball game has been over for three hours. With just two hours left on the air, the Easter Seal Telethon, Myles's "Festival of Love," has not "taken on a life of its own."

Quite the opposite. Indications are accumulating that the unthinkable may happen. No telethon ever sinks *below* last year's final total. Maybe it doesn't make this year's *goal*, maybe it doesn't register as *big* an increase as last year, but no telethon ever sinks *below* last year's.

This one is sinking. Last year's figure was $335,000. Myles's personal goal was almost $900,000.

With two hours left to go, the figure on the tote board is only $229,400, and Myles's advance gift pool is nearly exhausted.

Myles is nearly exhausted. He's watching Geraldo Rivera try to get the studio audience to sing *When the Saints Go Marching In* while Geraldo passes the Big Glass Cookie Jar around for dollars.

"Go out there and help him, Paul," Myles says despondently to an assistant emcee. "That's dying too."

Backstage people are getting irritable and wondering what went wrong.

Some people think the choice of Tony Curtis as emcee was not quite right. Tony had never done a telethon before, and his last well-known feature role was *The Boston Strangler*.

A youth who claims he raised $1,700 from a just-completed seventeen-hour dance marathon in Nassau is staggering around demanding that the winners' names be announced on TV.

The manager of a dance troupe is demanding that his act—canceled to make room for more direct appeals for phone pledges—be reinstated.

In the pledge-totalizing-and-verifying room an Easter Seal woman named Faith is gazing coldly at a thousand-dollar phone pledge a "hot-line hostess" has just rushed to her. (The rule is that all pledges over $25 must be verified by phone before they can be fed into the tote board.)

Faith seems to recognize the names on the pledge.

"*They'll* never make good on a thousand dollars to save their souls," says Faith.

Even Mr. Burger King is irritated. He has been waiting in the wings in his cumbersome Burger King costume for ten hours, since his early-morning appearance with the Bic Banana. He knows he's supposed to make one final presentation but he can't find out when.

The Bic Banana is puzzled. She doesn't know whether her father wants her to go on with Mr. Burger King for this final presentation or whether she's through with her banana costume for the night.

The father of the Bic Banana is Mr. Ron Shaw, national sales manager of Bic Pen Corporation, and he's out on the set now answering a phone on the "Celebrity Phone Panel."

Ron Shaw is the man who arranged the Bic Banana/Mr. Burger King/Easter Seals liaison. Before Bic, Ron Shaw was a Miami Beach nightclub comic. He used to do stand-up routines and pitches on the earliest Cerebral Palsy telethons down there, way back in the mid-fifties.

"I still do some of my old nightclub routines at sales-promotion conventions," he told me earlier in the evening.

And now he's figured out a way of doing sales promotion at telethons. He's dreamed up a complex promotional/charitable triple play for the Easter Seal Telethon. Here's how it works.

Bic sells 42,000 "Bic Clics" (with "Telethon '74" and the Easter Seal logo stamped on them) to the Easter Seal Society for ten cents apiece. ("They wholesale for twenty-two and a half cents each," Shaw says.) Easter Seals in turn gives them to Burger King, which offers them to the public for a 49-cent donation each. Burger King then donates the money to the Easter Seal Society.

Thus Bic gets Burger King to sell Bic Clics for Bic, thereby thinning down Bic's top-of-the-line inventory. Burger King gets promotional value from having Mr. Burger King on camera to make presentations to Easter Seals. Bic, needless to say, gets the same from the appearance of the Bic Banana and her father.

And Easter Seals, according to Ron Shaw, gets $20,000 if Burger King sells all 42,000 Bic Clics.

Forty-five minutes left to go. The figures on the tote board still haven't gone over $300,000. I'm standing out of camera range next to the row of seven crippled children in wheelchairs and braces who are lined up in front of the studio audience facing the tote board.

More and more frequently the celebrities, the satellite emcees, and Tony are "working" the kids: going over to the wheelchair lineup with a guest and letting the visible misfortune of the kids pump the pledges up.

"We don't show the parts that are left," says the woman standing next to me.

I recognize her as the advertising lady for the local Easter Seal chapter. She handled the phone next to mine when a shortage of celebrities about four in the morning caused us both to be pressed into service on the "Celebrity Phone Panel." I recall that while I was dealing with someone calling himself "The Prince of Gypsies of Newark," she was dealing with an obscene call.

She has been up all twenty-two hours and speaks in a tight-lipped rage. "The parts left," she repeats. "We don't show what these kids can do with the parts that are left of their twisted bodies. We don't show what Easter Seal does with what's left of their twisted bodies. These kids do art. They do hooked rugs, they do painting with their feet and toes."

She nods at the lineup of wheelchair kids. "But instead of showing that, we just have them sit there and look like twisted bodies."

With twenty-five minutes left the total is $275,790, still $60,000 below last year. The big question now is not whether the "Festival of Love" will fail to exceed last year's total, but by how much will it fail.

On camera things are getting flaky and frantic. Someone hands Tony a crumpled brown paper shopping bag. It's a big shopping bag with frayed twine handles, the kind in which old ladies in subways carry all their possessions.

"And here we have a little cheese from American Airlines for the kids," Tony announces, reading from a note he has been handed.

On cue the Telethon Band plays *S'Wonderful*. The studio audience applauds politely, and the camera follows Tony as he walks the shopping bag over to the line of kids in wheelchairs and braces. Something inside the bag rattles.

Tony reaches into the bag and comes out with a strange looking object. It is one of those gray crocks—a mini-crock actually—the kind that's usually filled with some processed cheddar cheese spread of the Wispride variety.

But unfortunately it's also one of those crocks with a maddening steel handle-and-lever apparatus sealing it.

Tony goes down the line of wheelchair kids—this particular group has been lined up almost three hours now—and hands them each a crock of cheese.

By the time Tony hands the last wheelchair kid her crock he can see that the first two kids in line have run into trouble trying to open theirs.

Tony returns to the first kid in the wheelchair line, takes the crock from him, and tries to pry it open for him. He gets nowhere. He gives it a twist. Nothing. Quickly Tony passes it back to the kid and flees to the tote board with the camera in pursuit.

For the remaining fifteen minutes of the telethon, Tony, Murray the K, and Mason Reese line up in front of the tote board begging for pledges, trying desperately to equal last year's mark. Meanwhile, the seven wheelchair kids are applying themselves to the mysterious crocks. They twist them, turn them, pry at them, pull at them, hand them back and forth among themselves. Some try to wrench the entire steel-wire apparatus off. Others try to slip the ceramic lid out from underneath the steel handle. The girl on the end, who has made the most determined attack, has succeeded only in pulling a rubber washer halfway out from underneath the lid of the crock from which it hangs uselessly. She is puzzling over what to do next.

At eight fifty-eight Tony announces the final pledge total: $310,000. About $25,000 *below* last year.

The "Festival of Love" goes off the air at nine. The parents of the wheelchair kids come on the set to wheel their children off. Each kid still has his crock. And the Wispride—or whatever it is—remains sealed within.

SECRETS OF THE LITTLE BLUE BOX

Since the statutory limitation has expired I can confess that during my travels in the invisible kingdom of the phone phreaks, I was in possession of one of those magical—and illegal—"little blue boxes." The one I had was designed to be sold to big-volume bookies at a retail price of $1,000—a price they would easily recoup with the limitless undetectable free calls they could make to odds-makers and bettors across the country.

It's hard to describe the excitement, exhilaration, the fever that overcomes you when you walk into a mild-mannered phone booth and transform yourself into Super Operator, the nervous system of the world at your command.

It's not merely the subversive pleasure of making unlimited free calls, it's the ability to make connections *that gives the little device its incredible appeal.*

Big volume buyers of blue boxes tended to be found in certain characteristically seventies subcultures: rock promoters, dope dealers, rolling-paper moguls, and the like (the only charge mega-salesman Bernie Cornfield ever was convicted of in the U.S. was possession and use of a blue box). A blue box permitted them to become remote-control traveling salesmen, letting their fingers do the walking on the blue-box buttons.

But the hard-core phone phreaks, the ones like the legendary "Captain Crunch," are more obsessed with the esthetics of connection making and the thrill of the chase than with salesmanship. For a time it seemed as if the phone phreaks might turn out to be the only successful revolutionary group to survive the seventies without working within the system. (They played *within the system.)*

Yet the phone company never ceased stalking these electronic con men, and the outcome of the continuing battle is still in doubt. Since this story was published the phone phreaks have achieved some spectacular victories. They've slipped into the White House phone system and awakened Richard Nixon from Watergate-troubled sleep with a four A.M. phone call. They've interrupted astronauts in midorbit and invented successor devices to the blue box, including the "red box," which effectively imitates the sound of coins dropping into a pay phone.

But there have been reverses. Captain Crunch has been arrested several times for his flamboyant exploits. Phone-company undercover security men try to play blind phone phreaks off against each other by turning some into informants with threats. And phone-company technology has been grinding away, devising special computer programs to sniff out patterns of blue-box activity, and accelerating its massive switch to all-electronic switching stations which, the phone company says, will frustrate phone phreaks for good. The phreaks say it isn't so.

My story revealed only a few of the frequency combinations that produced the magic twelve tones that put the phone system at one's command. In the years that followed its publication I've received a continuing stream of letters from potential phone phreaks seeking the remaining combinations. For those seeking such information, please don't write or call me (I've had to keep my own phone number unlisted ever since). The most up-to-date information on the phone-phreak underworld can be obtained from a newsletter called T.A.P. (152 W. 42 Street, Rm. 204, New York, N.Y. 10036). The editor of T.A.P. says his name is Alexander Graham Bell.

THE BLUE BOX IS INTRODUCED: ITS QUALITIES ARE REMARKED

I am in the expensively furnished living room of Al Gilbertson*, the creator of the "blue box." Gilbertson is holding one of his shiny black-and-silver "blue boxes" comfortably in the palm of his hand, pointing out the thirteen little red push buttons sticking up from the console. He is dancing his fingers over the buttons,

---

* His real name has been changed.

tapping out discordant beeping electronic jingles. He is trying to explain to me how his little blue box does nothing less than place the entire telephone system of the world, satellites, cables, and all, at the service of the blue-box operator, free of charge.

"That's what it does. Essentially it gives you the power of a super operator. You seize a tandem with this top button," he presses the top button with his index finger and the blue box emits a high-pitched cheep, "and like that"—cheep goes the blue box again—"you control the phone company's long-distance switching systems from your cute little Princess phone or any old pay phone. And you've got anonymity. An operator has to operate from a definite location: the phone company knows where she is and what she's doing. But with your beeper box, once you hop onto a trunk, say from a Holiday Inn 800 [toll-free] number, they don't know where you are, or where you're coming from, they don't know how you slipped into their lines and popped up in that 800 number. They don't even know anything illegal is going on. And you can obscure your origins through as many levels as you like. You can call next door by way of White Plains, then over to Liverpool by cable, and then back here by satellite. You can call yourself from one pay phone all the way around the world to a pay phone next to you. And you get your dime back too."

"And they can't trace the calls? They can't charge you?"

"Not if you do it the right way. But you'll find that the free-call thing isn't really as exciting at first as the feeling of power you get from having one of these babies in your hand. I've watched people when they first get hold of one of these things and start using it, and discover they can make connections, set up crisscross and zig-zag switching patterns back and forth across the world. They hardly talk to the people they finally reach. They say hello and start thinking of what kind of call to make next. They go a little crazy." He looks down at the neat little package in his palm. His fingers are still dancing, tapping out beeper patterns.

"I think it's something to do with how small my models are. There are lots of blue boxes around, but mine are the smallest and most sophisticated electronically. I wish I could show you the prototype we made for our big syndicate order."

He sighs. "We had this order for a thousand beeper boxes from a syndicate front man in Las Vegas. They use them to place bets coast to coast, keep lines open for hours, all of which can get expensive if you have to pay. The deal was a thousand blue boxes for $300 apiece. Before then we retailed them for $1,500 apiece, but $300,000 in one lump was hard to turn down. We had a manufacturing deal worked out in the Philippines. Everything ready to go. Anyway, the model I had ready for limited mass production was small enough to fit inside a flip-top Marlboro box. It had flush touch panels for a keyboard, rather than these unsightly buttons sticking out. Looked just like a tiny portable radio. In fact, I had designed it with a tiny transistor receiver to get one AM channel, so in case the law became suspicious the owner could switch on the radio part, start snapping his fingers, and no one could tell anything illegal was going on. I thought of everything for this model— I had it lined with a band of thermite which could be ignited by radio signal from a tiny button transmitter on your belt, so it could be burned to ashes instantly in case of a bust. It was beautiful. A beautiful little machine. You should have seen the faces on these syndicate guys when they came back after trying it out. They'd hold it in their palm like they never wanted to let it go, and they'd say, 'I can't believe it. I can't believe it.' *You* probably won't believe it until you try it."

THE BLUE BOX IS TESTED: CERTAIN CONNECTIONS ARE MADE

About eleven o'clock two nights later Fraser Lucey has a blue box in the palm of his left hand and a phone in the palm of his right. He is standing inside a phone booth next to an isolated shut-down motel off Highway 1. I am standing outside the phone booth.

Fraser likes to show off his blue box for people. Until a few weeks ago when Pacific Telephone made a few arrests in his city, Fraser Lucey liked to bring his blue box* to parties. It never failed: a few cheeps from his device and Fraser became the center of attention at the very hippest of gatherings, playing phone tricks and doing request numbers for hours. He began to take orders for his manufacturer in Mexico. He became a dealer.

Fraser is cautious now about where he shows off his blue box. But he never gets tired of playing with it. "It's like the first time every time," he tells me.

Fraser puts a dime in the slot. He listens for a tone and holds the receiver up to my ear. I hear the tone.

Fraser begins describing, with a certain practiced air, what he does while he does it.

---

* This particular blue box, like most blue boxes, is not blue. Blue boxes have come to be called "blue boxes" either 1) because the first blue box ever confiscated by phone-company security men happened to be blue, or 2) to distinguish them from "black boxes." Black boxes are devices, usually a resistor in series, which, when attached to home phones, allow all incoming calls to be made without charge to one's caller.

"I'm dialing an 800 number now. Any 800 number will do. It's toll free. Tonight I think I'll use the - - - - - [he names a well-known rent-a-car company] 800 number. Listen. It's ringing. Here, you hear it? Now watch."

He places the blue box over the mouthpiece of the phone so that the one silver and twelve black push bottons are facing up toward me. He presses the silver button—the one at the top—and I hear that high-pitched beep.

"That's 2,600 cycles per second to be exact," says Lucey. "Now, quick, listen."

He shoves the earpiece at me. The ringing has vanished. The line gives a slight hiccough, there is a sharp buzz, and then nothing but soft white noise.

"We're home free now," Lucey tells me, taking back the phone and applying the blue box to its mouthpiece once again. "We're up on a tandem, into a long-lines trunk. Once you're up on a tandem, you can send yourself anywhere you want to go." He decides to check out London first. He chooses a certain pay phone located in Waterloo Station. This particular pay phone is popular with the phone-phreaks network because there are usually people walking by at all hours who will pick it up and talk for a while.

He presses the lower left-hand corner button which is marked "KP" on the face of the box.

"That's Key Pulse. It tells the tandem we're ready to give it instructions. First I'll punch out KP 182 START, which will slide us into the overseas sender in White Plains." I hear a neat clunk-cheep. "I think we'll head over to England by satellite. Cable is actually faster and the connection is somewhat better, but I like going by satellite. So I just punch out KP Zero 44. The Zero is supposed to guarantee a satellite connection and 44 is the country code for England. Okay . . . we're there. In Liverpool actually. Now all I have to do is punch out the London area code which is 1, and dial up the pay phone. Here, listen, I've got a ring now."

I hear the soft quick purr-purr of a London ring. Then someone picks up the phone. "Hello," says the London voice.

"Hello. Who's this?" Fraser asks.

"Hello. There's actually nobody here. I just picked this up while I was passing by. This is a public phone. There's no one here to answer actually."

"Hello. Don't hang up. I'm calling from the United States."

"Oh. What is the purpose of the call? This is a public phone, you know."

"Oh. You know. To check out, uh, to find out what's going on in London. How is it there?"

"It's five o'clock in the morning. It's raining now."

"Oh. Who are you?"

The London passerby turns out to be an R.A.F. enlistee on his way back to the base in Lincolnshire, with a terrible hangover after a thirty-six-hour pass. He and Fraser talk about the rain. They agree that it's nicer when it's not raining. They say good-bye and Fraser hangs up. His dime returns with a nice clink.

"Isn't that far *out*," he says grinning at me. "London. Like that."

Fraser squeezes the little blue box affectionately in his palm. "I told ya this thing is for real. Listen, if you don't mind I'm gonna try this girl I know in Paris. I usually give her a call around this time. It freaks her out. This time I'll use the - - - - - [a different rent-a-car company] 800 number and we'll go by overseas cable, 133; 33 is the country code for France, the 1 sends you by cable. Okay, here we go. . . . Oh damn. Busy. Who could she be talking to at this time?"

A state police car cruises slowly by the motel. The car does not stop, but Fraser gets nervous. We hop back into his car and drive ten miles in the opposite direction until we reach a Texaco station locked up for the night. We pull up to a phone booth by the tire pump. Fraser dashes inside and tries the Paris number. It is busy again.

"I don't understand who she could be talking to. The circuits may be busy. It's too bad I haven't learned how to tap into lines overseas with this thing yet."

Fraser begins to phreak around, as the phone phreaks say. He dials a leading nationwide charge card's 800 number and punches out the tones that bring him the Time recording in Sydney, Australia. He beeps up the Weather recording in Rome, in Italian of course. He calls a friend in Boston and talks about a certain over-the-counter stock they are into heavily. He finds the Paris number busy again. He calls up "Dial a Disc" in London, and we listen to *Double Barrel* by David and Ansil Collins, the number-one hit of the week in London. He calls up a dealer of another sort and talks in code. He calls up Joe Engressia, the original blind phone-phreak genius, and pays his respects. There are other calls. Finally Fraser gets through to his young lady in Paris. They both agree the circuits must have been busy, and criticize the Paris telephone system. At two thirty in the morning Fraser hangs up, pockets his dime, and drives off, steering with one hand, holding what he calls his "lovely little blue box" in the other.

YOU CAN CALL LONG DISTANCE
FOR LESS THAN YOU THINK

"You see, a few years ago the phone company made one big mistake," Gilbertson explains two days later in his apartment. "They were careless enough to let some technical journal publish the actual frequencies used to create all their multi-frequency tones. Just a theoretical article some Bell Telephone Laboratories engineer was doing about switching theory, and he listed the tones in passing. At - - - - - [a well-known technical school] I had been fooling around with phones for several years before I came across a copy of the journal in the engineering library. I ran back to the lab and it took maybe twelve hours from the time I saw that article to put together the first working blue box. It was bigger and clumsier than this little baby, but it worked."

It's all there on public record in that technical journal written mainly by Bell Lab people for other telephone engineers. Or at least it was public. "Just try and get a copy of that issue at some engineering-school library now. Bell has had them all red-tagged and withdrawn from circulation," Gilbertson tells me.

"But it's too late. It's all public now. And once they became public the technology needed to create your own beeper device is within the range of any twelve-year-old kid, any twelve-year-old *blind* kid as a matter of fact. And he can do it in *less* than the twelve hours it took us. Blind kids do it all the time. They can't build anything as precise and compact as my beeper box, but theirs can do anything mine can do."

"How?"

"Okay. About twenty years ago A.T.&T. made a multi-billion-dollar decision to operate its entire long-distance switching system on twelve electronically generated combinations of six master tones. Those are the tones you sometimes hear in the background after you've dialed a long-distance number. They decided to use some very simple tones—the tone for each number is just two fixed single-frequency tones played simultaneously to create a certain beat frequency. Like 1,300 cycles per second and 900 cycles per second played together give you the tone for digit 5. Now, what some of these phone phreaks have done is get themselves access to an electric organ. Any cheap family home-entertainment organ. Since the frequencies are public knowledge now—one blind phone phreak has even had them recorded in one of those talking books for the blind—they just have to find the musical notes on the organ which correspond to the phone tones. Then they tape them. For instance, to get Ma Bell's tone for the number 1, you press down organ keys F^5 and A^5 [900 and 700 cycles per second] at the same time. To produce the tone for 2 it's F^5 and C^6 [1100 and 700 c.p.s.]. The phone phreaks circulate the whole list of notes so there's no trial and error anymore."

He shows me a list of the rest of the phone numbers and the two electric organ keys that produce them.

"Actually, you have to record these notes at 3¾ inches-per-second tape speed and double it to 7½ inches-per-second when you play them back, to get the proper tones," he adds.

"So once you have all the tones recorded, how do you plug them into the phone system?"

"Well, they take their organ and their cassette recorder, and start banging out entire phone numbers in tones on the organ, including country codes, routing instructions, 'KP' and 'Start' tones. Or, if they don't have an organ, someone in the phone-phreak network sends them a cassette with all the tones recorded, with a voice saying 'Number one,' then you have the tone, 'Number two,' then the tone and so on. So with two cassette recorders they can put together a series of phone numbers by switching back and forth from number to number. Any idiot in the country with a cheap cassette recorder can make all the free calls he wants."

"You mean you just hold the cassette recorder up to the mouthpiece and switch in a series of beeps you've recorded? The phone thinks that anything that makes these tones must be its own equipment?"

"Right. As long as you get the frequency within thirty cycles per second of the phone company's tones, the phone equipment thinks it hears its own voice talking to it. The original granddaddy phone phreak was this blind kid with perfect pitch, Joe Engressia, who used to whistle into the phone. An operator could tell the difference between his whistle and the phone company's electronic tone generator, but the phone company's switching circuit can't tell them apart. The bigger the phone company gets and the further away from human operators it gets, the more vulnerable it becomes to all *sorts* of phone phreaking."

A GUIDE FOR THE PERPLEXED

"But wait a minute," I stop Gilbertson. "If everything you do sounds like phone-company equipment, why doesn't the phone company charge you for the call the way it charges its own equipment?"

"Okay. That's where the 2,600-cycle tone comes in. I better start from the beginning."

The beginning he describes for me is a vision of the phone system of the continent as thousands of webs, of long-line trunks radiating from each of the hundreds of toll switching offices to the other toll switching offices. Each toll switching office is a hive compacted of thousands of long-distance tandems constantly whistling and beeping to tandems in far-off toll switching offices.

The tandem is the key to the whole system. Each tandem is a line with some relays with the capability of signaling any other tandem in any other toll switching office on the continent, either directly one-to-one or by programming a roundabout route through several other tandems if all the direct routes are busy. For instance, if you want to call from New York to Los Angeles and traffic is heavy on all direct trunks between the two cities, your tandem in New York is programmed to try the next best route, which may send you down to a tandem in New Orleans, then up to San Francisco, or down to a New Orleans tandem, back to an Atlanta tandem, over to an Albuquerque tandem, and finally up to Los Angeles.

When a tandem is not being used, when it's sitting there waiting for someone to make a long-distance call, it whistles. One side of the tandem, the side "facing" your home phone, whistles at 2,600 per second toward all the home phones serviced by the exchange, telling them it is at their service, should they be interested in making a long-distance call. The other side of the tandem is whistling 2,600 c.p.s. into one or more long-distance trunk lines, telling the rest of the phone system that it is neither sending nor receiving a call through that trunk at the moment, that it has no use for that trunk at the moment.

When you dial a long-distance number the first thing that happens is that you are hooked into a tandem. A register comes up to the side of the tandem facing away from you and presents that side with the number you dialed. This sending side of the tandem stops whistling 2,600 into its trunk line. When a tandem stops the 2,600 tone it has been sending through a trunk, the trunk is said to be "seized," and is now ready to carry the number you have dialed—converted into multi-frequency beep tones—to a tandem in the area code and central office you want.

Now when a blue-box operator wants to make a call from New Orleans to New York he starts by dialing the 800 number of a company which might happen to have its headquarters in Los Angeles. The sending side of the New Orleans tandem stops sending beep tones to a tandem it has discovered idly whistling 2,600 cycles in Los Angeles. The receiving end of that L.A. tandem is seized, stops whistling 2,600, listens to the beep tones which tell it which L.A. phone to ring, and starts ringing the 800 number. Meanwhile a mark made on the New Orleans office accounting tape notes that a call from your New Orleans phone to the 800 number in L.A. has been initiated and gives the call a code number. Everything is routine so far.

But then the phone phreak presses his blue box to the mouthpiece and pushes the 2,600-cycle button, sending 2,600 out from New Orleans tandem to the L.A. tandem. The L.A. tandem notices 2,600 cycles are coming over the line again and assumes that New Orleans has hung up because the trunk is whistling as if idle. The L.A. tandem immediately ceases ringing the L.A. 800 number. But as soon as the phreak takes his finger off the 2,600 button, the L.A. tandem assumes the trunk is once again being used because the 2,600 is gone, so it listens for a new series of digit tones —to find out where it must send the call.

Thus the blue-box operator in New Orleans now is in touch with a tandem in L.A. which is waiting like an obedient genie to be told what to do next. The blue-box owner then beeps out the ten digits of the New York number which tell the L.A. tandem to relay a call to New York City. Which it promptly does. As soon as your party picks up the phone in New York, the side of the New Orleans tandem facing you stops sending 2,600 cycles to you and starts carrying his voice to you by way of the L.A. tandem. A notation is made on the accounting tape that the connection has been made on the 800 call which had been initiated and noted earlier. When you stop talking to New York a notation is made that the 800 call has ended.

At three the next morning, when the phone company's accounting computer starts reading back over the master accounting tape for the past day, it records that a call of a certain length of time was made from your New Orleans home to an L.A. 800 number and, of course, the accounting computer has been trained to ignore these toll-free 800 calls when compiling your monthly bill.

"All they can prove is that you made an 800 toll-free call," Gilbertson the inventor concludes. "Of course, if you're foolish enough to talk for two hours on an 800 call, and they've installed one of their special antifraud computer programs to watch out for such things, they may spot you and ask you why you took two hours talking to Army Recruiting's 800 number when you're 4-F. But if you do it from a pay phone, they *may* discover something peculiar the next day—if they've got a blue-box hunting program in their computer—but you'll be a long time gone from the pay phone by then. Using a pay phone is almost guaranteed safe."

"What about the recent series of blue-box arrests all across the country—New York, Cleveland, and so on?" I asked. "How were they caught so easily?"

"From what I can tell, they made one big mistake: they were seizing trunks using an area code plus 555-1212 instead of an 800 number. Using 555 is easy to detect because when you send multi-frequency beep tones off 555 you get a charge for it on your tape and the accounting computer knows there's something wrong when it tries to bill you for a two-hour call to Akron, Ohio, information, and it drops a trouble card which goes right into the hands of the security agent if they're looking for blue-box users.

"Whoever sold those guys their blue boxes didn't tell them how to use them properly, which is fairly irresponsible. And they were fairly stupid to use them at home all the time.

"But what those arrests really mean is that an awful lot of blue boxes are flooding into the country and that people are finding them so easy to make that they know how to make them before they know how to use them. Ma Bell is in trouble."

And if a blue-box operator or a cassette-recorder phone phreak sticks to pay phones and 800 numbers, the phone company can't stop them?

"Not unless they change their entire nationwide long-lines technology, which will take them a few billion dollars and twenty years. Right now they can't do a thing. They're screwed."

CAPTAIN CRUNCH DEMONSTRATES HIS FAMOUS UNIT

There is an underground telephone network in this country. Gilbertson discovered it the very day news of his activities hit the papers. That evening his phone began ringing. Phone phreaks from Seattle, from Florida, from New York, from San Jose, and from Los Angeles began calling him and telling him about the phone-phreak network. He'd get a call from a phone phreak who'd say nothing but, "Hang up and call this number."

When he dialed the number he'd find himself tied into a conference of a dozen phone phreaks arranged through a quirky switching station in British Columbia. They identified themselves as phone phreaks, they demonstrated their homemade blue boxes which they called "M-F-ers" (for "multi-frequency," among other things) for him, they talked shop about phone-phreak devices. They let him in on their secrets on the theory that if the phone company was after him he must be trustworthy. And, Gilbertson recalls, they stunned him with their technical sophistication.

I ask him how to get in touch with the phone-phreak network.

He digs around through a file of old schematics and comes up with about a dozen numbers in three widely separated area codes.

"Those are the centers," he tells me. Alongside some of the numbers he writes in first names or nicknames: names like Captain Crunch, Dr. No, Frank Carson (also a code word for free call), Marty Freeman (code word for M-F device), Peter Perpendicular Pimple, Alefnull, and The Cheshire Cat. He makes checks alongside the names of those among these top twelve who are blind. There are five checks.

I ask him who this Captain Crunch person is.

"Oh. The Captain. He's probably the most legendary phone phreak. He calls himself Captain Crunch after the notorious Cap'n Crunch 2,600 whistle." (Several years ago, Gilbertson explains, the makers of Cap'n Crunch breakfast cereal offered a toy-whistle prize in every box as a treat for the Cap'n Crunch set. Somehow a phone phreak discovered that the toy whistle just happened to produce a perfect 2,600-cycle tone. When the man who calls himself Captain Crunch was transferred overseas to England with his Air Force unit, he would receive scores of calls from his friends and "mute" them—make them free of charge to them—by blowing his Cap'n Crunch whistle into his end.)

"Captain Crunch is one of the older phone phreaks," Gilbertson tells me. "He's an engineer who once got in a little trouble for fooling around with the phone, but he can't stop. Well, this guy drives across country in a Volkswagen van with an entire switchboard and a computerized super-sophisticated M-F-er in the back. He'll pull up to a phone booth on a lonely highway somewhere, snake a cable out of his bus, hook it onto the phone and sit for hours, days sometimes, sending calls zipping back and forth across the country, all over the world. . . ."

Back at my motel, I dialed the number he gave me for "Captain Crunch" and asked for G - - - - T - - - - - , the name he uses when he's not dashing into a phone booth beeping out M-F tones faster than a speeding bullet, and zipping phantomlike through the phone company's long-distance lines.

When G - - - - T - - - - - answered the phone and I told him I was preparing a story for *Esquire* about phone phreaks, he became very indignant.

"I don't do that. I don't do that anymore at all. And if I do it, I do it for one reason and one reason only. I'm learning about a system. The phone company is a System. A computer is a System. Do you understand? If I do what I do, it is only to explore a System. Computers. Systems. That's my bag. The phone company is nothing but a computer."

A tone of tightly restrained excitement enters the Captain's voice when he starts talking about Systems. He begins to pronounce each syllable with the hushed deliberation of an obscene caller.

"Ma Bell is a system I want to explore. It's a beautiful system, you know, but Ma Bell screwed up. It's terrible because Ma Bell is such a beautiful system, but she screwed up. I learned how she screwed up from a couple of blind kids who wanted me to build a device. A certain device. They said it could make free calls. I wasn't interested in free calls. But when these blind kids told me I could make calls into a computer, my eyes lit up. I wanted to learn about computers. I wanted to learn about Ma Bell's computers. So I built the little device. Only I built it wrong and Ma Bell found out. Ma Bell can detect things like that. Ma Bell knows. So I'm strictly out of it now. I didn't do it. Except for learning purposes." He pauses. "So you want to write an article. Are you paying for this call? Hang up and call this number."

He gives me a number in an area code a thousand miles north of his own. I dial the number.

"Hello again. This is Captain Crunch. You are speaking to me on a toll-free loop-around in Portland, Oregon. Do you know what a toll-free loop-around is? I'll tell you."

He explains to me that almost every exchange in the country has open test numbers which allow other exchanges to test their connections with it. Most of these numbers occur in consecutive pairs, such as 302 956-0041 and 956-0042. Well, certain phone phreaks discovered that if two people from anywhere in the country dial those two consecutive numbers they can talk together just as if one had called the other's number, with no charge to either of them, of course.

"Your voice is looping around in a 4A switching machine up there in Canada, zipping back down to me," the Captain tells me. "My voice is looping around up there and back down to you. And it can't ever cost anyone money. The phone phreaks and I have compiled a list of many many of these numbers. You would be surprised if you saw the list. I could show it to you. But I won't. I'm out of that now. I'm not out to screw Ma Bell. I know better. If I do anything it's for the pure knowledge of the System. You can learn to do fantastic things. Have you ever heard eight tandems stacked up? Do you know the sound of tandems stacking and unstacking? Give me your phone number. Okay. Hang up now and wait a minute."

Slightly less than a minute later the phone rang and the Captain was on the line, his voice sounding far more excited, almost aroused.

"I wanted to show you what it's like to stack up tandems. To stack up tandems." (Whenever the Captain says "stack up" it sounds as if he is licking his lips.)

"How do you like the connection you're on now?" the Captain asks me. "It's a *raw* tandem. A *raw* tandem. Ain't nothin' up to it but a tandem. Now I'm going to show you what it's like to stack up. Blow off. Land in a faraway place. To stack *that* tandem up, whip back and forth across the country a few times, then shoot on up to Moscow.

"Listen," Captain Crunch continues. "Listen. I've got a line tie on my switchboard here, and I'm gonna let you hear me stack and unstack tandems. Listen to this. I'm gonna blow your mind."

First I hear a super rapid-fire pulsing of the flutelike phone tones, then a pause, then another popping burst of tones, then another, then another. Each burst is followed by a beep-kachink sound.

"We have now stacked up four tandems," said Captain Crunch, sounding somewhat remote. "That's four tandems stacked up. Do you know what that means? That means I'm whipping back and forth, back and forth twice, across the country, before coming to you. I've been known to stack up twenty tandems at a time. Now, just like I said, I'm going to shoot up to Moscow."

There is a new, longer series of beeper pulses over the line, a brief silence, then a ring.

"Hello," answers a far-off voice.

"Hello. Is this the American Embassy Moscow?"

"Yes, sir. Who is this calling?" says the voice.

"Yes. This is test board here in New York. We're calling to check out the circuits, see what kind of lines you've got. Everything okay there in Moscow?"

"Okay?"

"Well, yes, how are things there?"

"Oh. Well, everything okay, I guess."

"Okay. Thank you." They hang up, leaving a confused series of beep-kachink sounds hanging in mid-ether in the wake of the call before dissolving away.

The Captain is pleased. "You believe me now, don't you? Do you know what I'd like to do? I'd like to call up your editor at *Esquire* and show him *just* what it sounds like to stack and unstack tandems. I'll give him a show that will *blow his mind*. What's his number?"

I ask the Captain what kind of device he was using to accomplish all his feats. The Captain is pleased at the question.

"You could tell it was special, couldn't you? Ten pulses per second. That's faster than the phone company's equipment. Believe me, this unit is *the* most famous unit in the country. There is no other unit like it. Believe me."

"Yes, I've heard about it. Some other phone phreaks have told me about it."

"They have been referring to my, ahem, unit? What is it they said? Just out of curiosity, did they tell you it was a highly sophisticated computer-operated unit, with acoustical coupling for receiving outputs and a switchboard with multiple-line capability? Did they tell you that the frequency tolerance is guaranteed to be not more than .05 percent? The amplitude tolerance less than .01 decibel? Those pulses you heard were perfect. They just come faster than the phone company. Those were high-precision op-amps. Op-amps are instrumentation amplifiers designed for ultra-stable amplification, super-low distortion and accurate frequency response. Did they tell you it can operate in temperatures from $-55\,°C$ to $+125\,°C$?"

I admit that they did not tell me all that.

"I built it myself," the Captain goes on. "If you were to go out and *buy* the components from an industrial wholesaler it would cost you at least $1,500. I once worked for a semiconductor company and all this didn't cost me a cent. Do you know what I mean? Did they tell you about how I put a call completely around the world? I'll tell you how I did it. I M-F-ed Tokyo inward, who connected me to India, India connected me to Greece, Greece connected me to Pretoria, South Africa, South Africa connected me to South America, I went from South America to London, I had a London operator connect me to a New York operator, I had New York connect me to a California operator who rang the phone next to me. Needless to say I had to shout to hear myself. But the echo was far out. Fantastic. Delayed. It was delayed twenty seconds, but I could hear myself talk to myself."

"You mean you were speaking into the mouthpiece of one phone sending your voice around the world into your ear through a phone on the other side of your head?" I asked the Captain. I had a vision of something vaguely autoerotic going on, in a complex electronic way.

"That's right," said the Captain. "I've also sent my voice around the world one way, going east on one phone, and going west on the other, going through cable one way, satellite the other, coming back together at the same time, ringing the two phones simultaneously and picking them up and whipping my voice both ways around the world and back to me. Wow. That was a mind blower."

"You mean you sit there with both phones on your ear and talk to yourself around the world," I said incredulously.

"Yeah. Um hum. That's what I do. I connect the phones together and sit there and talk."

"What do you say? What do you say to yourself when you're connected?"

"Oh, you know. Hello test one two three," he says in a low-pitched voice.

"Hello test one two three," he replies to himself in a high-pitched voice.

"Hello test one two three," he repeats again, low-pitched.

"Hello test one two three," he replies, high-pitched.

"I sometimes do this: *Hello* hello *hello* hello, *hello*, hello," he trails off and breaks into laughter.

WHY CAPTAIN CRUNCH HARDLY EVER TAPS PHONES ANYMORE

Using internal phone-company codes, phone phreaks have learned a simple method for tapping phones. Phone-company operators have in front of them a board that holds verification jacks. It allows them to plug into conversations in case of emergency, to listen in to a line to determine if the line is busy or the circuits are busy. Phone phreaks have learned to beep out the codes which lead them to a verification operator, tell the verification operator they are switchmen from some other area code testing out verification trunks. Once the operator hooks them into the verification trunk, they disappear into the board for all practical purposes, slip unnoticed into any one of the 10,000 to 100,000 numbers in that central office without the verification operator knowing what they're doing, and of course without the two parties to the connection knowing there is a phantom listener present on their line.

Toward the end of my hour-long first conversation with him, I asked the Captain if he ever tapped phones.

"Oh no. I don't do that. I don't think it's right," he told me firmly. "I have the power to do it but I don't. . . . Well one time, just one time, I have to admit that I did. There was this girl Linda, and I wanted to find out . . . you know. I tried to call her up for a date. I had a date with her the last weekend and I thought she liked me. I called her up, man, and her line was busy, and I kept calling and it was still busy. Well, I had just learned about this system of jumping into lines and I said to myself, 'Hmmm. Why not just see if it works. It'll surprise her if all of a sudden I should pop up on her line. It'll impress her, if anything.' So I went ahead and did it. I M-F-ed into the line. My M-F-er is powerful enough when patched directly into the mouthpiece to trigger a verification trunk without using an operator the way the other phone phreaks have to.

"I slipped into the line and there she was talking to another boyfriend. Making sweet talk to him. I didn't make a sound because I was so disgusted. So I waited there for her to hang up, listening to her making sweet talk to another guy. You know. So as soon as she hung up I instantly M-F-ed her up and all I said was, 'Linda, we're through.' And I hung up. And it blew her head off. She couldn't figure out what the hell had happened.

"But that was the only time. I did it thinking I would surprise her, impress her. Those were all my intentions were, and well, it really kind of hurt me pretty badly, and . . . and ever since then I don't go into verification trunks."

Moments later my first conversation with the Captain comes to a close.

"Listen," he says, his spirits somewhat cheered, "listen. What you are going to hear when I hang up is the sound of tandems unstacking. Layer after layer of tandems unstacking until there's nothing left of the stack, until it melts away into nothing. Cheep, cheep, cheep, cheep," he concludes, his voice descending to a whisper with each cheep.

He hangs up. The phone suddenly goes into four spasms: kachink cheep. Kachink cheep kachink cheep kachink cheep, and the complex connection has wiped itself out like the Cheshire cat's smile.

THE MF BOOGIE BLUES

The next number I choose from the select list of phone-phreak illuminati prepared for me by the blue-box inventor is a Memphis number. It is the number of Joe Engressia, the first and still perhaps the most accomplished blind phone phreak.

Three years ago Engressia was a nine-day wonder in newspapers and magazines all over America because he had been discovered whistling free long-distance connections for fellow students at the University of South Florida. Engressia was born with perfect pitch; he could whistle phone tones better than the phone-company equipment.

Engressia might have gone on whistling in the dark for a few friends for the rest of his life if the phone company hadn't decided to expose him. He was warned, disciplined by the college, and the whole case became public. In the months following media reports of his talent, Engressia began receiving strange calls. There were calls from a group of kids in Los Angeles who could do some very strange things with the quirky General Telephone and Electronics circuitry in L.A. suburbs. There were calls from a group of mostly blind kids in - - - -, California, who had been doing some interesting experiments with Cap'n Crunch whistles and test loops. There was a group in Seattle, a group in Cambridge, Massachusetts, a few from New York, a few scattered across the country. Some of them had already equipped themselves with cassette and electronic M-F devices. For some of these groups, it was the first time they knew of the others.

The exposure of Engressia was the catalyst that linked the separate phone-phreak centers together. They all called Engressia. They talked to him about what he was doing and what they were doing. And then he told them—the scattered regional centers and lonely independent phone phreakers—about each other, gave them each other's numbers to call, and within a year the scattered phone-phreak centers had grown into a nationwide underground.

Joe Engressia is only twenty-two years old now, but along the phone-phreak network he is "the old man," accorded by phone phreaks something of the reverence the phone company bestows on Alexander Graham Bell. He seldom needs to make calls anymore. The phone phreaks all call him and let him know what new tricks, new codes, new techniques they have learned. Every night he sits like a sightless spider in his little apartment receiving messages from every tendril of his web. It is almost a point of pride with Joe that *they* call *him*.

But when I reached him in his Memphis apartment that night, Joe Engressia was lonely, jumpy, and upset.

"God, I'm glad somebody called. I don't know why tonight of all nights I don't get any calls. This guy around here got drunk again tonight and propositioned me again. I keep telling him we'll never see eye to eye on this subject, if you know what I mean. I try to make light of it, you know, but he doesn't get it. I can hear him out there getting drunker and I don't know what he'll do next. It's just that I'm really all alone here. I just moved to Memphis, it's the first time I'm living out on my own, and I'd hate for it to all collapse now. But I won't go to bed with him. I'm just not very interested in sex and even if I can't see him I *know* he's ugly.

"Did you hear that? That's him banging a bottle against the wall outside. He's nice. Well forget about it. You're doing a story on phone phreaks? Listen to this. It's the *M F Boogie* blues."

Sure enough, a jumpy version of *Muskrat Ramble* boogies its way over the line, each note one of those long-distance phone tones. The music stops. A huge roaring voice blasts the phone off my ear: "AND THE QUESTION IS . . ." roars the voice, "CAN A BLIND PERSON HOOK UP AN AMPLIFIER ON HIS OWN?"

The roar ceases. A high-pitched operator-type voice replaces it. "This is Southern Braille Tel. & Tel. Have tone, will phone."

This is succeeded by a quick series of M-F tones, a swift "ka-chink" and a deep reassuring voice: "If *you* need home care, call the visiting-nurses association. First National time in Honolulu is four thirty-two P.M."

Joe back in his Joe voice again: "Are we seeing eye to eye? *'Si, si,'* said the blind Mexican. Ahem. Yes. Would you like to know the weather in Tokyo?"

This swift manic sequence of phone-phreak vaudeville stunts and blind-boy jokes manages to keep Joe's mind off his tormentor only as long as it lasts.

"The reason I'm in Memphis, the reason I have to depend on that homosexual guy, is that this is the first time I've been able to live on my own and make phone trips on my own. I've been banned from all central offices around home in Florida, they knew me too well, and at the University some of my fellow scholars were always harassing me because I was on the dorm pay phone all the time and making fun of me because of my fat ass, which of course I do have, it's my physical fatness program, but I don't like to hear it every day, and if I can't phone trip and I can't phone phreak, I can't imagine what I'd do, I've been devoting three quarters of my life to it.

"I moved to Memphis because I wanted to be on my own as well as because it has a Number 5 crossbar switching system and some interesting little independent phone-company districts nearby and so far they don't seem to know who I am so I can go on phone tripping, and for me phone tripping is just as important as phone phreaking."

Phone tripping, Joe explains, begins with calling up a central-office switch room. He tells the switchman in a polite earnest voice that he's a blind college student interested in telephones, and could he perhaps have a guided tour of the switching station? Each step of the tour Joe likes to touch and feel relays, caress switching circuits, switchboards, crossbar arrangements.

So when Joe Engressia phone phreaks he *feels* his way through the circuitry of the country. In this electronic garden of forking paths, he feels switches shift, relays shunt, crossbars swivel, tandems engage and disengage even as he hears—with perfect pitch—his M-F pulses make the entire Bell system dance to his tune.

Just one month ago Joe took all his savings out of his bank and left home, over the emotional protests of his mother. "I ran away from home almost," he likes to say. Joe found a small apartment house on Union Avenue and began making phone trips. He'd take a bus a hundred miles south into Mississippi to see some old-fashioned Bell equipment still in use in several states, which had been puzzling him. He'd take a bus three hundred miles to Charlotte, North Carolina, to look at some brand-new experimental equipment. He hired a taxi to drive him twelve miles to a suburb to tour the office of a small phone company with some interesting idiosyncrasies in its routing system. He was having the time of his life, he said, the most freedom and pleasure he had known.

In that month he had done very little long-distance phone phreaking from his own phone. He had begun to apply for a job with the phone company, he told me, and he wanted to stay away from anything illegal.

"Any kind of job will do, anything as menial as the most lowly operator. That's probably all they'd give me because I'm blind. Even though I probably knew more than most switchmen. But that's okay. I *want* to work for Ma Bell. I don't hate Ma Bell the way Gilbertson and some phone phreaks do. I don't want to screw Ma Bell. With me it's the pleasure of pure knowledge. There's something beautiful about the system when you know it intimately the way I do. But I don't know how much they know about me here. I have a very intuitive feel for the condition of the line I'm on, and I think they're monitoring me off and on lately, but I haven't been doing much illegal. I *have* to make a few calls to switchmen once in a while which aren't strictly legal, and once I took an acid trip and was having these auditory hallucinations as if I were trapped and these planes were dive-bombing me, and all of a sudden I *had* to phone phreak out of there. For some reason I had to call Kansas City, but that's all."

A WARNING IS DELIVERED

At this point—one o'clock in my time zone—a loud knock on my motel-room door interrupts our conversation. Outside the door I find a uniformed security guard who informs me that there has been an "emergency phone call" for me while I have been on the line and that the front desk has sent him up to let me know.

Two seconds after I say good-bye to Joe and hang up, the phone rings.

"Who were you talking to?" the agitated voice demands. The voice belongs to Captain Crunch. "I called because I decided to warn you of something. I decided to warn you to be careful. I don't want this information you get to get to the radical underground. I don't want it to get into the wrong hands. What would you say if I told you it's possible for three phone phreaks to saturate the phone system of the nation. Saturate it. Busy it out. All of it. I know how to do this. I'm not gonna tell. A friend of mine has already saturated the trunks between Seattle and New York. He did it with a computerized M-F-er hitched into a special Manitoba exchange. But there are other, easier ways to do it."

Just three people? I ask. How is that possible?

"Have you ever heard of the long-lines guard frequency? Do you know about stacking tandems with 17 and 2,600? Well, I'd advise you to find out about it. I'm not gonna tell you. But whatever you do, don't let this get into the hands of the radical underground."

(Later Gilbertson the inventor confessed that while he had always been skeptical about the Captain's claim of the sabotage potential of trunk-tying phone phreaks, he had recently heard certain demonstrations which convinced him the Captain was not speaking idly. "I think it might take more than three people, depending on how many machines like Captain Crunch's were available. But even though the Captain *sounds* a little weird, he generally turns out to know what he's talking about.")

"You know," Captain Crunch continues in his admonitory tone, "you know the younger phone phreaks call Moscow all the time. Suppose everybody were to call Moscow. I'm no right-winger. But I value my life. I don't want the Commies coming over and dropping a bomb on my head. That's why I say you've got to be careful about who gets this information."

The Captain suddenly shifts into a diatribe against those phone phreaks who don't like the phone company.

"They don't understand, but Ma Bell knows everything they do. Ma Bell knows. Listen, is this line hot? I just heard someone tap in. I'm not paranoid, but I can detect things like that. Well, even if it is, they know that I know that they know that I have a bulk eraser. I'm very clean." The Captain pauses, evidently torn between wanting to prove to the phone-company monitors that he does nothing illegal, and the desire to impress Ma Bell with his prowess. "Ma Bell knows the things I can do," he continues. "Ma Bell knows how good I am. And I am *quite* good. I can detect reversals, tandem switching, everything that goes on on a line. I have relative pitch now. Do you know what that *means*?

My ears are a $20,000 piece of equipment. With my ears I can detect things they can't hear with their equipment. I've had employment problems. I've lost jobs. But I want to show Ma Bell how good I am. I don't want to screw her, I want to work for her. I want to do good for her. I want to help her get rid of her flaws and become perfect. That's my number-one goal in life now." The Captain concludes his warnings and tells me he has to be going. "I've got a little action lined up for tonight," he explains and hangs up.

Before I hang up for the night, I call Joe Engressia back. He reports that his tormentor has finally gone to sleep—"He's not *blind* drunk, that's the way I get, ahem, yes; but you might say he's in a drunken stupor." I make a date to visit Joe in Memphis in two days.

A PHONE PHREAK CELL TAKES CARE OF BUSINESS

The next morning I attend a gathering of four phone phreaks in - - - - - (a California suburb). The gathering takes place in a comfortable split-level home in an upper-middle-class subdivision. Heaped on the kitchen table are the portable cassette recorders, M-F cassettes, phone patches, and line ties of the four phone phreaks present. On the kitchen counter next to the telephone is a shoe-box-size blue box with thirteen large toggle switches for the tones. The parents of the host phone phreak, Ralph, who is blind, stay in the living room with their sighted children. They are not sure exactly what Ralph and his friends do with the phone or if it's strictly legal, but he is blind and they are pleased he has a hobby which keeps him busy.

The group has been working at reestablishing the historic "2111" conference, reopening some toll-free loops, and trying to discover the dimensions of what seem to be new initiatives against phone phreaks by phone-company security agents.

It is not long before I get a chance to see, to hear, Randy at work. Randy is known among the phone phreaks as perhaps the finest con man in the game. Randy is blind. He is pale, soft, and pear-shaped, he wears baggy pants and a wrinkly nylon white sport shirt, pushes his head forward from hunched shoulders somewhat like a turtle inching out of its shell. His eyes wander, crossing and recrossing, and his forehead is somewhat pimply. He is only sixteen years old.

But when Randy starts speaking into a telephone mouthpiece his voice becomes so stunningly authoritative it is necessary to look again to convince yourself it comes from chubby adolescent Randy. Imagine the voice of a crack oil-rig foreman, a tough, sharp, weatherbeaten Marlboro man of forty. Imagine the voice of a brilliant performance-fund gunslinger explaining how he beats the Dow Jones by thirty percent. Then imagine a voice that could make those two sound like Stepin Fetchit. That is sixteen-year-old Randy's voice.

He is speaking to a switchman in Detroit. The phone company in Detroit had closed up two toll-free loop pairs for no apparent reason, although heavy use by phone phreaks all over the country may have been detected. Randy is telling the switchman how to open up the loop and make it free again:

"How are you, buddy. Yeah, I'm on the board out here in Tulsa, Oklahoma, and we've been trying to run some tests on your loop-arounds, and we find 'em busied out on both sides. . . . Yeah, we've been getting a 'BY' on them, what d'ya say, can you drop cards on 'em? Do you have 08 on your number group? Oh that's okay, we've had this trouble before, we may have to go after the circuit. Here, lemme give 'em to you: your frame is 05, vertical group 03, horizontal 5, vertical file 3. Yeah, we'll hang on here. . . . Okay, found it? Good. Right, yeah, we'd like to clear that busy out. Right. Now pull your key from NOR over to LCT. Yeah. I don't know why that happened, but we've been having trouble with that one. Okay. Thanks a lot, fella. Be seein' ya."

Randy hangs up, reports that the switchman was a little inexperienced with the loop-around circuits on the miscellaneous trunk frame, but that the loop has been returned to its free-call status.

Delighted, phone phreak Ed returns the pair of numbers to the active-status column in his directory. Ed is a superb and painstaking researcher. With almost Talmudic thoroughness he will trace tendrils of hints through soft-wired mazes of intervening phone-company circuitry back through complex linkages of switching relays to find the location and identity of just one toll-free loop. He spends hours and hours, every day, doing this sort of thing. He has compiled a directory of eight hundred "Band-six in-WATS numbers" located in over forty states. Band-six in-WATS numbers are the big 800 numbers—the ones that can be dialed into free from anywhere in the country.

Ed the researcher, a nineteen-year-old engineering student, is also a superb technician. He put together his own working blue box from scratch at age seventeen. (He is sighted.) This evening after distributing the latest issue of his in-WATS directory (which has been typed into Braille for the blind phone phreaks), he announces he has made a major new breakthrough:

"I finally tested it and it works, perfectly. I've got this switching matrix which converts any touch-tone phone into an M-F-er."

The tones you hear in touch-tone phones are *not* the M-F tones that operate the long-distance switching system. Phone phreaks believe A.T.&T. had deliberately equipped touch tones with a different set of frequencies to avoid putting the six master M-F tones in the hands of every touch-tone owner. Ed's complex switching matrix puts the six master tones, in effect puts a blue box, in the hands of every touch-tone owner.

Ed shows me pages of schematics, specifications, and parts lists. "It's not easy to build, but everything here is in the Heathkit catalog."

Ed asks Ralph what progress he has made in his attempts to reestablish a long-term open conference line for phone phreaks. The last big conference—the historic "2111" conference—had been arranged through an unused Telex test-board trunk somewhere in the innards of a 4A switching machine in Vancouver, Canada. For months phone phreaks could M-F their way into Vancouver, beep out 604 (the Vancouver code) and then beep out 2111 (the internal phone-company code for Telex testing), and find themselves at any time, day or night, on an open wire talking with an array of phone phreaks from coast to coast, operators from Bermuda, Tokyo, and London who are phone-phreak sympathizers, and miscellaneous guests and technical experts. The conference was a massive exchange of information. Phone phreaks picked each other's brains clean, then developed new ways to pick the phone company's brains clean. Ralph gave *M F Boogie* concerts with his home-entertainment-type electric organ, Captain Crunch demonstrated his round-the-world prowess with his notorious computerized unit and dropped leering hints of the "action" he was getting with his girl friends. (The Captain lives out or pretends to live out several kinds of fantasies to the gossipy delight of the blind phone phreaks who urge him on to further triumphs on behalf of all of them.) The somewhat rowdy Northwest phone-phreak crowd let their bitter internal feud spill over into the peaceable conference line, escalating shortly into guerrilla warfare; Carl the East Coast international phone relations expert demonstrated newly opened direct M-F routes to central offices on the island of Bahrain in the Persian Gulf, introduced a new phone-phreak friend of his in Pretoria, and explained the technical operation of the new Oakland-to-Vietnam linkages. (Many phone phreaks pick up spending money by M-F-ing calls from relatives to Vietnam G.I.'s, charging $5 for a whole hour of trans-Pacific conversation.)

Day and night the conference line was never dead. Blind phone phreaks all over the country, lonely and isolated in homes filled with active sighted brothers and sisters, or trapped with slow and unimaginative blind kids in straightjacket schools for the blind, knew that no matter how late it got they could dial up the conference and find instant electronic communion with two or three other blind kids awake over on the other side of America. Talking together on a phone hookup, the blind phone phreaks say, is not much different from being there together. Physically, *there* was nothing more than a two-inch-square wafer of titanium inside a vast machine on Vancouver Island. For the blind kids *there* meant an exhilarating feeling of being *in touch*, through a kind of skill and magic which was peculiarly their own.

Last April 1, however, the long Vancouver Conference was shut off. The phone phreaks knew it was coming. Vancouver was in the process of converting from a step-by-step system to a 4A machine and the 2111 Telex circuit was to be wiped out in the process. The phone phreaks learned the actual day on which the conference would be erased about a week ahead of time over the phone company's internal-news-and-shop-talk recording.

For the next frantic seven days every phone phreak in America was on and off the 2111 conference twenty-four hours a day. Phone phreaks who were just learning the game or didn't have M-F capability were boosted up to the conference by more experienced phreaks so they could get a glimpse of what it was like before it disappeared. Top phone phreaks searched distant area codes for new conference possibilities without success. Finally in the early morning of April 1, the end came.

"I could feel it coming a couple hours before midnight," Ralph remembers. "You could feel something going on in the lines. Some static began showing up, then some whistling wheezing sound. Then there were breaks. Some people got cut off and called right back in, but after a while some people were finding they were cut off and couldn't get back in at all. It was terrible. I lost it about one A.M., but managed to slip in again and stay on until the thing died . . . I think it was about four in the morning. There were four of us still hanging on when the conference disappeared into nowhere for good. We all tried to M-F up to it again of course, but we got silent termination. There was nothing there."

THE LEGENDARY MARK BERNAY TURNS OUT TO BE "THE MIDNIGHT SKULKER"

Mark Bernay. I had come across that name before. It was on Gilbertson's select list of phone phreaks. The California phone phreaks had spoken of a mysterious Mark Bernay as perhaps the first and oldest phone phreak on the West Coast. And in fact almost every phone phreak in the West can trace his origins either directly to Mark Bernay or to a disciple of Mark Bernay.

It seems that five years ago this Mark Bernay (a pseudonym he chose for himself) began traveling up and down the West Coast pasting tiny stickers in phone books all along his way. The stickers read something like "Want to hear an interesting tape recording? Call these numbers." The numbers that followed were toll-free loop-around pairs. When one of the curious called one of the numbers he would hear a tape recording pre-hooked into the loop by Bernay which explained the use of loop-around pairs, gave the numbers of several more, and ended by telling the caller, "At six o'clock tonight this recording will stop and you and your friends can try it out. Have fun."

"I was disappointed by the response at first," Bernay told me, when I finally reached him at one of his many numbers and he had dispensed with the usual "I never do anything illegal" formalities with which experienced phone phreaks open most conversations. "I went all over the coast with these stickers not only on pay phones, but I'd throw them in front of high schools in the middle of the night, I'd leave them unobtrusively in candy stores, scatter them on main streets of small towns. At first hardly anyone bothered to try it out. I would listen in for hours and hours after six o'clock and no one came on. I couldn't figure out why people wouldn't be interested. Finally these two girls in Oregon tried it out and told all their friends and suddenly it began to spread."

Before his Johnny Appleseed trip Bernay had already gathered a sizable group of early pre-blue-box phone phreaks together on loop-arounds in Los Angeles. Bernay does not claim credit for the original discovery of the loop-around numbers. He attributes the discovery to an eighteen-year-old reform-school kid in Long Beach whose name he forgets and who, he says, "just disappeared one day." When Bernay himself discovered loop-arounds independently, from clues in his readings in old issues of the *Automatic Electric Technical Journal*, he found dozens of the reform-school kid's friends already using them. However, it was one of Bernay's disciples in Seattle who introduced phone phreaking to blind kids. The Seattle kid who learned about loops through Bernay's recording told a blind friend, the blind kid taught the secret to his friends at a winter camp for blind kids in Los Angeles. When the camp session was over these kids took the secret back to towns all over the West. This is how the original blind kids became phone phreaks. For them, for most phone phreaks in general, it was the discovery of the possibilities of loop-arounds which led them on to far more serious and sophisticated phone-phreak methods, and which gave them a medium for sharing their discoveries.

A year later a blind kid who moved back east brought the technique to a blind kids' summer camp in Vermont, which spread it along the East Coast. All from a Mark Bernay sticker.

Bernay, who is nearly thirty years old now, got his start when he was fifteen and his family moved into an L.A. suburb serviced by General Telephone and Electronics equipment. He became fascinated with the differences between Bell and G.T.&E. equipment. He learned he could make interesting things happen by carefully timed clicks with the disengage button. He learned to interpret subtle differences in the array of clicks, whirrs, and kachinks he could hear on his lines. He learned he could shift himself around the switching relays of the L.A. area code in a not-too-predictable fashion by interspersing his own hook-switch clicks with the clicks within the line. Independent phone companies—there are nineteen hundred of them still left, most of them tiny island principalities in Ma Bell's vast empire—have always been favorites with phone phreaks, first as learning tools, then as Archimedes platforms from which to manipulate the huge Bell system. A phone phreak in Bell territory will often M-F himself into an independent's switching system, with switching idiosyncrasies which can give him marvelous leverage over the Bell System.

"I have a real affection for Automatic Electric equipment," Bernay told me. "There are a lot of things you can play with. Things break down in interesting ways."

Shortly after Bernay graduated from college (with a double major in chemistry and philosophy), he graduated from phreaking around with G.T.&E. to the Bell System itself, and made his legendary sticker-pasting journey north along the coast, settling finally in Northwest Pacific Bell territory. He discovered that if Bell does not break down as interestingly as G.T.&E., it nevertheless offers a lot of "things to play with."

Bernay learned to play with blue boxes. He established his own personal switchboard and phone-phreak research laboratory complex. He continued his phone-phreak evangelism with ongoing sticker campaigns. He set up two recording numbers, one with instructions for beginning phone phreaks, the other with latest news and technical developments (along with some advanced instruction) gathered from sources all over the country.

These days, Bernay told me, he has gone beyond phone-phreaking itself. "Lately I've been enjoying playing with computers more than playing with phones. My personal thing in computers is just like with phones, I guess—the kick is in finding out how to beat the system, how to get *at* things I'm not supposed to know about, how to *do* things with the system that I'm not supposed to be able to do."

As a matter of fact, Bernay told me, he had just been fired from his computer-programming job for doing things he was not supposed to be able to do. He had been working with a huge time-sharing computer owned by a large corporation but shared by many others. Access to the computer was limited to those programmers and corporations that had been assigned certain passwords. And each password restricted its user to access to only the one section of the computer cordoned off from its own information storager. The password system prevented companies and individuals from stealing each other's information.

"I figured out how to write a program that would let me read everyone else's password," Bernay reports. "I began playing around with passwords. I began letting the people who used the computer know, in subtle ways, that I knew their passwords. I began dropping notes to the computer supervisors with hints that I knew what I know. I signed them 'The Midnight Skulker.' I kept getting cleverer and cleverer with my messages and devising ways of showing them what I could do. I'm sure they couldn't imagine I could do the things I was showing them. But they never responded to me. Every once in a while they'd change the passwords, but I found out how to discover what the new ones were, and let them know. But they never responded directly to The Midnight Skulker. I even finally designed a program which they could use to prevent my program from finding out what it did. In effect I told them how to wipe me out, The Midnight Skulker. It was a very clever program. I started leaving clues about myself. I wanted them to try and use it, and then try to come up with something to get around that and re-appear again. But they wouldn't play. I wanted to get caught. I mean I didn't want to get caught personally, but I wanted them to notice me and admit that they noticed me. I wanted them to attempt to respond, maybe in some interesting way."

Finally the computer managers became concerned enough about the threat of information-stealing to respond. However, instead of using The Midnight Skulker's own elegant self-destruct program, they called in their security personnel, interrogated everyone, found an informer to identify Bernay as The Midnight Skulker, and fired him.

"At first the security people advised the company to hire me full-time to search out other flaws and discover other computer freaks. I might have liked that. But I probably would have turned into a double double agent rather than the double agent they wanted. I might have resurrected The Midnight Skulker and tried to catch myself. Who knows? Anyway, the higher-ups turned the whole idea down."

YOU CAN TAP THE F.B.I.'S CRIME CONTROL COMPUTER IN THE COMFORT OF YOUR OWN HOME, PERHAPS

Computer freaking may be the wave of the future. It suits the phone-phreak sensibility perfectly. Gilbertson, the blue-box inventor and a life-long phone phreak, has also gone on from phone-phreaking to computer-freaking. Before he got into the blue-box business Gilbertson, who is a highly skilled programmer, devised programs for international currency arbitrage.

But he began playing with computers in earnest when he learned he could use his blue box in tandem with the computer terminal installed in his apartment by the instrumentation firm he worked for. The print-out terminal and keyboard was equipped with acoustical coupling, so that by coupling his little ivory Princess phone to the terminal and then coupling his blue box on that, he could M-F his way into other computers with complete anonymity, and without charge; program and reprogram them at will; feed them false or misleading information; tap and steal from them. He explained to me that he taps computers by busying out all the lines, then going into a verification trunk, listening into the passwords and instructions one of the time sharers uses, and then M-F-ing in and imitating them. He believes it would not be impossible to creep into the F.B.I.'s crime-control computer through a local police computer terminal and phreak around with the F.B.I.'s memory banks. He claims he has succeeded in reprogramming a certain huge institutional computer in such a way that it has cordoned off an entire section of its circuitry for his personal use, and at the same time conceals the arrangement from anyone else's notice. I have been unable to verify this claim.

Like Captain Crunch, like Alexander Graham Bell (pseudonym of a disgruntled-looking East Coast engineer who claims to have invented the black box and now sells black and blue boxes to gamblers and radical heavies), like most phone phreaks, Gilbertson began his career trying to rip off pay phones as a teen-ager. Figure them out, then rip them off. Getting his dime back from the pay phone is the phone phreak's first thrilling rite of passage. After learning the usual eighteen different ways of getting his dime back, Gilbertson learned how to make master keys to coin-phone cash boxes, and get everyone else's dimes back. He stole some phone-company equipment and put together his own home switchboard with it. He learned to make a simple "bread-box" device, of the kind used by bookies in the thirties (bookie gives a number to his betting clients; the phone with that number is installed in some widow lady's apartment, but is rigged to ring in the bookie's shop across town; cops trace big betting number and find nothing but the widow).

Not long after that afternoon in 1968 when, deep in the stacks of an engineering library, he came across a technical journal with the phone tone frequencies and rushed off to make his first blue box, not long after that Gilbertson abandoned a very promising career in physical chemistry and began selling blue boxes for $1,500 apiece.

"I had to leave physical chemistry. I just ran out of interesting things to learn," he told me one evening. We had been talking in the apartment of the man who served as the link between Gilbertson and the syndicate in arranging the big $300,000 blue-box deal which fell through because of legal trouble. There has been some smoking.

"No more interesting things to learn," he continues. "Physical chemistry turns out to be a sick subject when you take it to its highest level. I don't know. I don't think I could explain to you how it's sick. You have to be there. But you get, I don't know, a false feeling of omnipotence. I suppose it's like phone-phreaking that way. This huge thing is there. This whole system. And there are holes in it and you slip into them like Alice and you're pretending you're doing something you're actually not, or at least it's no longer *you* that's doing what you were doing. It's all Lewis Carroll. Physical chemistry and phone-phreaking. That's why you have these phone-phreak pseudonyms like The Cheshire Cat, The Red King, and The Snark. But there's something about phone-phreaking that you don't find in physical chemistry." He looks up at me:

"Did you ever steal anything?"

Well yes, I—

"Then you know! You know the rush you get. It's not just knowledge, like physical chemistry. It's forbidden knowledge. You know. You can learn about anything under the sun and be bored to death with it. But the idea that it's illegal. Look, you can be small and mobile and smart and you're ripping off somebody large and powerful and very dangerous."

People like Gilbertson and Alexander Graham Bell are always talking about ripping off the phone company and screwing Ma Bell. But if they were shown a single button and told that by pushing it they could turn the entire circuitry of A.T.&T. into molten puddles, they probably wouldn't push it. The disgruntled-inventor phone phreak needs the phone system the way the lapsed Catholic needs the Church, the way Satan needs a God, the way The Midnight Skulker needed, more than anything else, response.

Later that evening Gilbertson finished telling me how delighted he was at the flood of blue boxes spreading throughout the country, how delighted he was to know that "this time they're really screwed." He suddenly shifted gears.

"Of course, I do have this love/hate thing about Ma Bell. In a way I almost *like* the phone company. I guess I'd be very sad if they were to go away or if their services were to disintegrate. In a way it's just that after having been so good they turn out to have these things wrong with them. It's those flaws that allow me to get in and mess with them, but I don't know. There's something about it that gets to you and makes you want to *get to it*, you know."

I ask him what happens when he runs out of interesting, forbidden things to learn about the phone system.

"I don't know, maybe I'd go to work for them for a while."

"In security even?"

"I'd do it, sure. I'd just as soon play—I'd just as soon work on either side."

Even figuring out how to trap phone phreaks? I said, recalling Mark Bernay's game.

"Yes, that might be interesting. Yes, I could figure out how to outwit the phone phreaks. Of course if I got too good at it, it might become boring again. Then I'd have to hope the phone phreaks got much better and outsmarted me for a while. That would move the quality of the game up one level. I might even have to help them out, you know, 'Well kids. I wouldn't want this to get around but did you ever think of—?' I could keep it going at higher and higher levels forever."

The dealer speaks up for the first time. He has been staring at the soft blinking patterns of lights and colors on the translucent tiled wall facing him. Actually there are no patterns: the color and illumination of every tile is determined by a computerized random-number generator designed by Gilbertson which ensures that that there can be no meaning to any sequence of events in the tiles.

"Those are nice games you're talking about," says the dealer to his friend. "But I wouldn't mind seeing them screwed. A telephone isn't private anymore. You can't say anything you really want to say on a telephone or you have to go through that paranoid bulls - - -.

'Is it cool to talk on the phone?' I mean, even if it is cool, if you have to ask 'Is it cool?' then it isn't cool. You know. Like those blind kids, people are going to start putting together their own private telephone companies if they want to really talk. And you know what else. You don't hear silences on the phone anymore. They've got this time-sharing thing on long-distance lines where you make a pause and they snip out that piece of time and use it to carry part of somebody else's conversation. Instead of a pause, where somebody's maybe breathing or sighing, you get this blank hole and you only start hearing again when someone says a word and even the beginning of the word is clipped off. Silences don't count— you're paying for them, but they take them away from you. It's not cool to talk and you can't hear someone when they don't talk. What the hell good is the phone? I wouldn't mind seeing them totally screwed."

THE BIG MEMPHIS BUST

Joe Engressia never wanted to screw Ma Bell. His dream had always been to work for her.

The day I visited Joe in his small apartment on Union Avenue in Memphis, he was upset about another setback in his application for a telephone job.

"They're stalling on it. I got a letter today telling me they'd have to postpone the interview I requested again. My landlord read it for me. They gave me some runaround about wanting papers on my rehabilitation status but I think there's something else going on."

When I switched on the forty-watt bulb in Joe's room—he sometimes forgets when he has guests—it looked as if there was enough telephone hardware to start a small phone company of his own.

There is one phone on top of his desk, one phone sitting in an open drawer beneath the desk top. Next to the desk-top phone is a cigar-box-size M-F device with big toggle switches, and next to that is some kind of switching and coupling device with jacks and alligator plugs hanging loose. Next to that is a Braille typewriter. On the floor next to the desk, lying upside down like a dead tortoise, is the half-gutted body of an old black standard phone. Across the room on a torn and dusty couch are two more phones, one of them a touch-tone model; two tape recorders; a heap of phone patches and cassettes; and a life-size toy telephone.

Our conversation is interrupted every ten minutes by phone phreaks from all over the country ringing Joe on just about every piece of equipment but the toy phone and the Braille typewriter. One fourteen-year-old blind kid from Connecticut calls up and tells Joe he's got a girl friend. He wants to talk to Joe about girl friends. Joe says they'll talk later in the evening when they can be alone on the line. Joe draws a deep breath, whistles him off the air with an earsplitting 2,600-cycle whistle. Joe is pleased to get the calls but he looked worried and preoccupied that evening, his brow constantly furrowed over his dark wandering eyes. In addition to the phone-company stall, he has just learned that his apartment house is due to be demolished in sixty days for urban renewal. For all its shabbiness, the Union Avenue apartment has been Joe's first home-of-his-own, and he's worried that he may not find another before this one is demolished.

But what really bothers Joe is that switchmen haven't been listening to him. "I've been doing some checking on 800 numbers lately, and I've discovered that certain 800 numbers in New Hampshire couldn't be reached from Missouri and Kansas. Now it may sound like a small thing, but I don't like to see sloppy work; it makes me feel bad about the lines. So I've been calling up switching offices and reporting it, but they haven't corrected it. I called them up for the third time today and instead of checking they just got mad. Well, that gets me mad. I mean, I do try to help them. There's something about them I can't understand—you want to help them and they just try to say you're defrauding them."

It is Sunday evening and Joe invites me to join him for dinner at a Holiday Inn. Frequently on Sunday evening Joe takes some of his welfare money, calls a cab, and treats himself to a steak dinner at one of Memphis's thirteen Holiday Inns. Memphis is the headquarters of Holiday Inn. Holiday Inns have been a favorite for Joe ever since he made his first solo phone trip to a Bell switching office in Jacksonville, Florida, and stayed in the Holiday Inn there. He likes to stay at Holiday Inns, he explains, because they represent freedom to him and because the rooms are arranged the same all over the country so he knows that any Holiday Inn room is familiar territory to him. Just like any telephone.

Over steaks in the Pinnacle Restaurant of the Holiday Inn Medical Center on Madison Avenue in Memphis, Joe tells me the highlights of his life as a phone phreak.

At age seven, Joe learned his first phone trick. A mean babysitter, tired of listening to little Joe play with the phone as he always did, constantly, put a lock on the phone dial. "I got so mad. When there's a phone sitting there and I can't use it . . . so I started getting mad and banging the receiver up and down. I noticed I banged it once and it dialed one. Well, then I tried banging it twice . . ." In a few minutes Joe learned how to dial by pressing the hook switch at the right time. "I was so excited I remember going 'whoo whoo' and beat a box down on the floor."

At age eight Joe learned about whistling. "I was listening to some intercept nonworking-number recording in L.A.—I was calling L.A. as far back as that, but I'd mainly dial nonworking numbers because there was no charge, and I'd listen to these recordings all day. Well, I was whistling 'cause listening to these recordings can be boring after a while even if they are from L.A., and all of a sudden, in the middle of whistling, the recording clicked off. I fiddled around whistling some more, and the same thing happened. So I called up the switch room and said, 'I'm Joe. I'm eight years old and I want to know why when I whistle this tune the line clicks off.' He tried to explain it to me, but it was a little too technical at the time. I went on learning. That was a thing nobody was going to stop me from doing. The phones were my life, and I was going to pay any price to keep on learning. I knew I could go to jail. But I had to do what I had to do to keep on learning."

The phone is ringing when we walk back into Joe's apartment on Union Avenue. It is Captain Crunch. The Captain has been following me around by phone, calling up everywhere I go with additional bits of advice and explanation for me and whatever phone phreak I happened to be visiting. This time the Captain reports he is calling from what he describes as "my hideaway high up in the Sierra Nevada." He pulses out lusty salvos of M-F and tells Joe he is about to "go out and get a little action tonight. Do some phreaking of another kind, if you know what I mean." Joe chuckles.

The Captain then tells me to make sure I understand that what he told me about tying up the nation's phone lines was true, but that he and the phone phreaks *he* knew never used the technique for sabotage. They only learned the technique to help the phone company.

"We do a lot of troubleshooting for them. Like this New Hampshire/Missouri WATS-line flaw I've been screaming about. We help them more than they know."

After we say good-bye to the Captain and Joe whistles him off the line, Joe tells me about a disturbing dream he had the night before: "I had been caught and they were taking me to a prison. It was a long trip. They were taking me to a prison a long long way away. And we stopped at a Holiday Inn and it was my last night ever at a Holiday Inn, and it was my last night ever using the phone and I was crying and crying, and the lady at the Holiday Inn said, 'Gosh, honey, you should never be sad at a Holiday Inn. You should always be happy here. Especially since it's your last night.' And that just made it worse and I was sobbing so much I couldn't stand it."

Two weeks after I left Joe Engressia's apartment, phone-company security agents and Memphis police broke into it. Armed with a warrant, which they left pinned to a wall, they confiscated every piece of equipment in the room, including his toy telephone. Joe was placed under arrest and taken to the city jail where he was forced to spend the night since he had no money and knew no one in Memphis to call.

It is not clear who told Joe what that night, but someone told him that the phone company had an open-and-shut case against him because of revelations of illegal activity he had made to a phone-company undercover agent.

By morning Joe had become convinced that the reporter from *Esquire*, with whom he had spoken two weeks ago, was the under-cover agent. He probably had ugly thoughts about someone he couldn't see gaining his confidence, listening to him talk about his personal obsessions and dreams, while planning all the while to lock him up.

"I really thought he was a reporter," Engressia told the Memphis *Press-Scimitar*. "I told him everything. . . ." Feeling betrayed, Joe proceeded to confess everything to the press and police.

As it turns out, the phone company *did* use an undercover agent to trap Joe, although it was not the *Esquire* reporter.

Ironically, security agents were alerted and began to compile a case against Joe because of one of his acts of love for the system: Joe had called an internal service department to report that he had located a group of defective long-distance trunks, and to complain again about the New Hampshire/Missouri WATS problem. Joe always liked Ma Bell's lines to be clean and responsive. A suspicious switchman reported Joe to the security agents who discovered that Joe had never had a long-distance call charged to his name.

Then the security agents learned that Joe was planning one of his phone trips to a local switching office. The security people planted one of their agents in the switching office. He posed as a student switchman and followed Joe around on a tour. He was extremely friendly and helpful to Joe, leading him around the office by the arm. When the tour was over he offered Joe a ride back to his apartment house. On the way he asked Joe—one tech man to another—about "those blue boxes" he'd heard about. Joe talked about them freely, talked about his blue box freely, and about all the other things he could do with the phones.

The next day the phone-company security agents slapped a

monitoring tape on Joe's line, which eventually picked up an illegal call. Then they applied for the search warrant and broke in.

In court Joe pleaded not guilty to possession of a blue box and theft of service. A sympathetic judge reduced the charges to malicious mischief and found him guilty on that count, sentenced him to two thirty-day sentences to be served concurrently, and then suspended the sentence on condition that Joe promise never to play with phones again. Joe promised, but the phone company refused to restore his service. For two weeks after the trial Joe could not be reached except through the pay phone at his apartment house, and the landlord screened all calls for him.

Phone phreak Carl managed to get through to Joe after the trial, and reported that Joe sounded crushed by the whole affair.

"What I'm worried about," Carl told me, "is that Joe means it this time. The promise. That he'll never phone-phreak again. That's what he told me, that he's given up phone-phreaking for good. I mean his entire life. He says he knows they're going to be watching so closely for the rest of his life he'll never be able to make a move without going straight to jail. He sounded very broken up by the whole experience of being in jail. It was awful to hear him talk that way. I don't know. I hope maybe he had to sound that way. Over the phone, you know."

He reports that the entire phone-phreak underground is up in arms over the phone company's treatment of Joe. "All the while Joe had his hopes pinned on his application for a phone-company job, they were stringing him along, getting ready to bust him. That gets me mad. Joe spent most of his time helping them out. The bastards. They think they can use him as an example. All of a sudden they're harassing us on the coast. Agents are jumping up on our lines. They just busted - - - - - -'s mute yesterday and ripped out his lines. But no matter what Joe does, I don't think we're going to take this lying down."

Two weeks later my phone rings and about eight phone phreaks in succession say hello from about eight different places in the country, among them Carl, Ed, and Captain Crunch. A nationwide phone-phreak conference line has been reestablished through a switching machine in - - - - - - - - , with the cooperation of a disgruntled switchman.

"We have a special guest with us today," Carl tells me.

The next voice I hear is Joe's. He reports happily that he has just moved to a place called Millington, Tennessee, fifteen miles outside of Memphis, where he has been hired as a telephone-set repairman by a small independent phone company. Someday he hopes to be an equipment troubleshooter.

"It's the kind of job I dreamed about. They found out about me from the publicity surrounding the trial. Maybe Ma Bell did me a favor busting me. I'll have telephones in my hands all day long."

"You know the expression, 'Don't get mad, get even'?" phone phreak Carl asked me. "Well, I think they're going to be very sorry about what they did to Joe and what they're trying to do to us."

THE EXALTATION OF RABBI BAAL HA TOV

When this story appeared a writer I know told me it wasn't really about Nixon's Second Inaugural Ball, but instead "a parable of the immigrant experience in America." Having reread it for the first time since then, I still maintain it was about the Inaugural Ball—it's all true for one thing—but I'd be a liar if I didn't say I liked the parable notion.

In any case, rereading the story did recall to me the delight it was to cover such events for The Voice *back then when the paper was still run by founding editor Dan Wolf. You could go to an event like the Inaugural Ball and not feel the need to write about how well the President danced and to which songs. The daily papers and the news-magazines would take care of that. This left you free to seek out peripheral epiphanies that reflected in some parabolic way the essence of the main event. You could, for instance, pick up on the song and dance of an overstimulated Hasidic rabbi and see the event through his wide eyes, and the wider eyes of the people he would encounter in his odyssey about the ballroom.*

The first time I sighted the old rabbi, he was bucking through the crowd on the dance floor, clutching a big black book to his chest, plunging and shifting through clusters of expensive Republicans with the reckless agility of a fine halfback.

This particular dance floor, here at the north end of the grand foyer of the Kennedy Center for the Performing Arts, is no ordinary dance floor. Less than fifteen minutes ago, on this floor—over there in front of the bandstand where the old rabbi is plugging away right now—the President and the First Lady waltzed together

—the very first time, the President had announced beforehand, that he had ever actually danced at an Inaugural Ball.

The President is gone now. The Lionel Hampton orchestra is temporarily silent. This historic dance floor is jammed with rich and powerful patrons of the $1,000 V.I.P. boxes, all of them arrayed in gleaming formal wear.

With his long, black Hasid coat hanging loose and his wide-brimmed Hasid hat pressed down tight, with his gray beard untrimmed and his lips grimly pursed, the old rabbi drew more than occasional stares of wonder as he pushed through the Republican elite.

The rabbi glanced appraisingly at the faces of each group he passed through, but kept his course set for one particularly distinguished-looking cluster of couples over at the far end of the bandstand.

As soon as he broke through to this elegant group, the rabbi grabbed one of them—a tall, silver-haired gentleman—by the elbow, pulled him around to face him, and began speaking to him with animation.

The silver-haired man shook his head gravely down at the rabbi, who was not much taller than five feet. At this point I arrived within hearing range, and the first thing I heard the rabbi say was: "So you're not George Bush. I thought you were George Bush. Okay, what are you, a senator?"

The man shook his head.

"No senator. Congressman? What? No congressman? Nothing?"

The rabbi sighed and shrugged.

He turned to the other gentlemen in the group. "How about you? You a senator or a congressman? No? You a celebrity of any kind? No? Look. George Bush. Can any of you give me George Bush?"

"I believe George Bush may not be at this particular ball," said the first gentleman somewhat frostily.

"Any other celebrities you got for me?" the rabbi pressed him, while holding up his big black book. "Look here, I got eighteen senators and an admiral signed today. Volpe, too, I got. I just shook hands with Volpe and he signed. Here, look." With a dramatic flourish the old rabbi flung open his big black book to its full size: two feet high and two feet wide.

"The book" turned out to be some kind of presentation album. Inside, on the left-hand side, was a two-foot photograph of President Nixon. Facing the smiling President, on the other side of the album, was what appeared to be a very long poem.

"This is my hymn," the rabbi told the politely attentive group. "I wrote this hymn for the President in celebration of the occasion of his inauguration. Look, the eighteen senators I got here."

The rabbi pointed to a column of autographs running down the inside margin of the hymn. "See, here's Kennedy, and here's Volpe, whom I just shook hands with. So now you see why I have to find George Bush to sign. Republican Chairman. When I get it all completely signed I will present it to the President at the White House, a hymn on occasion of his inauguration from Rabbi Baal Ha Tov."

At this point, Rabbi Baal Ha Tov noticed someone looking over his shoulder, taking notes on the text of his hymn.

"What is this, a reporter here? You want the words, go ahead. I can also send you my hymn 'Landmark of Achievement,' commemorating the Bicentennial, 1976. Who are you? Can you get me George Bush?"

I introduced myself to the rabbi. I told him I didn't think I could get him George Bush.

"Don't worry. I'll find him, George Bush. Meanwhile, you want to hear me sing the hymn for you? Look, here's Hatfield's signature. Pictures also I had taken with Hatfield."

I told the rabbi he didn't have to sing the hymn for me. But I asked him to explain the unusual opening section of the hymn. As it appeared in the big black album, the opening verse read like this:

INAUGURATION
COMMEMORATION
NATURALIZATION
MANIFESTATION
AFFIRMATION
EXULTATION
MEDIATION
CONGRATULATION
CELEBRATION
ADMIRATION
DEDICATION
PRESENTATION
AMERICANIZATION
ADULATION
PARTICIPATION
SALUTATION
APPRECIATION

"What's to explain?" the rabbi asked me. "That's the beginning of the hymn. Listen. I'll sing."

The rabbi proceeded to sing out each one of those seventeen words, one after the other, in a vaguely quavering cantorial style.

During the singing, the elegant Republican couples began edging away from the rabbi, presenting various elegant shoulder blades in back angles to him and me.

"You like it, huh?" said the rabbi to me when he finished singing the opening verse of his hymn. "As good as 'Ole Man River,' isn't it? Yeshiva students wrote the music for me. The poetry is mine. Did you know I am direct descendant Baal Shem Tov?"

"Wait a minute, there's only one Baal Shem Tov in the world at a time. You're not really him, are you?"

"I told you I'm Baal *Ha* Tov. Look," he said, pointing to the top of the hymn where it was written, "by Rabbi Baal Ha Tov."

"That's me, Baal Ha Tov. But I am descended from Baal Shem Tov. Also I have written twenty-four other songs about the President. I can send you copies for your newspaper story. Also—"

"Do you really like the President that much?"

"I like all Presidents. I am for Johnson. I am born 1901, I am for Coolidge, for Harding, too. Also Einstein. I have Einstein's endorsement. I went to visit Einstein in 1954. Hello, are you a senator, yes?"

The rabbi had caught hold of another elbow. The elbow belongs to another tall Republican gentleman in a burnished black tuxedo. He was passing by with a golden-haired woman in a jeweled turquoise gown when the rabbi waylaid him. There is another, equally resplendent, couple along with them.

"No senator, huh? No congressman? Any of you celebrities of any kind? Can you get me George Bush?"

Undismayed by negative answers to all these questions, the rabbi proceeds once again to display the interior of his big black album. He sings brief excerpts from the inaugural hymn. He shows off the accompanying autographs.

The golden-haired lady in the turquoise gown announces to the others in the group that she thinks the rabbi's gray beard is "adorable." She confides to the rabbi that her brother went to Israel once.

The rabbi beams at her, grabs her drink from her hand, and says: "Can I have some of your drink?"

Without waiting for a reply he takes a swallow of the drink, returns it to her, and pushes through the group toward an Oriental man wearing a Secret Service pin, whom the rabbi apparently mistakes for a waiter. "Hey, fella? Where do we get a drink? I want a drink," the rabbi informs the Oriental secret service man.

The agent waves vaguely toward the opposite end of the grand foyer. The rabbi returns to the foursome he has just left, and conducts a brief whispered conversation with the woman whose brother visited Israel. Something passes from her hand to his hand.

Leaving them behind, the rabbi makes his way back to me.

"Look, David, look," (Throughout the evening, the rabbi persists in calling me David, although I am quite sure I introduced myself as Ron.) The rabbi holds up a small pasteboard ticket before my eyes. It reads: "Good for one drink, Inaugural Ball, January 20, 1973."

"Where's the bar, David? Find the bar for me. I need a drink. This has been a great day for me. Here, you hold this book. I'm seventy-two years old and I've been going all day. First we find me the bar, then we look for Mr. Bush."

It takes a long time to get within sight of the bar. Every few feet of the way down the foyer, the rabbi stops a group of potential celebrities and asks for senators and congressmen and George Bush, grabs the heavy black album out of my hands, unfolds its wonders for them, and asks for "a taste" of their drinks.

He has several tastes. One generous group poured him a full glass of champagne. Two women in the champagne group embraced the rabbi tipsily, and asked their husbands to allow them to have their pictures taken with him. The rabbi disengages himself, plunges ahead, shoving the big black album back into my hand and downing the champagne.

We almost reached the bar. But suddenly the rabbi saw the medals.

An inaugural official rushed past us in the direction of the $1,000 V.I.P. boxes, carrying a stack of small, white gift packages. The top one was open, revealing a souvenir inauguration medal.

The rabbi grabbed the man's arm as he went by, nearly causing the entire stack of packages to buckle and spill.

"How about one for me?" the rabbi asked the harassed official. "Let me have one of those medals. I got a hymn to the President here."

"Souvenirs will be given to everyone *as they leave* tonight," the harried inaugural man told the rabbi, twisting out of his grasp.

"You hear that, David? Forget the drinks, David! Let's get those medals!" He bent his head down and pointed it back into the crowd.

I followed him as best I could. Halfway down the grand foyer, the rabbi made a right turn into what is known as "the Hall of State" and headed down toward the entrance a hundred yards away.

I caught up with the rabbi as he finished interrogating another medal-box courier in front of the Latvian Folk Group Performing Ensemble.

"David, let's go, David. Up ahead they give the medals and souvenir book, too. Look, David. I got someone waiting outside. A woman. I got to get rid of her."

"A woman?"

"She holds my things for me. I'll tell you what. I'll just give her five bucks, tell her to go away, then we get the medals. What do you think, David, let's go."

The rabbi led me forward to the very entrance of the concert hall, past the line of ticket takers and secret service agents to a cluster of chairs just inside the doors. He approached a kindly-looking middle-aged lady who was sitting on a folding chair, hands clasped in her lap, smiling sweetly at the approach of the rabbi.

The rabbi introduced the lady to me, grabbed the big black album from me, had a brief whispered conference with the lady, then turned and beat back into a growing commotion forming around a beleaguered hand truck piled high with boxes of souvenir medals. I watched the rabbi disappear into a growing crowd besieging the hand truck, clamoring for medals.

The lady smiled benevolently at the disappearing rabbi, and then looked up at me with her eyes shining. "He's a wonderful man, isn't he? I just take care of him. I'm not even Jewish, but I'm studying to convert. The rabbi's past seventy, you know. I just take care of him. Look, here's his letter from President Nixon and pictures from his visit to the White House."

She handed me a letter on White House stationery and some glossy photos. The photos showed the rabbi on the White House grounds showing a collage of presidential history he had created to a presidential secretary and a presidential gardener.

"Look what the President wrote," the lady said. "The rabbi gave the President an inscribed Bible and the President sent him this personal letter."

She points to a passage on the letter which is, sure enough, signed "Richard M. Nixon."

"It was most gracious of you to want me to have this symbolic and inspirational gift," the President wrote to the rabbi. "You may be sure it is one which will occupy a special place among my cherished mementos."

Suddenly the rabbi is back. His face is glowing, and he is bearing his big black album aloft in triumph.

"David. David. I just got now Bob Hope! Look, Bob Hope!"

"Did Bob Hope say anything to you?"

"He looked at my hymn and he told me 'that's the most wonderful piece of art I've ever seen.' Come with me, David, we'll get the dignitaries. We'll get the medals."

He turned to the woman. "You stay right here and wait," he instructed her. She smiled agreeably.

The rabbi pulled me off into the crowd.

"Listen, David, that woman. Forget her. She's just a maid. She is here today, gone tomorrow, you know what I mean, not worth writing about. Hello, hostess." The rabbi grabbed a young girl with an "official hostess" badge pinned to her dress. "Hostess, do you have any senators for me? Naval people? I have one admiral. Wait! Medals! I see medals. Hey, mister. Hey. You have a medal for me?"

The rabbi was off again, on the trail of another souvenir-box carrier, leaving me to grin foolishly at the startled "official hostess." This time I didn't try to follow the rabbi.

In fact, I didn't see the rabbi again till hours later. It was after one o'clock that morning, as the ball was coming to a close. When I emerged from the Kennedy Center Opera House into the grand foyer, after observing an exclusive Inaugural Ball performance of a group described in the Inaugural Ball programme as "The Philadelphia Chinatown YMCA Gordon Dragon Club."

Anyway, there was the rabbi, dashing madly through the grand foyer, album in hand, with a strange look compounded of bliss and near hysteria on his face.

The rabbi caught sight of me and grabbed my arm. "Ah, David, David. Wonderful. Sammy Davis I am going to get. Sammy Davis. Party at Hilton. Two doctors with car waiting to take me."

The rabbi paused to catch his breath. The bliss faded: hysteria bloomed.

"David! The woman. I have to find that woman! We have to get to the car! Two doctors waiting to take me to Sammy Davis. Where is that woman?"

"You mean the—"

"Yes. The one with my things. She's got the merchandise. I left the medals with her. Where did I leave her? I can't find the right hall. Two doctors are waiting with a car. Help me, David. Find the woman."

I led the rabbi through the grand foyer in the direction of the Hall of Nations. Once on the way, hysteria faded and bliss blossomed.

"David. Mayor Washington I got. And a naval man I got. David. I am more exalted tonight than even the President. When the Mayor Washington signed, they lifted me up on their hands to him. I tell you, David, I am so exalted tonight. And now Sammy Davis."

As we pass by the Baltimore Estonian Women's Chorus, a giggling young woman seems to recognize the rabbi, reaches out and pulls him into her arms, kisses him, and whispers something in his ear.

Muttering something about Sammy Davis and doctors, the rabbi pulls away from the woman and continues his charge down the hall.

"You see, David, everyone knows me—the women and the men. Hello, are you the Governor? No? David, where is that woman?"

At last we reached the lady with the sweet smile. Urgently, the rabbi explains the doctors' situation to her, pulls her to her feet.

"Help, hurry. They're with a car at the Opera House entrance. At the Washington Hilton is the party. Sammy Davis I'll get. Maybe even George Bush do you think? Hurry, David. Which way?"

The rabbi refuses to take a short cut outside the center from the Concert Hall entrance. Instead, we march up the Hall of Nations against the tide, make a right into the grand foyer and proceed into the Hall of State, and make another right and head down the Hall of State to the Opera House entrance.

The rabbi becomes slightly frantic at the length of this journey. When at last we arrive at the Opera House door, the rabbi looks wildly around at the exiting throng.

He cannot find the two doctors. Not even one.

"Are you sure this is the right entrance, David? They said Opera House. Is this Opera House?"

I assure the rabbi it is Opera House.

The rabbi lunges into the crowd, leaving me and the woman behind. We see him bobbing and weaving through the tide of departures, then turning and struggling back, sad-eyed.

"They said here, the doctors. Maybe outside. Come. They will be in a car outside waiting."

Outside there is the roar and jumble of buses and official White House limousines. The rabbi prowls up and down the crowded curbside.

No doctors.

"They must have waited a long time and left, the doctors. They must want us to meet them at the Hilton Hotel with Sammy Davis. A party till four in the morning they said. They'll be waiting for us there. Come, David, find us a bus to the Hilton."

I found him a bus that was headed downtown. The bus was crowded, but there was one seat left. The rabbi took it, folded his arms around his big black album, and shut his eyes. The sweet-faced lady stood next to his seat, smiling down upon him.

Ten minutes passed. The bus frequently revved its engines, but did not move an inch. It seemed to have become trapped against the curb by a formation of other buses, most of which were them-selves motionless.

I pushed my way off the bus and started walking. That was the last I saw of the Rabbi Baal Ha Tov.

THE CORPSE AS BIG AS THE RITZ

Old Cecil B. De Mille said it himself. Playing himself in Sunset Boulevard, *De Mille gazes upon aging screen star Norma Desmond leaving the studio lot, her deluded dreams of a spectacular comeback still intact, and pronounces: "No one should underestimate the damage to the human spirit that can be done by a dozen press agents working overtime."*

This is a story about the obverse side of that pronouncement—the damage that the life of promotion and self-promotion wreaks upon the self of the promoter.

Press agents are not generally considered romantic figures, but David Whiting was more than a press agent for Sarah Miles, and this is a romance of a sort—a destructive relationship between a dreamer of Gatsbylike pretensions and a movie star that only one of the two thought was love. I think when the story first appeared many people might have read it mainly to find out whether one of the big stars in this movie-set mystery had gotten away with murder. Specifically, had Burt Reynolds somehow caused the mysterious "star-shaped wound" that was found on the dead body of star-struck David Whiting as he lay on the tiles of Sarah Miles's motel room bathroom? (To set the record straight, I don't think Burt did.) The preoccupation with such questions obscured the fact that this is not a story about stars, but about the short, unhappy life of a would-be star maker, as strange and mysterious a character in his own way as Tommy the Traveler, with an equally secret self.

Sergeant Forrest Hinderliter of the Gila Bend (Arizona) Police had been up since two in the morning with a dead body and a shaky story. He'd found the body—a black man with a bullet hole in his back—lying on the floor in Apartment 44 of the North Euclid Avenue project at the western edge of town. He'd also found a woman there, and this was her story:

She woke up after midnight to find a man on top of her, making love to her. She'd never seen the man before. She told him to get off and get out; she warned him she was expecting another man. A car pulled up outside and flashed its lights. A minute later the other man came through the door. Explanations were inadequate. In the scuffle a gun was drawn, a .38 revolver. A shot went off, the first visitor died.

An accident, the woman told Sergeant Hinderliter, the gun had gone off by accident. An accident, the other man, the one who owned the .38, told the sergeant.

Sergeant Hinderliter had the body tagged and carted off to Phoenix for an autopsy. He took statements until six thirty in the morning, then returned to the station house to check in for his regular Sunday tour of duty.

He was drinking black coffee at Birchfields's Café at six minutes past noon when the phone rang. It was Mrs. Steel, the station-house dispatcher, on the line. She had just taken a call from a man at the Travelodge Motel. There was a dead body in room 127, it was reported, an overdose of something.

Up until 1965 Gila Bend showed up frequently in National Weather Summaries as having registered the highest daily temperature in America. One hundred twenty in the shade was not unusual. Occasionally Gila Bend was referred to as the hottest place in America.

It was hot in Gila Bend, but not that hot, the Mayor of Gila Bend confided to me one evening at the Elks Club bar. Someone in Gila Bend had been doing some fooling around with the thermometer readings to make Gila Bend look a few degrees hotter than it was. In 1965, the Weather Bureau did some checking and put a stop to the matter. Since then Gila Bend has been just another hot place.

There's an old narrow-gauge railroad that runs south from the town to the open-pit copper mines near the Mexican border. The Phelps Dodge Corporation uses the railroad to run copper anodes from their foundries up to the Southern Pacific freight siding at Gila Bend. Hollywood Westerns occasionally use the railroad's ancient steam locomotive and the cactus wastes surrounding the tracks for "location" work.

On January 28, 1973, an MGM production company shooting

The Man Who Loved Cat Dancing, a high-budget, middlebrow Western starring Sarah Miles, Burt Reynolds, and Lee J. Cobb, arrived at Gila Bend. Forty members of the cast and crew checked into the Travelodge Motel on the eastern edge of town.

There was no pulse. The skin had cooled. Pale blotches on the hands, the neck, and the forehead suggested to Sergeant Hinderliter that death had come to the body several hours before he had. Rigor mortis, in its early stages, had stiffened the arms which were wrapped around an empty polyethylene wastebasket. It was twelve thirty P.M.

The young man lay curled up on his left side on the floor of the partitioned-off "dressing-room" area of Travelodge room 127. His nose touched the metal strip which divided the carpeted dressing-room floor from the tiled floor of the bathroom. His feet stuck out beyond the end of the partition.

The capsules were big and red. There were about a dozen, and most of them lay in two groups on the floor. Burt Reynolds would later testify he saw pills lying on top of the dead man's arm.

The sergeant wondered why the man on the floor had decided to collapse and die in what was clearly a woman's bedroom: the vanity counter above the body teemed with vials of cosmetics, a woman's wardrobe packed the hangers, a long brown hairpiece streamed across a nearby suitcase. As he stepped out to his squad car Sergeant Hinderliter felt a hand on his arm. The hand belonged to an MGM official.

"He'd been drinking," the MGM man told the sergeant in a confidential tone. "He'd been drinking, he swallowed a lot of pills, he took a bunch of pills and he was dead. He took an overdose," the man said.

The sergeant asked the MGM person for the dead man's name and position.

The name was David Whiting, he told the sergeant. "He was Miss Miles's business manager. You see, that was Miss Miles's room he was in. It was Miss Miles who found him, but . . ."

"Where is Miss Miles?" the sergeant asked.

"She's over there in 123, Mr. Poll's room, now, but she's much too upset to talk. She's had a terrible experience, you can understand, and . . ."

"Yes, he was my business manager," the sergeant recalls Miss Miles telling him a few minutes later. "He was my business manager, but all he wanted to do was f—— me all the time and I wasn't going to be f——ed by him."

Sergeant Hinderliter is a mild-mannered and mild-spoken cop.

He has a round open face, a blond crew cut, and a soft Arizona drawl. His dream at one point in his life was to earn a mortician's license and open a funeral home in Gila Bend, but after four years' study he dropped out of morticians' school to become a cop because he missed dealing with warm bodies. In his off-duty hours Sergeant Hinderliter is a scoutmaster for Troop Number 204. He recalls being somewhat surprised at Miss Miles's language. "Now I've heard that kind of talk sitting around with some guys," he told me. "But I never heard a lady use those words." (Later, as we shall see, Miss Miles denied she had used those words.)

Miss Miles was stretched out on one of the twin beds in room 123, her head propped up by pillows. Her face was flushed, her eyes streaked and wet. She was upset, she told the sergeant, but she was willing to talk.

I might as well tell you the whole story, she said.

The sergeant took notes, and this is the whole story she told that afternoon, as he remembers it:

It all started at the Pink Palomino café. There were a dozen of them there, movie people; they had driven thirty-six miles to the Palomino for a kind of prebirthday party for Burt Reynolds who was to turn thirty-eight the next day, Sunday, February 11.

She had driven to the Pink Palomino with Burt Reynolds, but she left early and drove back to Gila Bend with Lee J. Cobb. She had wanted a ride in Cobb's impressive new car—a Citroën on the outside, a powerful Maserati racing engine within. Back at the Travelodge she proceeded to the cocktail lounge. She had one drink. She danced.

It was close to midnight when she started back to her own room. Halfway there she decided to stop by and apologize to Burt for failing to return to Gila Bend with him.

When she entered room 135, Reynolds's room, she found a Japanese masseuse there too. Sarah asked permission to remain during the massage. The Japanese woman rubbed, Sarah talked. Around three A.M. she left and walked around the rear of the building to her own room. As soon as she stepped into the room, she told the sergeant, David Whiting jumped out of the dressing room and grabbed her.

Whiting demanded to know where she'd been and whom she'd been with. She told him it was none of his business. He slapped her. She screamed. From the next room, the nanny Sarah had hired to look after her five-year-old son rushed into Sarah's room through a connecting door.

Sarah told the nanny to call Burt. David Whiting released Sarah and ran outside. Burt Reynolds arrived shortly thereafter and took

Sarah back to his room where she spent the remainder of the morning.

Sometime later that Sunday morning, it may have been eight o'clock, it may have been ten, Sarah left Reynolds's room and returned to the nanny's room, number 126. She spoke briefly with the nanny, reentered her own room to use the bathroom, and found David Whiting's body on the floor. She gasped, ran back to the nanny's room, and told her to call Burt.

Gila Bend Coroner Mulford T. "Sonny" Winsor IV was still in bed Sunday afternoon when the dispatcher called him with news of the Travelodge death. He too had been up all night with the shooting death in the Euclid Street project. He had some questions. Had the dead black man, in fact, been a total stranger to the woman and the man with the .38, or had there been a more complicated relationship?

Coroner Winsor—he is also Justice of the Peace, Town Magistrate, Registrar of Vital Statistics, and a plumbing contractor on the side—wasted no time with the second body, the one he found at the Travelodge. There was nothing in room 127 to suggest anything but suicide. He rounded up a coroner's jury, including three Gila Bend citizens he found eating in the Travelodge Coffee Shop, and took them into room 127 to view the body for the record.

Next Coroner Winsor looked for some piece of identification for the death certificate, some proof that the dead man was in fact David Whiting. He bent over the body on the floor and reached into the pockets of the dark trousers. Nothing. Nothing in the right front pocket. He rolled the body gently over to look in the left front. There—no ID, but a key—a Travelodge key to room 127, Sarah's room, the room in which the young man died.

Coroner Winsor decided to check the young man's own room for identification. He ran back through the rain to the motel office, learned that David Whiting was registered to room 119, and ran back with a key.

He saw bloodstains as soon as he crossed the threshold of 119. There was blood on the pillow at the head of one of the twin beds. There was blood on the bath towel at the foot of the bed. There was blood, he soon discovered, clotted upon wads of toilet tissue in the bathroom. There was blood, he discovered later, on a Travelodge key on the other bed. It was a key for room 126, the nanny's room.

The death of David Whiting suddenly became a more complex affair. Had he been beaten before he died? The coroner called the chief of police over to room 119. The chief of police took one look and decided to call in the professionals from the Arizona State Police. There was the possibility of assault, even murder, to consider now.

Sarah Miles had a boil. The year was 1970 and Sarah Miles had come to Hollywood to do publicity for *Ryan's Daughter*. She had two appointments that afternoon: the first at noon with the show-business correspondent of *Time*, the next at three o'clock with a *Vogue* photographer. It was the *Vogue* appointment which worried her: *Vogue* wanted to feature her as one of the three most beautiful women in the world, and there, on her cheek, was a stubborn boil.

So she was not in an especially good mood as she sat in her bungalow at the Beverly Hills Hotel, waiting for the man from *Time* to arrive. Nor had her mood improved thirty minutes later when he finally showed up.

He wore a dark, three-piece English-cut suit, a luxuriously proper Turnbull and Asser shirt. He flashed a burnished-gold Dunhill lighter and a burnished-bronze hothouse tan. He removed a bottle from his suit coat, announced that it contained his personal Bloody Mary mix, and began the interview by discoursing at length upon the inadequacies of all other Bloody Marys. His name was David Whiting. He was twenty-four years old.

The subject of Sarah's boil came up. David Whiting confessed that he too had, on occasion, trouble with his skin. However, he told Sarah, he knew the *very best dermatologist in Hollywood*, and knew of an extraordinary pill for boils. Take one and ten minutes later, he promised Sarah, her boil would vanish.

He disappeared for ten minutes and returned with a bottle of the magic boil pills. She took one. The boil lasted much longer than ten minutes. The interview did not. As she went off to be the most beautiful woman in the world for *Vogue*, she assumed she had seen the last of David Whiting.

The next evening they met again. He requested the meeting, but despite his strange performance the first time, she didn't turn him down. She was amused by his pomposity, intrigued by his intelligence. She began calling him "Whiz Kid."

A few days later she was sitting in the V.I.P. lounge of the L.A. airport awaiting a flight to New York when David Whiting showed up and announced that he was taking the same flight. He secured the seat next to her. The next morning in New York he showed up in her suite at the Sherry Netherland. He took a room on the same floor. She never encouraged him, she says, but neither did she tell him to get lost.

Maybe it was the Vuitton luggage.

"He always had to have the best," she remembers. "All his doctors were the best doctors, his dentist was the very best dentist, Henry Poole was the very best tailor in London, everything with David had to be the best. If your agent wasn't the very best agent, then you had to change; if your doctor wasn't right, change, and he couldn't understand me because nothing I had was the best. . . . He'd spend hours at a restaurant choosing the best wines. . . . Suddenly he'd say to me, 'Do you have Vuitton luggage?' and I honestly had never heard of it. I said what was that word, and he said, '*Vuitton!* Come on! Don't pretend with me.'"

She wasn't pretending, she said. "It was funny. He was a *joke* in that he made people laugh. He was the sort of person you could send up . . . But David was the first person who awakened me to what was the best and what wasn't the best."

Then came the Working Permit Crisis. There was panic in the Sherry Netherland suite. For ten days Sarah had been unable to appear on American television because her working permit had not come through. A small army of MGM PR people scurried in and out of her suite reporting new delays and new failures, receiving scornful tongue lashings from Sarah.

"I began to get quite angry. I remember calling Jim Aubrey, the head of MGM you know, and telling him this is ridiculous, I've been here ten days, and this is ridiculous, all the money that's being wasted through these silly, interminable delays. And David Whiting was in the room with all these others and he started going, 'What's the matter? What happened? What happened? Working permit? Good God!' And he went straight to the phone and rang up a number and in half an hour my working permit arrived. . . . Literally in one telephone call I had a working permit which these other people hadn't been able to get for ten days. And I sort of thought, hmmmm, that's not bad. . . ."

Then there was the eye infection. "I came up with an eye infection and couldn't go on the Frost show . . . and he said, 'Oh, don't worry, I'll see to that,' and he took me across New York to an eye specialist, who gave me special stuff that cleared up my eyes. He was terribly efficient in certain areas, really terrifically efficient. Then he'd go over the top. Whenever he'd done something good, he'd get euphoric, and he'd suddenly go higher and higher and higher until he suddenly thought he was some sort of Sam Spiegel-cum-President-of-America and he'd go berserk in thinking he was terrific."

He followed her everywhere in New York. He was going to get *Time* to do a cover story on her. He arranged a lunch with Henry

Grunwald, editor of *Time*, for her. Things didn't go smoothly. "You f——ed the whole thing up. You f——ed the whole thing," David screamed at her when she reported back to him. He continued to follow her.

A few days later he waved good-bye to her at Kennedy Airport as she took off for England, her country home, her husband, and her child. The next morning he knocked at the front door of her country home in Surrey. He was stopping by on his way to a skiing holiday, he told her. He stayed for a year.

Sergeant Hinderliter didn't see the "star-shaped wound," as it came to be called, the first time he looked at David Whiting's body. Nor had he seen blood. But when he returned to room 127, Sarah's room, he was startled to see a pool of blood seeping out onto the tiles of the bathroom floor. The body seemed to be bleeding from the head.

Sergeant Hinderliter found the "star-shaped wound" at the back of the head, to the right of the occipital point. The wound had apparently stopped bleeding sometime after death, and resumed when the coroner rolled the body over to search for identification.

This "stellate or star-shaped contused laceration one inch in diameter . . . is the kind of injury we frequently see in people who fall on the back of the head," the autopsy doctor would testify at the coroner's inquest.

"This, of course, does not preclude," he added, "the possibility of the decedent having been pushed. . . ."

There were other marks on the body. Two "superficial contused scratches" on the middle of the abdomen. One "superficial contused abrasion" on the lower abdomen. Several scratches on the hands. There were "multiple hemorrhages"—bruises—on the chest and the left shoulder.

"Would those be consistent with someone having been in a scuffle or a fight?" the autopsy doctor was asked at the inquest.

"Yes," said the autopsy doctor.

But despite the suggestive marks on the outside of David Whiting's body, the cause of death, the autopsy doctor concluded, was to be found within.

A CATALOG OF THE VARIOUS DRUGS IN SARAH MILES'S BEDROOM AS COMPILED BY DETECTIVE BARNEY HAYES AND CHEMIST JACK STRONG OF THE ARIZONA STATE POLICE

Item One: some pills, multivitamin preparation
Item Two: capsules, antibiotic drug

Item Three: capsules, Serax Oxazepan, for treatment of anxiety
    and depression
Item Four: A—capsules of Dalmane which is a hypnotic and
    B—some capsules which were not identified
Item Five: tablets, Methaqualone, which is a hypnotic antihista-
    mine combination
Item Six: some capsules, Ampicillin Trihydrate, which is an anti-
    biotic
Item Seven: some further capsules which were not identified
Item Eight: some pills, Compazine, a tranquilizer
Item Nine: A—yellow tablets, Paredrine, which is a hypotensive
    and
    B—some gray pills, Temaril, an antipruritic and anti-
    histaminic
Item Ten: tablets of Donnatal which is antispasmodic and sedative
Item Eleven: white tablets, a yeast
Item Twelve: a liquid, an anticough mixture

One item was missing from the scene. Burt Reynolds told Sergeant
Hinderliter that when he had been summoned by Sarah to look at
the body, he had noticed a pill bottle clenched in one of David
Whiting's fists. He had pried it loose, Reynolds said, and rushed in
to Sarah who was, by then, in room 123. He had shown her the
bottle and asked her, "Do you know what these are?" She was too
upset to reply, he said.

    The pill bottle disappeared. Burt Reynolds doesn't remember
what he did with it. He might have thrown it away in room 123,
he said. He might have had it in his hand when he returned to 127,
the room with the body in it. He remembers seeing a prescription-
type label of some sort on it, but he doesn't remember what the
label said. The pill bottle was never found.

And the pills on the arm: nobody seems to have explained the pills
on the arm. David Whiting may have knocked some pills on the
floor, but there would be no easy way for him to knock pills down
onto his own arm while lying curled up on the floor. No one else
in the case has admitted knocking them down onto his arm, or
dropping them there.

There are other unanswered questions about the pills David took
on his last night. Item Five on the list of Sarah's drugs is a pill
called Mandrax. Mandrax is the English trade name for a formula-
tion of two drugs. One—the main ingredient—is Methaqualone,
which is described in medical literature as a "hypnotic," and as

such occupies the drowsy middle ground between the barbiturates and the tranquilizers. The second ingredient in Mandrax tablets is a small amount of diphenhydramine which, under the more familiar trade name Benadryl, is marketed as an antihistamine and mild depressant.

American drug companies sell pure Methaqualone—without the Benadryl—under several trade names, including the one which had become a household word by the time David Whiting died: Quaalude.

The autopsy doctor found Methaqualone in David Whiting's body. (There were 410 milligrams in his stomach, 7.4 mg. in his liver and .88 mg. per hundred milliliters—about 45 mg. altogether—in his bloodstream.) The doctor also found some Benadryl in his blood, along with half a drink's worth of alcohol and "unquantitated levels" of a Valium-type tranquilizer.

Where did that Methaqualone come from? Because of the presence of the Benadryl, it is possible to surmise that the pills David Whiting swallowed were Mandrax, rather than an American version of Methaqualone. Sarah Miles would later testify at the coroner's inquest that she "believed" she found "a few"—she was not sure how many—pills from Item Five, her Mandrax supply, missing after David Whiting's death. Sarah would also testify that she believed David Whiting no longer had a Mandrax prescription of his own because, she says, David's London doctor had taken David off the drug. But if David Whiting did take Mandrax that night it still cannot be said with absolute certainty that the tablets he swallowed did come from Sarah Miles's "Item Five."

Nor is there any certainty about the number of tablets David Whiting swallowed that night. Adding up the quantities of Methaqualone found in his stomach, blood, and liver, one finds a total of less than 500 milligrams. Since each Mandrax tablet contains only 250 milligrams of Methaqualone, it would seem that the residue of perhaps two, and no more than three, tablets was present in David Whiting's system at the time of his death. But there is no data available on how long he had been taking Methaqualone before that evening, nor whether he had developed a tolerance or sensitivity to the drug.

Was there enough Methaqualone in David Whiting's body to kill him? The autopsy doctor, you will recall, found less than one milligram per hundred milliliters in his blood. According to one traditional authority—*The Legal Medicine Annual* of 1970—it takes three times that amount, three milligrams per hundred milliliters, to kill an average man. However, about the time David

Whiting died, the literature on Methaqualone had entered a state of crisis. The Great American Quaalude Craze of 1972 had produced a number of overdose deaths, and, consequently, a number of new studies of the kill-levels of the drug. The results of one of those studies—summarized in an article in a publication called *Clinical Chemistry*—was making the rounds of the autopsy world at the time of David Whiting's death. The *Clinical Chemistry* article challenged the traditional 3-milligram kill-level, and suggested that less Methaqualone than previously suspected could cause death.

The Maricopa County autopsy doctor who first examined David Whiting cited these new, lower figures, plus the combined depressant effect of Benadryl, alcohol, and the "unquantitated levels" of another tranquilizer to explain why two or three tablets' worth of Methaqualone could have killed David Whiting. He called the old figures "insufficient and antiquated evidence."

But affidavits from a leading pharmacologist and a leading forensic pathologist introduced at the inquest by David Whiting's mother challenged the certainty of the original autopsy doctor's conclusion, especially his willingness to abandon the traditional authorities. "These reports have not been established in the literature," one of the affidavits said.

So great is the conflict between the new and old figures that a certain small dose cited in the new study as a poisonous "minimum toxic level" qualifies as a "therapeutic dose" under the old system.

These uncertainties placed David Whiting's final Mandrax dose in a disputed netherland between therapy and poison, leaving unanswered the questions of whether he took the tablets to calm down or to kill himself, or whether he killed himself trying to calm down.

Some items found in David Whiting's Travelodge room (number 119):
—fifty-nine photographs of Sarah Miles
—a large leather camera bag stamped with a LIFE decal, four expensive Nikons inside
—a six-month-old *Playboy* magazine, found lying on the bottom sheet of the unmade, bloodstained bed, as if he had been reading it while he waited for the bleeding to stop
—a piece of luggage—a medium-sized suitcase—lying open but neatly packed on the other bed, as if in preparation for a morning departure and a two-day trip
—two bottles of Teacher's Scotch, one nearly empty, on the night table between the beds. Also a can of Sprite

—an Olivetti portable typewriter with the ribbon and spools ripped out and lying tangled next to it

—a book called *The Mistress*, a novel, the film rights to which David Whiting had purchased on behalf of Sarah Miles. He wanted her to play the title role.

—a copy of a screenplay called *The Capri Numbers*, a romantic thriller David Whiting had been working on with an English actor. Sarah Miles was to play the part of Jocylin. In the screenplay's preliminary description of Jocylin we learn that "this story will teach her the meaning of 'there's a vulgarity in possession: it makes for a sense of mortality.' "

—a Gideon Bible. The Bible is not mentioned in police reports, but when I stayed in David Whiting's motel room a month after his death, I looked through the Bible and found three widely separated pages conspicuously marked, and one three-page section torn out.

The upper-right-hand corner of page 23 has been dog-eared. On page 23 (Genesis: 24-25) we read of, among other things, the death and burial of Sarah.

The lower-left-hand corner of page 532 has been dog-eared. It contains Psalms 27 and 28—each of which is headed, in the Gideon edition, "A Psalm of David." In these two psalms, David pleads with God not to abandon him. ("Hide not thy face far from me; put not thy servant away in anger . . . leave me not, neither forsake me.") David declares he wants to remain "in the land of the living" but warns that "if thou be silent to me I become like them that go down into the pit."

The upper-left-hand corner of page 936 has been dog-eared. The Last Supper is over. Christ, alone on the Mount of Olives, contemplating his imminent crucifixion, asks God, "If thou be willing, remove this cup from me." He prays feverishly ("his sweat was as it were great drops of blood"), then descends to his disciples, whereupon Judas betrays him with a kiss.

Torn out of the Gideon Bible in David Whiting's motel room are pages 724 to 730. Consulting an intact Gideon Bible, I discovered that those pages record the climactic vision of the destruction of Babylon from the final chapters of the Book of Jeremiah, and the despairing description of the destruction of Jerusalem from the beginning of Lamentations.

"I shall make drunk her princes and her wise men," says the Lord in regard to his plans for the rulers of Babylon, ". . . and they shall sleep a perpetual sleep and not wake." "I called for my lovers but they deceived me . . . my sighs are many and my heart is faint," says the weeper in the torn-out pages of Lamentations.

Police found no suicide note.

Four months after he moved into Mill House, her country home in Surrey, David Whiting threatened to kill himself, Sarah Miles told me. The threat was powerful enough, she says, to prevent her and her husband from daring to ask him to leave for six more months.

Just what was David Whiting doing, living in the household of Mr. and Mrs. Robert Bolt, Mill House, Surrey, anyway?

At first he was just stopping off on his way to a European ski resort. Then he was staying awhile to gather more material for his *Time* story. His "angle" on this story, he told them, was going to be "the last happy marriage" or something like that. He did not believe in happy marriages, didn't believe they could exist anymore, yet here Sarah and Robert Bolt had what appeared to be a happy marriage and he wanted to find out just what it was they had.

Then David thrust himself into the *Lady Caroline Lamb* project, a kind of family enterprise for Robert Bolt and Sarah. When David arrived in the summer of 1971, *Lamb* was only a screenplay. Robert Bolt—the forty-nine-year-old playwright who wrote *A Man for All Seasons* and several David Lean screenplays—had written it, he wanted Sarah to star in it, he wanted to direct it himself. He was having trouble getting the money for it.

As soon as David arrived he jumped in, started calling producers, money people, studios, agents. He whisked Sarah off to Cannes, rented a villa there for the film festival the better to make "contacts." He went to work on her finances, clearing up a "huge overdraft" in Sarah's account. He talked her into getting new lawyers, new accountants, new agents. He flattered Robert Bolt about his writing, Sarah about her acting. He quit his job at *Time* to devote himself to helping them make *Lamb*, he told them. He persuaded Sarah to make him her business manager, which meant he got ten percent of whatever she got. He persuaded Robert and Sarah to give him a salaried job in their family film company— Pulsar Productions Ltd. On the Pulsar stationery he became "David Whiting, Director of Publicity and Exploitation."

Lamb is a triangle. A year after he moved in with Robert Bolt and Sarah, David Whiting produced a publicity book about the film. This is how he describes that triangle:

There is Lady Caroline, to be played by Sarah Miles: "On fire for the dramatic, the picturesque . . . a creature of impulse, intense sensibility and bewitching unexpectedness," David wrote. "On those for whom it worked she cast a spell which could not be resisted. . . . Such a character was bound finally to make a bad wife." She ends up dying "for love." "And so at the end of her short life, she achieved the ultimate gesture which all her life she has been seeking."

Then there is her husband William Lamb, ultimately to become Lord Melbourne, the Whig Prime Minister: "A Gentleman, self-controlled and decent," David wrote. "A capacity for compromising agreeably with circumstance . . . When Caroline threw herself into her notorious affair with Lord Byron, William refused to take it seriously. . . . He detected in Byron all that was specious in the poet's romantic posturing . . . he was not jealous but his spirit was wounded."

And finally there was Byron: "He was a raw nerve-ridden boy of genius," David wrote, "a kind of embodied fantasy . . . emerged from obscurity . . . born to nobility and relative poverty. With his pale face, extreme good looks and pouting expression . . . the public was entranced with the personality of its twenty-four-year-old author. Nevertheless," twenty-four-year-old David Whiting added, his "divine fire gleamed fitfully forth through a turmoil of suspicion and awkwardness. His sophistication was a mask for shyness. . . . At the most elementary level he was a poseur."

Halfway into an interview with Sarah Miles I read her that passage about Byron from David's book about *Lamb*, and asked her if that was, perhaps, David Whiting writing about himself.

"I think he got that from Lord David Cecil, actually," she said. "Most of it you'll find is from other books, I'm afraid."

I tried again: "What I mean is, did he see the family he moved into at Surrey as a kind of reflection of the Lamb triangle?"

"The Lamb triangle? I see what you mean. It hadn't crossed my mind until you said it. Maybe you're right, I hadn't thought of it like that at all."

At this point I felt compelled to ask directly, and yet if possible with some delicacy, the question that had been on my mind.

"It seems, uh, a probably fortuitous coincidence that this *Lamb* thing was going on at the same time David was, uh, well, what *was* your, what was his relationship, was he sexually possessive or . . . ?"

"Nope," Sarah interrupted briskly. "Not a bit. You see, this is the area which is weird. He never made a pass at me, he never spoke of me sexually, it was just a sort of"—pause—"I don't quite know how to put it—it seems so self-*bragg*ing, you know, to say the things he said—I can't really, because I don't really—I think he, he wanted to put me up *there*, because it would sort of excuse himself from any sort of reality. I think if he had really made an ordinary mundane *pass* and been rejected, it would have ruined this other image that he had. You know what I mean, I mean if at one time we really *had* had an affair, it would have probably been the best thing for David. I mean he probably would have realized that I was just an ordinary girl like the rest of them."

At this point I thought of what Sergeant Hinderliter had told me Sarah had told *him* on the afternoon of the death, about David Whiting "always wanting to f—— me all the time. . . ."

Now that statement did not imply that Sarah Miles had, in fact, slept with David Whiting. It did however raise the question in my mind about whether David Whiting had or had not ever made "a mundane pass" at Sarah, and I felt I had to ask her about it.

"Sarah, uh, I feel I have to ask you this, it's, uh, a difficult question," I faltered, toward the close of the interview. "But, uh, this sergeant in Gila Bend told me that you told him that all David Whiting wanted to do . . ." I repeated what the sergeant had quoted her as saying.

She skipped, at most, one third of a breath.

"There have been some *extraordinary* reports from those police-men, I mean there really have." She gave a small sigh. "I mean I don't understand what this is *about*. Well I went back into the room, well, there's a whole area in there the police were . . . *very odd indeed*, and I don't *understand*, I mean that quote. . . . What time? When?"

I told her when the sergeant said he heard it.

"I mean, can you imagine, can you imagine me saying this to a policeman, that anyone in their right mind could say that. . . ."

"I can imagine you being upset and—"

"But to say *that*! I'm terribly sorry but I'm not the liar in this case."

It was not sex David Whiting wanted so desperately, Sarah told me, it was family. He'd never had a real family before, he'd told the Bolts. His parents divorced when he was a child, he'd hardly seen his father, who, he said, was some sort of director of Pan Am, a position which gave David the right to fly the world for next to nothing. He'd been a child prodigy, he told them, and his mother had sent him off to one boarding school after another. He'd had some unpleasant years in boarding schools. He was too smart for any of them, but they'd treated him badly. Once he said he had been forced to submit to a spinal injection to cure a "learning deficiency" because he'd been stubbornly pretending he didn't know how to read. So painful was this spinal injection that he'd immediately picked up a volume of Shakespeare and started to perform from it just to forestall repetition of that pain. He'd gone to the finest prep school in Washington, D.C., with the sons of the famous and powerful. He'd become an extraordinary ladies' man among the debutante daughters of the famous and the powerful, he told them. He dropped names of his conquests.

His prep-school classmates thought he would become President, he told the Bolts. But what he wanted to be, he told them, was the greatest producer there ever was. At an early age he had taken off from school to make movies in the Libyan desert and the hot spots of Europe. He had been the youngest man ever appointed full-fledged *Time* correspondent, but he had given all that up for Sarah and Robert and for what they could become under his management. He wanted to make Sarah the greatest star there ever was. For all that, he told them, but also for their home, and for the feeling of being part of a family at last.

But after three months things started to go wrong in this family. David became dissatisfied with mere "publicity-and-exploitation" duties. He wanted to do more. Nobody understood how good he was, nobody gave him a chance to show how much he could do. He decided to show them. Without the consent of the producer of *Lamb* he arranged a deal to produce a movie of his own—a documentary about the making of *Lamb*. This didn't go over well with the real producer. He made enemies. He started staying up in his room for days at a time, according to Sarah, worrying about his skin problem, his weight problem, his falling-hair problem, claiming all the while that he was working on scripts and deals, but failing to do his publicity work on time. Finally, according to Sarah, he was fired from his publicity job. She was the only one to take his side, she says. She kept him on as business manager, but both she and Robert suggested to David that he might be happier and get more work done if he moved out of their country home into Sarah's London town house.

It was at this point, September, 1971, according to Sarah, that David told them that if they ever forced him to leave their family he'd kill himself.

She found it hard to take this threat lightly, Sarah says. Twice before she'd been threatened that way, and twice before she'd ended up with a dead body on her hands. Sarah tells the story of the first two suicides.

First there was Thelma. Thelma had gone through Roeder, the exclusive Swiss finishing school, with Sarah. Since then Thelma had gone through hard times and electroshock treatment. She'd read a newspaper report that Sarah had taken a town house at

18 Hasker Street, Chelsea; she showed up there one day and asked to move in for a while.

Thelma stayed three years. She moved her young son in with her. Sarah gave her a "job" to earn her stay—walking Sarah's Pyrenean mountain dog—but Thelma forgot about it half the time. At night, according to Sarah, "she turned the place into a brothel," admitting a stream of men into her basement quarters. Finally, after Thelma had taken two messy overdoses, Robert Bolt came into Sarah's life and told her she had to get rid of Thelma.

"I told Robert if I chucked her out she'd kill herself," Sarah recalls. "And Robert said, 'Christ, Sarah, grow up. They all say that but not all of them do it.' Robert got to arguing with Thelma one day and said, 'Look, for Christ sake Thelma, can't you see what you're doing to Sarah? If you really mean business you'll jump.' "

Sarah asked Thelma to leave. Thelma jumped.

Then there was Johnny. Sarah had been kicked out of her Chelsea town house because of the obtrusive behavior of her Pyrenean mountain dog. Sarah and Robert had married and were moving to a country home in Surrey. Johnny came along. He was a landscape gardener and owner of three Pyrenean mountain dogs. "I decided to sublease the Chelsea house to him. I thought it would be a very funny joke, having been kicked out for one, to move in somebody with *three* Pyrenean mountain dogs. That tickled me. I liked that," Sarah says.

Johnny was very well dressed, and told the Bolts he was very well off. "But I let him have it for almost nothing, he was 'a friend, we'd have him up for weekends, he was a very charming fellow, he was a queer but a very nice man—boy."

After nine months Johnny hadn't paid a cent of rent.

"Robert told me, 'Sarah, you're crazy to let this go on. . . . Go up there and get the money.' So on a Friday I went up. The house looked lovely . . . he had a fantastic deep freeze, fantastic food, new carpets—he lived very high."

She asked him for the money. He said of course he'd give it to her—the very next day.

The next morning, back at her country home, she received a telephone call from a policeman. "He asked me if I were Sarah Miles, and did I own 18 Hasker Street, and I said yes, and he said Mr. Johnny W—— has put his head in the oven, he's gassed himself to death. . . ."

In mid-February of 1972, David Whiting moved into 18 Hasker Street.

On the second day of March, 1972, David Whiting was rushed

to St. George's Hospital, London, unconscious, dressed only in his underwear, suffering from an overdose of drugs. After his release, Sarah and Robert took him back again.

One evening later that year David Whiting was drinking in London with a woman writer who was preparing a story about Sarah Miles. He began confiding in her about his dream. Robert Bolt was nearing fifty, he observed, while he, David Whiting, was only half that age. He could wait, he told her, wait for Robert Bolt to die, and then he knew Sarah would be his at last. The woman writer seemed to think David Whiting was being deadly serious.

Not enough people die in Gila Bend to support a funeral home. So when the autopsy doctor in Phoenix completed his work on David Whiting, he sewed the body back up and shipped it to Ganley's funeral establishment in Buckeye—thirty miles north of Gila Bend—to await claiming by next of kin.

There was some question about next of kin. David Whiting had filled in the next-of-kin blank on his passport with the name "Sarah Miles." No other next of kin had stepped forward. For three days no one seemed to know if David Whiting's parents were dead or alive. Finally on Wednesday the Gila Bend chief of police received a call from a woman on the East Coast who said she had once been engaged to David Whiting. Among other things she told the chief the name of a person on the West Coast who might know how to reach the mother. After several further phone calls, the chief finally learned of a certain Mrs. Campbell of Berkeley, California.

On Thursday, February 15, a small gray-haired woman stepped off the Greyhound bus in Buckeye, Arizona. She proceeded to Mr. Ganley's establishment on Broadway and introduced herself to Mr. Ganley as Mrs. Louise Campbell, the mother of David Whiting. She persuaded Mr. Ganley to drive her into Gila Bend to see the chief of police.

There was trouble in the chief's office that day. As soon as she walked in Mrs. Campbell demanded to know how the chief had located her. No one was supposed to know where she was. She demanded to be told who had tipped him off. The chief asked her about David Whiting's father. She told him they had been divorced long ago. She told him that three weeks before David's death the father had suffered a near-fatal heart attack and was not to be contacted under any circumstances. Her present husband, David's stepfather, was spending the winter in Hawaii for his poor health and she didn't want him contacted either. She said she wanted David Whiting's personal property. The chief told her he couldn't release it to her until after the completion of the inquest, scheduled for February 27. He agreed to allow her to select a suit for David to be buried in.

"The chief opened up the suitcase and she grabbed everything she could and ran outside to the car with it, clutching it in her arms," Mr. Ganley recalls with some bemusement. . . . "Oh, she went running from one room to the other in the police station and finally the chief said, 'Get her the hell out of here, will you?' She grabbed everything she could get before they could stop her. I was picking out certain belongings in which to bury him. She just grabbed them. . . ."

Ten days later, Mrs. Campbell reappeared at Mr. Ganley's funeral home. It was nine o'clock at night. She was accompanied by an unidentified man.

She asked Mr. Ganley to take the body out of the refrigerator. She wanted to examine it, she said.

Mr. Ganley protested, "I said, 'Well, lady, why don't you take him into the County Mortuary . . . we don't like to show a body like this, he isn't clothed, he's covered with, uh . . . he's been in the refrigerator.' She said, 'Well, that's all right.' "

Mr. Ganley took the body out of the refrigerator and wheeled it out for Mrs. Campbell's inspection.

"She wanted to know if all his organs were there," Mr. Ganley recalled. "She said, 'Could you open him up?' I said no, we won't do that. Well, she wanted to know if the organs were there and I said well I presume they are."

A few days later Mrs. Campbell showed up at Ganley's funeral home again, this time with a different man, whom she introduced as a pathologist from a neighboring county. Again she demanded that the body be brought out of the refrigerator for inspection. Again, with reluctance, Mr. Ganley wheeled it out.

Mr. Ganley asked this pathologist if he had any documentary proof that Mrs. Campbell was, in fact, the boy's mother.

"He told me that he just assumed that she was. So I said well, okay, go ahead. So he opened him up and checked the organs, to see if they had all been returned after the first autopsy."

It was during this session, Mr. Ganley recalled, that Mrs. Campbell did some checking of her own. She examined the star-shaped wound on the back of the head and found it sewn up. She complained to Mr. Ganley about that.

"She asked me why we did that, and I said, well, to keep it from leaking all over the table. And she said, 'Don't do anything else to it.' And then she'd probe up in there with her finger."

"She actually put her finger in it?"

"Oh yeah . . . She never expressed one bit of grief except when

I first saw her and she sobbed . . . well, one night she kissed him and said poor David or something."

How badly had David Whiting beaten Sarah Miles? You will recall that Sergeant Hinderliter remembers Sarah telling him on the afternoon of the death that David Whiting had "slapped" her. It was the sergeant's impression that Sarah meant she had been slapped just once. He had asked her where Whiting had slapped her. She had pointed to the left side of her head. The sergeant does not recall seeing any marks, or any bruises, or any blood. Eleven days later Sarah told the police and the press that David Whiting had given her "the nastiest beating of my life."

This is how she described it.

"He started to throw me around the room like they do in B movies. . . . This was the most violent ever in my life. I was very frightened because all the time I was saying, 'Hold your face, Sarah, because you won't be able to shoot next day' . . . he was beating me on the back of my head . . . there were sharp corners in the room and he kept throwing me against them . . . I was just being bashed about . . . he was pounding my head against everything he could . . . it was the nastiest beating I've ever had in my life. It was even nastier because it was my friend you see."

A lot had happened between the Sunday afternoon of February 11 when Sarah told Sergeant Hinderliter about being slapped and the evening of February 22 when she told the Arizona State Police about the "nastiest beating."

On Monday morning, February 12, an MGM lawyer named Alvin Cassidy took an early plane from L.A. to Phoenix, drove out to Gila Bend, and advised members of the cast and crew of *The Man Who Loved Cat Dancing* that it would not be wise to talk to detectives from the State Police without the advice of counsel. MGM people stopped talking.

On Monday afternoon the cast and crew of *Cat Dancing* began checking out of the Travelodge and heading for a new location two hundred miles southeast in the town of Nogales on the Mexican border.

On Monday evening Rona Barrett broke the story on her nationally syndicated Hollywood gossip show.

Rona had sensed something funny going on the night before when she attended the Directors' Guild premiere of *Lady Caroline Lamb*. Someone had given Rona a tip that Robert Bolt, who was attending the premiere of his film, had received a "very upsetting phone call."

Monday morning Rona began talking to her sources in Gila

Bend. By Monday evening she was able to tell her national audience of a report that Sarah Miles had been beaten up in her motel room by her business manager, a former *Time* correspondent. Rona called it "the alleged beating"—alleged because, according to Rona's sources on location, Sarah Miles was "on the set the next day showing no signs of having been attacked."

On Wednesday of that first week, MGM hired two of the best criminal lawyers in Arizona—John Flynn of Phoenix and Benjamin Lazarow of Tucson—to represent Sarah, Burt, and the nanny.

The MGM legal armada at first succeeded in working out a deal with the detectives. Sarah, Burt, and a few others would tape-record informal, unsworn statements about the night of the death, and answer, with the help of their attorneys, questions put to them by detectives. The detectives and the County Prosecutor made no pledge, but MGM hoped, through this taping device, to avoid having Sarah and Burt and the rest of the cast subpoenaed to testify publicly at the forthcoming coroner's inquest.

These recorded interviews with the detectives, which have come to be known as the "Rio Rico tapes," took place on Thursday, February 22, at the Rio Rico Inn of Nogales, Arizona, where the MGM people were quartered. Sarah's description of the violent, nasty beating, quoted above, comes from one of these tapes.

The deal fell through. Gila Bend Justice of the Peace Mulford Winsor, who was to preside at the inquest, was not satisfied with this absentee-testimony arrangement. He issued subpoenas for Sarah, Burt, Lee J. Cobb, the nanny, and the two other MGM people, commanding them to appear in person in Gila Bend on February 27 to take the stand and testify.

MGM's legal forces promptly went to court. They asked that the subpoenas be quashed on the ground that appearances at the inquest would subject the six people to "adverse publicity and public display."

On February 27, just a few minutes before the inquest was about to open in Gila Bend, Justice of the Peace Winsor was served with a temporary restraining order barring him from calling Sarah or Burt to testify. Justice Winsor decided to proceed with the inquest without them, and called Sergeant Hinderliter to the stand as the first witness.

But the movie company had not counted on the determination of tiny, gray-haired Mrs. Campbell, who turned out to be a shrewd operator despite her fragile, grief-stricken appearance.

Early that morning in Phoenix Mrs. Campbell had hired her own lawyer, presented him with a thousand-dollar retainer, and told him to contest the MGM injunction. Then she caught the first bus out to Gila Bend. On the bus she sat next to a reporter for the London *Sun* who was on his way out to cover the inquest. She introduced herself to the English reporter as a correspondent for a Washington, D.C., magazine and asked him for the details of the case. She wanted to know whether it were possible to libel a dead man.

When she arrived at the courthouse, a one-story concrete all-purpose administrative building, Mrs. Campbell began passing out to the press Xeroxed copies of a document which she said was David Whiting's last letter to her, a document which proved, she said, that David Whiting was neither unhappy nor suicidal. (While this "last letter" certainly did not give any hint of suicidal feelings, neither did it give a sense of much intimacy between mother and son. David Whiting began the letter by announcing that he was sending back his mother's Christmas present to him, and went on to request that she send instead six pairs of boxer shorts. "I find the English variety abominably badly cut," he wrote. "Plaids, stripes, and other bright colors would be appreciated, and I suggest you unwrap them, launder them once, and airmail them to me in a package marked 'personal belongings.' ")

Next Mrs. Campbell approached Justice Winsor and asked him to delay the start of the inquest until her lawyer, who she said was on his way, could be present to represent her. She didn't give up when he refused and opened the inquest. She continued to interrupt the proceedings in her quavering voice with pleas for a recess to await the appearance of her lawyer. At one point Justice Winsor threatened to have her removed.

It came down to a matter of minutes. By midafternoon the two men from the County Attorney's office conducting the inquest had called their last witness, and the Justice of the Peace was about to gavel the inquest to a close and send the coroner's jury out to decide the cause of David Whiting's death. At the last minute, however, the judge received a phone call from the presiding Justice of the Superior Court in Phoenix. Mrs. Campbell had secured an order preventing the coroner's jury from beginning its deliberations until a full hearing could be held on the question of whether Sarah, Burt, and the nanny should be forced to appear in person to testify. Justice Winsor recessed the inquest, and Mrs. Campbell walked out with her first victory. She'd only just begun. On March 7, after a full hearing, the court ruled in her favor and ordered Sarah, Burt, and the nanny to appear at the inquest. Finally, on March 14, the three of them returned to Gila Bend and took the stand, with Mrs. Campbell seated in the front row of the courtroom taking notes.

There were strange stories circulating about Mrs. Campbell. There was a rumor that she might not be the boy's mother at all.

Other than the "last letter," she hadn't shown any identification to Mr. Ganley. The copy of the last letter she was handing around showed no signature. Mrs. Campbell said she herself had written the word "David" at the bottom of the copy. She had left the original with the signature at home, she said. "Naturally I treasure it . . . that's why I didn't bring it."

Mrs. Campbell refused to give me her home address or phone number. She insisted on keeping secret the whereabouts of both David Whiting's real father and his stepfather, her present husband. She implied that anyone attempting to contact the real father, who was recovering from a recent heart attack, might cause his death: she was protecting him from the news, she said.

She described herself as a free-lance science writer, as a former writer for *Architectural Forum*, as a member of the faculty of the University of California at Berkeley, and as retired. She insisted at first that her married name was spelled without a "p" in the middle. Then suddenly she began insisting that it was spelled with a "p."

She described herself frequently as "a woman without means," and a "woman living on a fixed income," but she hired four of the top lawyers in the State of Arizona to work on the case. She claimed to have flown to England with her aging mother to visit David a few months before he died.

"My only interest in this whole affair is to protect the name of my son," she maintained. "He was not a suicidal type, he was not the type to beat up women."

She was curiously silent about certain areas and curiously ill-informed about others. There was his marriage, for instance. Mrs. Campbell led me to believe that I was the first person to tell her that her son had been married. This revelation took place in the Space Age Lodge, a motel next to the Gila Bend Courthouse building, a motel distinguished by the great number of "life-sized" Alien Beings crawling over its roofs and walls. The second session of the inquest—the one at which Sarah and Burt had finally testified—had just come to an end and Mrs. Campbell was seated at a table in the Space Age Restaurant handing out copies of various affidavits to reporters and occasionally responding to questions.

"Mrs. Campbell, has David's ex-wife been in touch with you?" I asked.

"His what?" she demanded sharply.

"His ex-wife, the one who—"

"David was never married," she said firmly.

"What about the London *Express* story which said he was

married to a Pan Am stewardess, and that he used her Pan Am discount card to fly back and forth to England?"

"What wife? What are you talking about? Where did you read that? I never heard of any marriage."

(It is possible that she may have been feigning surprise here, although to what purpose is not clear. The mother of the girl he married told me she herself was certain her daughter never married David Whiting. Nevertheless there *is* a marriage certificate on file with the Registrar of Vital Statistics, Cook County, Illinois, which records the marriage of David Andrew Whiting to Miss Nancy Cockerill on January 29, 1970. Apparently there was a divorce also, because the wife is now remarried and living in Germany.)

Later that same day I had a long talk with Mrs. Campbell in the coffee shop of the Travelodge Motel, where she was staying during the inquest.

He was born in New York City on either August 25 or 26, she told me. "I'm not sure which is the right one, but I remember we always used to celebrate it on the wrong day." She leaps quickly to prep school. "He did so well at St. Albans that he was admitted to Georgetown University on a special program after his junior year and . . ."

When I asked her where David lived, and where he went to school before prep school, she cut off my question. "I don't see what that has to do with anything. I prefer not to tell you." She proceeded to attempt to convince me to drop my story on David Whiting and instead write an "exposé" of one of the Arizona lawyers hired by MGM, and "how these attorneys use their power and influence in this state." She would give me inside information, she said.

"It was always expected that David would go to Harvard," she began again when I declined to drop the story and returned to the subject of David Whiting. "For a boy of David's ability it was perfectly obvious he was headed for Harvard."

He didn't make it. Something about too many debutante parties, and not quite terrific grades in his special year at Georgetown. David Whiting went to tiny Haverford College instead. He majored in English there and wrote an honors thesis "on F. Scott Fitzgerald or Hamlet, I can't remember," Mrs. Campbell told me.

"There was a line from *The Great Gatsby* I do remember," she told me. "That was David's favorite book, and it's a line I think applies to what I saw here today. It was about the kind of people who always have others around to clean up the mess they leave."

I later checked the Scribner edition of *The Great Gatsby*: "They were careless people, Tom and Daisy—they smashed up things and creatures and then retreated back into their money or their vast carelessness, or whatever it was that kept them together, and let other people clean up the mess they had made."

A Fitzgerald Story of Sorts:

She met him at Mrs. Shippens' Dancing Class. Her name was Eleanor, and she was a granddaughter of F. Scott Fitzgerald and Zelda. He was—well, she never knew who he was, in the sense of family, but it was assumed that the dancing students at Mrs. Shippens' were from the finest families of Washington, Virginia, and Eastern Shore society. He certainly acted the part. His name was David Whiting.

When the male pupils at Mrs. Shippens' reached a certain age, they were placed on Miss Hetzel's list. Miss Hetzel's list was a register of eligible males worthy of being called upon to serve as escorts and dancing partners at the finest debuts and cotillions.

Eleanor met him again at a Hunt Cup weekend. She found him sometimes witty, sometimes amusingly pretentious in his efforts to be worldly. In November, 1963, she wrote him inviting him to be her escort at a holiday dance at Mrs. Shippens'. She still has his letter of reply, because of a curious device he employed in it.

Centered perfectly between the lines of his letter to her were the unmistakable impressions of what seemed to be a letter to another girl. This ghostly letter in-between-the-lines was filled with tales of nights of drinking and lovemaking in expensive hotel suites with a girl named "Gloria." Eleanor is certain there was no Gloria, that the whole thing was an elaborate fake designed to impress her, if not with its truth, at least with its cleverness.

"He was always worrying about the way he looked—we'd be dancing or something and he'd always be checking with me how he looked, or giving me these, you know, aristocratic tips about how *I* looked, or *we* looked."

And how did he look?

"Well, he was very fat at first, I think."

"Fat?"

"Oh, quite tremendous. I mean pretty heavy. He'd make jokes about himself. But then all that changed. He spent a summer in North Africa and Libya with a movie production company. He came back from that summer looking much more thin and intense," she remembers. "He came back and all he was talking about was taking over that movie company, and oh, he had great dreams. I remember taking a walk with him—we were at some party and we were both nervous, and we took a walk through this garden and he just went on and on, just—it was the first time I'd seen him thin and he was talking about how he was gonna take over that movie company, and how great he'd been and how he was going to be a producer. . . . He'd always talked about movies, he could name every movie and every movie star that was in them—I mean, some people do that but he was *good*, he knew them *all*."

She drifted away from him—"He was never my boyfriend or anything," she says pointedly—and didn't hear from him for almost two years when one day she got a phone call in her dorm at Sarah Lawrence.

It was David Whiting, then a student at Haverford. "Well, I hadn't seen him and I didn't know where he was at school, and he said, 'Will you come and see me, I'm at Princeton.' So I took the bus down. I got there I guess about nine in the morning, and called him up and he said could I come over to the room—I didn't know it wasn't his room—so I walked in and he just poured this tall glass of straight gin and no ice and said, 'Will you have some?' And I said, 'No, I don't really think I'm in the mood, I was sort of wondering what we're gonna do today,' and he said, 'Well, I think we'll stay in the room until tonight when we'll go over to some clubs.' I could sort of see the day's program unfolding. . . ."

For the next two hours he tried to convince her to sleep with him. "It could be really boring the way he talked about himself so much and how his ego would be damaged if I didn't sleep with him. I remember it was this scene of me sitting up, you know, every once in a while, and we'd talk and we'd stretch out and I'd say, 'Well, I'm going,' and he'd *throw* me down. And he finally got in a real bad mood, and I went."

"Did he ever admit to you that he was just posing as a Princeton student?"

"Oh yes, at the end I think he did."

"Did he think he could get away with it?"

"Well, I guess if we'd never left the room he could have."

Some Last Effects of David Whiting: an inventory of items left behind from his eighteen-month career as Hollywood correspondent for *Time*.

—One 275-watt Westinghouse sunlamp. Left in a file cabinet in his old office in the *Time* suite on Roxbury Drive in Beverly Hills, across from the "House of Pies." "He used to come in after midnight and sit for hours with the sunlamp on—I don't know if he was working or what," the *Time* switchboard operator recalls. Once he didn't turn it off. "I came in in the morning one day and I smelled smoke, and I checked in David's office, and it was his sunlamp. He'd left sometime early in the morning, and he'd just put it in his drawer without turning it off. It was smoldering in there, he might have set the place on fire."

—One pocket memo book with the notation "Cannes No. 6" scrawled in Magic Marker on the front cover. From the same file cabinet. Not long after he had been transferred to the Hollywood job, David Whiting took off for Cannes to "cover" the film festival. A Paris correspondent for *Time* had been under the impression *he* had been assigned to cover it. There was some dispute. The Paris man filed the story. David Whiting took many notes. Interviews with producers, directors, starlets. Memos to himself. A sample memo to himself from "Cannes No. 6":

> General Memo:
> -morn. look good
> -pics
> -people

—One magazine story, written under an interesting pseudonym, for *Cosmopolitan*. The pseudonym is "Anthony Blaine," a synthesis of Amory Blaine and Anthony Patch, the heroes, respectively, of Fitzgerald's first two novels, *This Side of Paradise* and *The Beautiful and Damned*. The *Cosmopolitan* story by "Anthony Blaine" is about Candice Bergen. He met her in Cannes in 1970. He fibbed about his age to her, he played the worldly bon vivant for her, he followed her to Spain where she was making a movie, he continued to see her back in Beverly Hills. He was possessed with her, he told friends. He was just a good friend to her, she told me.

—One box kite, still in the possession of Paula Prentiss. David Whiting was doing a story for *Time* about Paula and her husband, Dick Benjamin. The angle was going to be the idea of a happy marriage, he told them. He visited them a second time in their apartment in New York, and "there was a big change from the first time we met him, I could tell something was wrong," Paula recalls, "that he needed something from us. He wouldn't come out and say it, but we could tell, he'd sit and drink martinis and pop pills all the time. But we did have some good moments with him. I remember he brought us a box kite and he took us out on the beach and showed us how to fly it." (The story about Dick and Paula never appeared in *Time*. It did show up in the November, 1971, issue of *Cosmopolitan*, this time under David Whiting's real name. *Cosmopolitan* also published a David Whiting story about Sarah Miles, the one he had been "researching" when he began following Sarah around for *Time*. The story, published in December, 1971, is titled *Sarah Miles: The Maiden Man-Eater* and the subtitle reads: "She uses words that would make a construction worker blush, but from her they sound refined.")

—One list of all the girls David Whiting had ever kissed. "I walked into his office one day and he had his big debutante album out—it had all his invitations and dance programs, and dashing photos of David and the debs," a woman who writes for *Time* recalls. "And he was working on a list he told me was a list of all the girls he'd ever kissed—just kissed, that was enough—and he was going to add it to the album I think."

—One Bekins Warehouse storage number, the index to the artifacts David Whiting left behind when he left for England. Included are some of his many Savile Row suits he decided not to bring back to London with him. "Let me tell you about his suits," the friend who has custody of the Bekins number told me. "He used to fly to London—on his wife's Pan Am card, of course—fly there on a Thursday to have a fitting done. He'd come back Monday, then fly back again the next weekend for the final fitting and bring back the suit."

—One copy of *The Crack-Up* by F. Scott Fitzgerald, a battered, underlined paperback bequeathed to a woman he knew. Two passages have been cut out with a razor blade. One of the underlined passages: "I didn't have the two top things: great animal magnetism or money. I had the second things, though: good looks and intelligence. So I always got the top girl."

A passage cut out with a razor blade: the fourth verse from a poem called "The Thousand-and-First Ship," a Fitzgerald attempt at a modern version of Keats's "La Belle Dame Sans Merci": "There'd be an orchestra/ Bingo! Bango!/ Playing for us/ To dance the tango,/ And people would clap/ As we arose,/ At her sweet face/ And my new clothes."

They checked into the Gila Bend Travelodge on Monday, January 29. At first David Whiting took the room adjoining Sarah's. Hers was number 127, his 126; an inner door connected the two. He didn't last there very long. Rooms 126 and 127 are in the section of the motel most remote from traffic. They could be reached only by walking back from the highway, past the Travelodge bar, past the length of the larger two-story rooming unit, all the way to the rear of the parking lot and around the back of a smaller, single-story row of Travelodge cubicles. The bedroom windows of numbers 126 and 127 face nothing; they look north upon miles and miles of cactus and mesquite waste. Closer at hand to numbers 126 and 127 is the Travelodge garbage shed.

On Friday, February 2, four days after David and Sarah checked into these adjoining rooms, David was forced to move. Sarah's five-year-old son Thomas and the nanny hired to care for him were arriving from England that evening. So, on Friday afternoon, nine days before his death, David Whiting moved out of number 126 and into number 119, a room across the parking lot in the two-story motel building.

He seems to have chosen this place of exile with some care. The view, for instance, had two peculiar advantages. For one, the line of sight for someone looking straight out the bedroom window of number 119 runs straight across a short span of parking lot and then directly along the walkway in front of the row of rooms he left behind, right past the doors to numbers 126 and 127. No one entering or leaving Sarah's room could escape the notice of an observer looking out the window of number 119.

The other, more subtle advantage to this observation post had to do with the placement of a staircase. A broad openwork staircase of wood planks and iron bars descends from the second floor of motel rooms above number 119 and touches ground on the sidewalk in front of the room, forming a slanting screen in front of the bedroom window. Outsiders in the Travelodge parking lot can't see through the confusing lattice of horizontal steps, diagonal banisters, and vertical railing supports to the bedroom window of 119 behind it. But someone peeking out from *within* the bedroom window of 119, from behind this sheltering screen, can see quite well, although at first it is something like looking out from within a confusingly barred cage.

Sarah says she never knew where David had moved. She'd never bothered to find out, having no occasion to visit him.

But she knew he was watching her. Keeping track of her movements. She'd return from a day on the set and as soon as she walked into her room, the phone would ring and he'd want to know what she'd be doing that night, and with whom.

He had been acting extraordinarily possessive from the moment they arrived at Gila Bend. She hadn't been prepared for anything quite like it. Before they'd left England he'd seemed in better shape than he'd been in a long time. He'd been working on a screenplay, he'd been going out with women, he'd been less obsessed with managing her personal life.

"But as soon as we touched down in America he was back to square one," she says. "He was the old David again."

Sarah speculates it might have something to do with the way she worked. "When I'm on a picture I'm—see, he had known me as a girl who lived in the country, who loved horses, and who lived a quiet life," Sarah told the inquest. "When I get on a film I like to get to know everybody. The wranglers—I never met wranglers before. Christ, they're marvelous people, you know. I mean I want to spend all my time with cowboys."

So Sarah went out at night. Going out in Gila Bend didn't mean going far. It meant eating at Mrs. Wright's Colonial Dining Room, next door to the Travelodge, then walking back across the parking lot to the Travelodge Cocktail Lounge for drinking and dancing to a country-and-western jukebox. For Sarah—according to Gila Bend locals who hung around with the cast and crew—going out meant dancing a lot, flirting, tossing off four-letter words in a merry way. (A *Women's Wear* profile of Sarah, published a week before David Whiting's death, features a picture of Sarah perched in a sex-kittenish pose on one of the black Naugahyde banquettes in the Travelodge Cocktail Lounge. *The Lady with the Truck-driver's Mouth* is the title of the story.)

Meanwhile David Whiting stayed in. At first she'd invite him to come to the bar with her, Sarah says, but he'd refuse and stay in his room and watch for her return. He kept to himself, remote from everyone but Sarah, and Sarah began keeping her distance from him. Waitresses at the Travelodge Coffee Shop recall David Whiting coming in alone night after night, sitting at the counter, and ordering, night after night, a shrimp cocktail and a club sandwich.

During the day he'd haunt the shooting set in the desert, a dark and formal figure amidst the real and costumed cowboys and the casual MGM production officials. He'd have one of his Nikons with him, and he'd hover around Sarah clicking off stills. Or he'd have some papers he wanted her to look at, other papers he'd want her to sign. He began getting on the nerves of the MGM people. There are reports he'd been getting on Sarah's nerves.

The first big fight broke out in room 127 on the evening of Tuesday, February 6. The nanny was in the middle of it. Janie Evans is her name, she is twenty-three years old, dark haired, dark eyed, and rather sexy. She had been hired for this Gila Bend trip one week before Sarah and David left England. Sarah had hired her on the recommendation of David Whiting, and there is good reason to believe that David Whiting and the soon-to-be nanny had been seeing each other before the hiring.

In any case David and the nanny had mutual friends in London, and one of them was a woman named Tessa Bradford, and it was a curious story about David and this Tessa Bradford that led to the Tuesday-night fight.

The nanny had been talking to Sarah about David. That winter in London, the nanny told Sarah, David had developed an obsession for Tessa Bradford. He had haunted her house, followed her car, called her at all hours, rented a Mercedes limousine to take her to the theater. After all this Tessa Bradford had dropped him, the nanny told Sarah. She had thought David was crazed.

That Tuesday night in room 127 Sarah asked David about the story. He became enraged, rushed into room 126, dragged the nanny back to Sarah's room demanding that she "tell the truth."

"Why didn't you tell the truth? Why did you say it was a Mercedes when it was only a mini cab? Why did you say I kept phoning her, I only phoned her five times," Janie Evans recalls him yelling.

Then he turned on Sarah. He grabbed her. "He had her—his hand on her neck like this," the nanny testified at the inquest, "wallowing her head backward and forward, and I shouted at him and Sarah pushed at him, and he went through the door and she threw a vase right after him . . . it didn't hit him, it smashed on the concrete outside."

"He got upset that I didn't get upset about him seeing another woman," Sarah explains. "But I couldn't take his private life seriously."

Other things started going wrong for David Whiting. On Wednesday, February 7, the producer of *Cat Dancing*, Martin Poll, approached David on the set. As usual David had been recording Sarah's performance with his Nikon. Poll hinted strongly that David's presence was not entirely welcome.

"He wasn't in anyone's way," Poll told me, "but for myself I like to have a very private set and it was a closed set from the beginning of the picture, and it was distracting to have photographs taken all the time."

"Did you ask him to stay off then, or what was the actual conversation?" I asked Poll.

"I am really not interested in sitting on the griddle," was all Poll answered.

On Thursday, February 8, Sarah saw David Whiting for the next to last time.

"He came into my room that evening and his face was ashen and white, and more sallow than I've ever seen it. And he put the script on the bed and he said, 'I've just read it and it's no good at all. I can't write anything.' "

After that, nobody remembers seeing David Whiting outside his motel room.

On Friday morning David Whiting called the motel manager to complain about the reception on his TV. He was getting sound but no picture, he said. But when the motel manager came to the door of number 119 to see about getting David his picture back, he found the DO NOT DISTURB card hanging from the doorknob. He kept checking, the manager recalls, but the DO NOT DISTURB sign never came down.

There are indications that David Whiting was trying to get out of Gila Bend. Thursday night he placed a call to a woman in Washington, D.C. He talked to her for eighty-four minutes. They had been engaged once. He had continued to confide in her after he left her behind for Hollywood. That night he told her that "the particular situation there in Gila Bend was over for him," she recalls. He didn't sound overjoyed about things, but neither did he sound suicidal, she says. He did say he wanted to see her and talk to her "about this situation in Gila Bend and about him and me." He talked about flying to Washington to see her.

Two nights later, Saturday night, about an hour before midnight David Whiting received a call from a friend in Beverly Hills. The friend wanted to know if David was going to attend the Directors' Guild premiere of *Lamb* Sunday evening. "No," David told the friend, "Sarah and I think it will be a bummer."

Nevertheless, David told his friend, he was thinking of leaving Gila Bend for Hollywood sometime in the middle of the next week.

David's voice sounded slurred that night, the friend recalls.

"It sounds like you're into a couple of reds," he told David.

"No," David replied. "Mandrax."

Burt Reynolds wanted a massage. It was close to midnight when he returned from the Pink Palomino, picked up his phone, and asked the desk to ring the room of the Japanese masseuse.

Reynolds was staying in room 135. It was in the same single-story block of cubicles as Sarah's room. The two rooms were no more than six or eight yards apart, almost back to back, in fact. However, as close as they were physically, it was still necessary to go all the way around the building to get from one to the other, and going around the building meant passing directly in front of David Whiting's screened-in bedroom window.

The Japanese masseuse was staying in room 131. Her name was Letsgo (an Americanization of her Japanese first name, Retsuko) Roberts, and she had been summoned to the Travelodge on Friday afternoon to tend to Sarah, who had suffered a bruising fall from a horse. Letsgo and Sarah got along so well that she was plucked from her regular tour of duty at a place called The International Health Spa in Stockdale, Arizona, and installed in a room at the Travelodge.

About midnight on Saturday Letsgo received a phone call from Burt.

He asked her to come over to room 135 and work on him. When Letsgo walked into Burt's room she found Sarah there, she told me. She had the feeling the two of them had been drinking.

"They were kind of—kind of, you know, not drunk—but kind of happy, you know, after drink," Letsgo recalls.

Burt, attired in a white terry-cloth dressing gown, proceeded to lie on the bed, and Letsgo proceeded to give him a two-hour massage.

Meanwhile Sarah chatted with Burt. She apologized for leaving the party early with Lee J. Cobb. She told him about an old boy-friend of hers. He told her about an old girl friend of his. Sarah turned on the TV, watched a British film; she ate an apple and a banana; she lay down next to Burt on the double bed and dozed off, according to Letsgo.

About two A.M. the masseuse offered to walk Sarah back to her room, but Burt told her he'd see that Sarah got back safely. The masseuse left.

An hour and fifteen minutes later Burt walked Sarah around the back of the building to her room.

Back in his own room, Burt had hardly slipped off his clothes and slipped into bed when the phone rang. It was the nanny. She was saying something about Sarah being beaten up, something about David Whiting. He heard a scream over the phone, Burt told Sergeant Hinderliter the following afternoon. He heard no scream over the phone, Burt testified at the inquest four weeks later.

Scream or no scream, Burt put his clothes back on and headed around the building for Sarah's room. It was at this moment that the paths of Burt Reynolds and David Whiting may have crossed. David's violent encounter with Sarah had just come to an end. He ran out of her room just about the time the nanny called Burt for help. If David Whiting was proceeding to his own room while Burt was on his way to Sarah's, David and Burt might have met in the parking lot at the northwest corner of the building.

When Burt first told the story of the events of that night to Sergeant Hinderliter, he did not mention encountering David Whiting or anyone else on his way to Sarah's room.

Ten days later in the "Rio Rico tapes" and then again on the witness stand at the inquest—much to the surprise of Sergeant Hinderliter—Burt testified that he did see "someone" as he was heading around that corner.

"It was to my left as I came around. . . . I saw someone going in the door, and the door slammed very hard behind him. . . . At the time I didn't know whose room it was, nor could I identify him since I'm not very good at identifying backs, but it looked like a man, and the door slammed behind him. Later I found out, the next day, that that was David Whiting's room."

And then, a few minutes later, leading the wounded Sarah back to his own room, something caught Burt's eye. "As I rounded the corner to go to my room I saw the drapes open and close," in the window of the same room whose door had slammed behind a man a few minutes ago. There was no light on in the room behind the drapes, he told the inquest, a detail which makes his observation of the moving drapes all the more acute, since the window of that room is well-screened from view by a staircase.

At this point, Sarah testified at the inquest, Burt told her, "If I was not as mature as I am now, I would lay him out."

The following afternoon, after the body of David Whiting had been discovered, the masseuse heard this story from Sarah. Sarah and Burt were back in Burt's room. "Mr. Reynolds wanted to go down and fight him, Mr. Whiting, but Sarah, she stopped him. . . ." the masseuse told me. "She told Mr. Reynolds it would cause more trouble."

Sarah testified that shortly after she arrived at Burt's room she became worried about the well-being of the man who had beaten her. She told Burt she wanted to call up David Whiting "to see if he was all right." It was not physical injury she was concerned about, it was injury to David's *feelings*, she says. "Because whenever he has hit me he has always been so ashamed afterward, so remorseful. . . ."

But Sarah did not make the call. Burt advised her to "deal with everything in the morning," and she went to sleep. Had she in fact made that call she might have saved his life.

Not much is known of the movements of David Whiting that night. Sarah did give David a call early in the evening to inform him that Burt had invited her to attend the birthday celebration at the Pink Palomino in Ajo. Sarah says she invited David to come along and that David refused. He was in his room at eleven P.M. calling Hollywood. It is reasonable to speculate that he stayed up waiting, as usual, for Sarah's return. He may have spent these hours peering out from behind his sheltered observation post. In the absence of anyone crossing his line of sight, the picture outside his bedroom window consisted of the empty walkway past Sarah's room and a blank brick wall, the narrow end of the one-story unit containing Sarah's room.

At night the management of the Gila Bend Travelodge switches on an intense blue spotlight implanted among the dwarf yucca palms which line that blank stucco wall. The blue spot illuminates the sharp green spears of the yucca palms and casts confusingly colored shadows of their fanlike arrays upon the wall, an effect apparently intended to create an air of tropical mystery in the Travelodge parking lot.

If David Whiting had been watching at just the right moment, he might have seen Sarah cross the parking lot from the Travelodge Cocktail Lounge and head toward Burt Reynolds's room.

Three things are known for sure. Sometime before three thirty A.M. David Whiting entered Sarah Miles's bedroom. Sometime after she encountered him there, he returned to his own room, where he left bloodstains. And sometime before noon the next day, he returned to Sarah's room and died.

He had a key to Sarah's room. "I kept on saying, 'David, are you taking my keys, because they're not here anymore,'" Sarah told the inquest. "And he said, 'I don't need to take keys. You know me, I can pick a lock.' He was very proud of the fact that he could pick locks." Nevertheless a key to Sarah's room, number 127, was the only item found on him after his death.

The only witness to the goings-on in room 127 was the nanny, Janie Evans. "I think you'll find that the nanny is the key to this whole thing," Sarah's lawyer in the case, Benjamin Lazarow of Tucson, Arizona, told me, as he slipped a tape cassette—one of the "Rio Rico tapes"—into his Sony. "You listen to this cassette with the nanny on it. Listen to how scratchy and worn out it sounds. You know why? It's because the detectives kept playing it over and over again. They were *very* interested in the nanny's story."

The first thing she saw in room 127 that night, says the nanny, on the tape, was Sarah lying on the floor with David Whiting on top of her bashing her head on the floor. "That'll teach you!" David was yelling at Sarah, the nanny says. (Ten days before the "Rio Rico tapes," on the afternoon following the death, the nanny had told Sergeant Hinderliter that Whiting had slapped Sarah, but that she didn't know if she had actually seen it or not.)

The nanny ran over and tried to pull Whiting off Sarah, she said. She failed, and finally, responding to Sarah's plea, picked up the phone and called Burt.

When Burt arrived, the nanny returned to her bed in room 126.

Twenty minutes later she was dozing off when she heard noises in Sarah's room. It sounded like someone opening and closing a drawer in there, she says. She called out, "Sarah?" but no one answered. This led her to assume that David Whiting had returned. "I was scared. I mean he had been violent. I didn't want to see him so I didn't say anything more."

She went back to sleep, she says.

After he finished playing the "Rio Rico tapes," Attorney Lazarow took out a tape he made on his own of an interview with the nanny. At the end of the interview, Lazarow suddenly asked her a peculiar question:

"Did you hit David Whiting over the head with anything?"

She did not, she replied. I wondered what had prompted Lazarow to ask the question in the first place.

"Oh, I don't know," Lazarow said. "Maybe I was just trying to shake her, see if there was something she was leaving out of her story. We were trying to figure out how he might have gotten that star-shaped wound, and we figured maybe it happened when the nanny was trying to pull Whiting off Sarah during the fight, but both she and Sarah said no."

The star-shaped wound on the back of David Whiting's head has yet to be explained away.

An MGM lawyer attempted to explain it away by suggesting that in a fit of rage David Whiting simply smashed the back of his head against a wall. Others suggest that David Whiting was, literally, star struck that night, and that Burt Reynolds was the star. Reynolds has a reputation in Hollywood for an explosive temper and an itch to fight. Before the death, he regaled Gila Bend locals with tales of past punch-outs, adding that he had decided to leave that part of his life behind now that he had become a big star. A woman who knew Reynolds intimately for years told me that he used to blame it on his spleen. His spleen had been removed after a high-school football injury, and ever since then he'd been unable to control his violent temper because, he said, the spleen had some thing to do with controlling the rush of adrenaline. All of which helps explain why Reynolds became such an obvious target for suspicion; none of it is evidence.

Spleen or no spleen, if Reynolds *had* lost control of his temper and given Whiting a beating, it seems likely that the body would show more evidence of violence than it did.

According to Dr. Robert Wright, who performed autopsy number two on the body of David Whiting, the most violent interpretation that can be made from a reading of the marks left upon the body is this: someone grasped Whiting firmly by the shoulders, shook him, and either shoved him back against a wall causing him to hit his head, or threw him down causing him to strike his head on the ground.

State Police crime-lab people found no evidence on either the walls or the bathroom floors of rooms 119, 126, and 127 to suggest that a bloody bashing had taken place in any of those rooms. (The bedroom floors are carpeted.)

The parking lot outside is covered with asphalt. If it happened, it could have happened out there in the parking lot. But a hard rain swept through Gila Bend in the early morning hours of that Sunday. Any bloodstains that might have been left upon the parking-lot asphalt would have been washed away. The mystery of where and how, and by whose hands, if any, David Whiting received his star-shaped wound remains unsolved.

Does it matter? Dr. Wright thinks it matters. Dr. Wright is a forensic pathologist for the Coroner's Office of the City and County of San Francisco, and a professor of forensic pathology at the University of California Medical Center. He was called upon by Mrs. Campbell, David's mother, to perform an autopsy after she had the body shipped out of Arizona and installed in the refrigerator of a funeral home in Berkeley, just one day before the third and final session of the inquest.

"The force of the impact to the head," Dr. Wright declared in his autopsy summary, "could well have caused a temporary loss of consciousness (a brain concussion), and may have caused him to behave in a stuporous fashion, and to be unmindful of his subsequent acts."

He could have been knocked silly, in other words, and in that state of silliness taken two or three too many pills, killing himself unintentionally. It was a borderline overdose. David Whiting might have been unaware he was crossing the border.

Dr. Wright's conclusion must, of course, be weighed against the milder conclusion of the original autopsy doctor who had not been selected by the boy's mother. But his report does give some substance to something the mother said to me in the coffee shop of the Travelodge.

"The horrible part is, severe-intoxication doses of this drug can produce deep coma. And the horrible thing is if these people thought he was dead—the pulse would have been faint—they could have been drunk or high, suppose they didn't know how to take a pulse—they could have sat around for hours, while his life ebbs away."

The nanny woke up at seven thirty in the morning, she said.

She was very cold. She walked through the connecting door into Sarah's room and found the outside door wide open to the chill morning air. She shut the outside door and headed back for the inner door into her own room.

The nanny said she never saw a body in the course of this little expedition. When Sergeant Hinderliter came upon the body about twelve thirty he found the legs from the knees down sticking out beyond the end of the dressing-room partition. Walking back from closing the outside door that morning, the nanny was walking straight toward the end of the dressing-room partition and, presumably, straight toward the protruding legs of David Whiting. There was light: the lights were still on in the room from the night before. But she was drowsy, the nanny said, and she saw no body.

This means one of three things:

The body was not there.

The body was there and the nanny did not, in fact, see it.

The body was there, dead or alive, the nanny saw it and went back to sleep without reporting it. Or else she reported it to someone, and that someone waited four hours before reporting it to the police.

Which leads to another unresolved question: how long before she reported it did Sarah find the body?

"At one time she told me she went back to her room at eight o'clock in the morning," Sergeant Hinderliter told me, recalling his interview with Sarah the day of the death. "And the next time she turned around and said it was ten o'clock. I didn't question her on the time at that time because she was upset, and because at the time of my interview I was just working on a possible drug overdose."

Eleven days later, in the "Rio Rico tapes," and then again at the inquest, Sarah said it was around eleven fifteen when she returned to her room and found the body.

Sarah was on the witness stand. The Deputy County Attorney had just led her gently through her account of the death, eliding over any discussion of her stay with Burt Reynolds.

Now came the moment many of those following the case closely had been waiting for. The Deputy County Attorney seemed to be approaching, gently of course, the subject of Sarah's Sunday-afternoon statement to Sergeant Hinderliter. People wanted to know, for instance, whether Sarah had been slapped or beaten.

"Now, do you remember talking to the policeman that came the next morning?" the Deputy County Attorney asked her, meaning Sergeant Hinderliter, and afternoon, not morning.

"Well, I was terribly shook up the next morning. Do you mean the policeman?"

Yes, said the Deputy County Attorney, he meant the policeman.

"By the time I saw the policeman I had heard that Mr. Whiting was dead," Sarah replied. "This was when I was in a bad way."

"Do you recall that conversation with the officer at all?" the Deputy County Attorney asked.

"No. I just told him what had happened."

"But you remember what you told him at this time?" the Deputy County Attorney persisted.

At precisely this point Sarah burst into tears.

"The truth," she sobbed urgently. "The same as I'm giving you now, I think."

The courtroom was silent. At his desk, the Deputy County Attorney looked down at his hands as if in remorse for having trespassed the bounds of decency with his ferocious questioning. From his bench, the Justice of the Peace leaned over toward Sarah and patted her hand comfortingly. When Sarah had wiped the tears from her eyes, the Deputy County Attorney started an entirely new line of questioning and did not venture near the subject again.

There was one final moment of high melodrama at the inquest. The questioning was over, and Sarah, face flushed and stained with tears, asked to make two final statements. First, she declared, she had never resisted testifying before the inquest. "I was bulldozed by my husband, producers, Burt Reynolds, MGM," she said. "I wanted to go as soon as I could . . . and I was not allowed to do this and for this I feel a grudge."

And second, she said, there was the matter of David Whiting's body, still languishing at that time in Mr. Ganley's refrigerator wrapped up in a sheet. (As of this writing, about three months after his death, the body is still languishing unburied in the refrigerator of the Bayview mortuary in Berkeley, "awaiting further tests" and further word from Mrs. Campbell, who hasn't been heard from in some time, an employee of the mortuary told me.)

"I hear from my attorney," Sarah told the Gila Bend courtroom, "that somebody doesn't want to bury this boy and that the state is going to bury him."

Sarah rose up in the witness stand, eyes wet. "*Well, I would like to bury him!*" she cried. With that, she rushed from the courtroom.

Sarah Miles never contacted him, Mr. Ganley told me. "No sir.

I've never heard from Miles or anyone of that type. In fact," said Mr. Ganley, "they weren't even interested in David Whiting after his death."

I asked him what he meant by that, and he told me this story.

It was the afternoon of the death. Mr. Ganley was in room 127 with the body of David Whiting, helping the investigators prepare it for shipment to the County Morgue in Phoenix for an autopsy.

"Miss Miles was in the room next door, and she sent word over she wanted to come in and get a dress because they were having a party up at the bar and she wanted to get up there. And the investigators wouldn't let her have the dress. They told her when they were through with the room she could get anything she wanted out of it."

"But that was what she wanted—a party dress?"

"Yeah, she wanted to go to the Elks Club, they were having a barbecue for Reynolds's birthday," Mr. Ganley said.

Meanwhile, Burt Reynolds was in his room talking with a couple of his friends, trying to decide whether to go to that Elks Club party or not. The party was for him, of course, and he would disappoint a lot of the Gila Bend people if he didn't show up. But then, there had been that unfortunate death, and that made it hard for him to feel like celebrating.

Finally, according to one of the people in the room with Burt, the decision came down to this. "Burt said something like if it had been an accident, that was one thing, then it was tragic, you know, and it was no time to party. But if it was suicide, if this guy was so worthless he didn't have the guts to face life, then why spoil the party?"

Burt went to the party.

THE FRIENDS OF BOBBY ZAREM

In an age in which most of what passes for "public relations" has been institutionalized into the corporate bureaucracies of "leisure conglomerates," Bobby Zarem is one of the last of the old-fashioned lone operators, a self-made man with a self-created aura about him. The fact that his wares are as effete and ephemeral as celebrity and glamour should not obscure his kinship with the old-fashioned traveling salesman. His shrewd sense of how to turn such insubstantial qualities as personality and image into marketable commodities is the trademark of the seventies version of that familiar American figure. His specialty is the ability to make the sophisticates of the media, to whom he's selling his bill of goods, think they're not being sold something, or at least to disguise it so subtly that they think of Bobby more as a lovable social director than a salesman. Still there is poignancy in Bobby's insistence that all these people, "The Friends of Bobby Zarem," are really friends, not just customers. Unlike most salesmen, he's not content with the sale; he needs to believe he's sold himself, too.

Bobby Zarem looks a bit like the Wizard of Oz. Not the awesome apparition that terrified the Munchkins. More like the real Wiz, the nervous little guy discovered behind the curtain manipulating the grand illusion.

Like the Wiz, Bobby Zarem is an image maker, and the Big Apple is his Emerald City. In the past three years Bobby has become the hottest new phenomenon in the world of celebrity entertainment public relations.

The forty-year-old Savannah-born Yale-educated publicist made his reputation with his wizardry staging a special kind of promotion: New York movie-premiere parties, those magical media events that glitter like elaborate ice sculptures for one evening then melt away into the night.

Ephemeral as they are, these parties are not all for fun; they can play a significant role in the economic future of the film they're thrown for and the studio financing it. One of Bobby's events can transform the opening of a twenty-million-dollar studio turkey with awful reviews into "news" of a sort—daily paper and TV coverage, stories in the newsmagazine "personality" sections, all of which creates "awareness" of the movie as a phenomenon apart from its quality, gives it enough media momentum to minimize the effect of critics.

Bobby did it for *Tommy*, the big-budget rock musical. His celebrated black tie formal dinner for socialites and stars, the one he staged down in the Fifty-seventh Street subway station (carpeted and damasked for the occasion), is one of those lavish "Zarem events," as they've come to be called, that have made Zarem himself a media phenomenon.

"People talked about the *Tommy* party as though it were an *entity*," Bobby recalls proudly. "I mean *Vogue* wrote a few months later that everybody was trying to have '*Tommy* parties.' "

Despite the success of his spectacular *Tommy*-style Zarem events (the weight lifter-studded party that pumped *Pumping Iron*; the "Speakeasy theme" party at 21 for *Lucky Lady*; the party for *The Ritz*, a movie about gay baths, at the Four Seasons; the spectacular wedding of Sly Stone at Madison Square Garden), Bobby Zarem is not merely a master of the massive revel. He also specializes in carefully orchestrating a series of intimate pre-release screenings of a movie for celebrities and opinion makers to build "awareness" for an upcoming release. And he's a whiz at creating the nonspectacular but quietly classy, cunningly wrought premiere party—the kind that depends for its success not upon its expansiveness but its exclusivity—the stellar magnitude of the fortunate few socialites and celebrities on Zarem's guest list and the radiant residue of free publicity the pictures of the party in the morning papers provide. Bobby describes, for instance, how one crucial photo of Jackie Kennedy at the premiere party simply *made The Front* a big picture.

Bobby wants to make clear that he wasn't asking Jackie to this premiere to *use* her for that reason. "I mean, she knows that she is being asked to a screening because she's thought of as being terrific, and not because, uh, somebody wants to *use* her." Bobby says, characteristically beginning with a circumlocutory apology.

"Her associating with this specific film gave it a certain, uh—
awareness—respectability that I'm not saying it didn't deserve, but
might not have gotten if she hadn't been there and been
photographed."

Zarem's uncanny ability to get the most chic celebrities, the
"SSTs" (the word *Women's Wear Daily* has decreed to replace the
outmoded, subsonic jet set), together with some of the most
sophisticated and powerful media people at his "events" has
mystified many. Are all these "fabulous fabulous people," as he
calls them, his "great great friends"? Or are both groups, the
celebrities and the media people, there because of some professional quid pro quo? By getting press people and the SSTs
together in the floating social club of Zaremevents—by elevating
the press to SST status—has Zarem managed to blur, however
artfully, the border line between public relations and journalism?

Whatever his secret, it's been successful. Increasingly when a
big movie studio heads east for New York with a big budget at
stake and a lot riding on the opening publicity blitz, they'll
jettison their own in-house PR people and turn the premiere over
to Zarem.

And most recently Bobby has been venturing into image-making
for clients outside the movie world. Late last year the sovereign
State of New York was looking for someone to do a promotion
campaign for a new television commercial in the "I Love New
York" series, this one a Broadway show-centered pitch for New
York City tourism: a promotion for a promotion and a party to
celebrate it. They turned to Zarem. Bobby persuaded them the
premiere had to be a Valentine's Day Event and required not one
but two parties: an "I Love New York" Valentine's Day luncheon
at Tavern on the Green (another Zarem client) and an "I Love
New York" Valentine's evening disco dance at Studio 54.

Intrigued by the notion of Bobby Zarem (whom I'd never met
before), taking on the reality-stricken countenance of New York
City (could he do for the Big Apple what he'd done for Marisa
Berenson?), I spent some time watching Bobby Zarem promote.

The first time I walked into his modest Madison Avenue offices
it was evening, and I found Bobby dressed with offhand preppy
sloppiness in a torn sweater with a red bandanna around his neck.
He was cleaning some marijuana, complaining about his upcoming
migraine (he gets one every Sunday, he says), and worrying that
his service might not ring through if he got a call from Carrie
Fisher, the *Star Wars* princess, who is (with Margaux Hemingway
and Gilda Radner) one of the cosponsors of the V-Day disco
dance.

Bobby seemed nervous and sensitive about this Valentine's Day promotion task when I first talked to him. Later I would come to realize that he seems nervous and sensitive about almost everything. Nervous about his migraines. Sensitive about his own image. Nervous about whether people really like him for himself or for his parties. He shares this nervousness with an analyst three times a week, and thirty times a day with just about everyone else who calls him.

But this first night I spoke to him he seemed particularly nervous about the St. Valentine's Day job. It was an important step for the still fledgling fortunes of Bobby Zarem Inc., the firm he formed when he left public relations industry titan Rodgers and Cowan to go into business for himself.

In addition, Bobby's got some stiff competition for his Valentine's Day promotion. Although the luncheon has clear sailing ahead—undivided media attention and the presence of the Mayor and Governor as well as the stars of Bobby's guest list—two rival Valentine's Day promotions threaten to turn February 14 into a great three-way Love Feast face-off.

First there's the Valentine's Day charity benefit for the Myasthenia Gravis Foundation. Ordinarily a charity for an obscure disease would pose no threat to a Zarem promotion, but this one's got a heavily social guest list with the promise of at least one Kennedy in attendance, and what's worse they've stolen a leaf from Bobby's *Tommy* party concepts—they're staging a black tie formal dinner dance on the main concourse of Grand Central Station—a cinch for at least one picture and caption that Bobby might have captured for his own event.

But that's not the most serious competition. The biggest threat is the New York Citizens Committee Ball at the Hilton. It has no imaginative location concept going for it, but the guest list will be formidable: the Mayor and Governor will be there, Liza Minnelli will entertain, and—it has been promised—Liza will climax the evening by dancing with Mayor Koch. Bobby knows that's the picture everyone's going to want in the morning editions, and Bobby's not confident his disco dance can beat it. He's got Margaux Hemingway, Carrie Fisher, and Gilda Radner co-hosting his "I Love New York" Valentine's night dance at Studio 54. The multiple host technique, a Zarem specialty he's refined to an art, will draw the attention of three constituencies, the size of the party is impressive, but word is out on the gossip circuit that Bobby wanted Liza for *his* event, that Liza refused, and now Bobby's disgruntled that despite an uncontested triumph for his lunch, his second party will not be, as they say, the "A" party of the evening.

Which perhaps explains why he got so upset about the picture of Miss Yonkers that accompanied what seemed to be a fine plug for his parties.

It is evening, ten days before the Valentine's Day battle. Bobby is sitting at a front table at Elaine's, a kind of nighttime office for him, since so many clients, potential clients, and entertainment-world journalists hang out there. Bobby's in the middle of discoursing to me about the essence of his art ("I don't think of my works as paintings as much as sculptures you see . . .") when someone comes in with the Night Owl edition of *The News* and ruins his evening.

There on page seven is what seems a nice paragraph plugging "I Love New York" Valentine's Day parties, but Bobby barely reads it. He's too upset by the picture accompanying it.

"What's she doing there?" he exclaims, pointing to the young woman with a "Miss Yonkers" sash around her bathing suit. Since Bobby's promo is sponsored by New York State, the picture editor innocently chose a Miss New York State bathing suit shot to accompany it. "She has nothing to do with my event," he complains. "That's exactly the wrong impression. How could that happen?

"It's all wrong. Just entirely the wrong image," he continues. Especially with the competition he's facing, Bobby must create an elegant image of his event if he wants his SST friends to grace the place. There must be an aura of exclusivity and glamour. The beauty queen picture suggests the exclusivity and glamour of a supermarket opening.

"I wish it hadn't run at all," Bobby moans.

It is high noon, St. Valentine's Day, and there is no love lost between rival publicists about to do battle in the Great St. Valentine's Day PR War.

Up in Bobby Zarem's Madison Avenue offices, his staff has convened for a final run-through for the tense hours to come, and the specter of dirty tricks by the opposition suddenly arises.

Bobby is on the phone explaining this dramatic new development to an associate. "I got a call last night," Bobby says. "Someone said that Liza Minnelli had been told Local 802 was going to picket Studio 54 tonight. I think it's a phony tip. First of all, Liza was not even invited. She was never on our list. Why would someone call her and tell her something like that unless they wanted to spread the rumor and make other people stay away who *were* invited?"

Bobby thinks he detects the fine hand of a competitor behind this dirty trick.

He suspects "a fairly low grade PR rep who's been trying to jettison our event by planting false items in the paper because they've got another one. This isn't the first time they've tried to plant false items. They put one in saying Woody Allen was coming to my event and then had someone call him up, and since he didn't know anything about it, he said he was not coming to ours, he was going to theirs. They've been trying to harm us but it's cool, it's fine," he concludes without much conviction.

Calls are placed to various authorities to check out the 802 picket tip while Bobby and his staff tend to last minute table-seating shifts for the upcoming luncheon. Gilda has decided at the last minute she wants to go to the lunch as well as the disco dance.

"Why don't we put her at table twenty-two. That's a good table," one assistant suggests. "She'll like them."

"But we've got some gaps developing in table nine since Adolph and Betty [Green and Comden] have to leave after fifty minutes for a rehearsal," Bobby says.

"Well," another assistant queries, "should we consider them to be *gaps* or should we consider them *there*, because if they're gaps we can shift Gilda from table twenty-two to their table. But do you think table fourteen looks weak right now?"

Clearly this is a subtle and intricate social science, this table-seating shifting. Zarem prides himself on the "chemistry" of a table, on his virtuosity in the art of social collage, and again one is reminded how illuminating such apparent trivia as Zarem table settings will be to future historians of the seventies. Just as historians of the reign of Queen Elizabeth seize upon a shadowy behind-the-scenes figure like Simon Forman the court astrologer and find in his coded diaries of charts and consultations a more accurate picture of the nexus of power in the royal household, so too will Bobby Zarem seating charts be seized upon someday to illuminate the real mechanics of social status in the seventies in New York. For Zarem is the court astrologer of today's entertainment royalty, and his seating charts are sensitive zodiacs that register the subtle shifts in the chic constellations of the fame game.

Finally the seatings are pronounced perfect. "It's going to be a good event this lunch." Bobby concludes the meeting. "With that little bit of snow in the park the Tavern will look like something out of nineteenth-century Russia."

"The reason it will be good," says an assistant with a less

romantically inclined sensibility, "is because there's not one extraneous piece of dreck at any of those tables." Meaning people who weren't celebrities or rich or useful in some way, or who squeaked by that terrible judgment because they were writing a story about Bobby. "Not one extraneous piece of *dreck*," she repeats with satisfaction.

How did Bobby Zarem arrive at this eminence, able to judge with a terrible swift word whether one is an "extraneous piece of dreck" or a "fabulous fabulous person" (most people in his milieu seem to fall into one of those categories)? How did someone who grew up in sleepy Savannah establish himself as arbiter and stage manager for these most inside of all New York events?

He says he grew up feeling like a sensitive lonely outsider. Not because he was Jewish in the Deep South (Savannah, Bobby says, was founded in part by Jewish debtors in the seventeenth century and has a history of tolerance). No, he was just a shy kid, he says, who spent a lot of time watching movies and fell in love with the blissful musical comedy image of New York he'd get in films like *On the Town*. But the real New York was as remote from Savannah as Kansas from Oz until a serious illness forced his father to go off to see the medical specialists of Manhattan. Bobby remembers a winter he went north to New York to be with his ailing father. Bobby stayed at the Waldorf, and while he waited in vain for the ineffectual magic of the medical wizards to revive his father, he escaped to the refuge of the playhouses and the unfailing wizardry wrought by the musical comedy stage. It is not surprising considering the circumstances that he became hooked on the healing harmonies of the exhilarating fantasy worlds. Nor should it be surprising that he speaks of the theatrical quality of his media events as a therapeutic response to an ailing culture. The essential ingredient that makes a Zarem event special, says Zarem, is "a mental energy that I create—to take the place of a real one that doesn't exist. It's the creation of the fantasy to replace the vitality that maybe isn't there."

Which is why Bobby's media events are frequently more memorable than the movies or celebrities they're designed to publicize; they're therapeutic in the way medicine shows are—the pitchman lifts the spirit more than the potion he's pitching. For one night for a few privileged people, Bobby Zarem can stage-manage the illusion that the ailing city is one big musical comedy.

It was musical comedy, says Bobby, that caused him to graduate third to last in his class at Andover. Too hooked on Comden and Green's *Two on the Aisle* to study, he says. While good test scores got him placed on the waiting list at Yale, it required an archetypal act of self-promotion to get himself into the entering class. "It was September and I hadn't heard from them so I sent them a telegram saying I would be showing up at the admissions office the next day and wait there with my bags until they let me in. I got a telegram back the next day officially accepting me." Although Bobby claims to have been lonely and unhappy in New Haven, spending most of his time hanging around the Shubert Theater escaping into the theater, he nevertheless was selected for membership in Scroll and Key, next to Skull and Bones the oldest and most elite senior secret society on campus.

When he wound up in New York after graduation in 1958, Bobby began to gather about him a growing network of friends— not a secret society, more like a social club, a very elite social club. The Friends of Bobby Zarem.

Bobby broke into the PR business doing promotional work for a firm that booked classical music tours. Although he spent most of his time out of New York going from town to town traveling-salesman fashion to set up local bookings, he was working for the most distinguished clients in the entertainment business and dealing with the socialites who run the benefit concerts. When he moved over to work for Joseph E. Levine and later Rodgers and Cowan on movie promotion, Bobby's soft-spoken self-deprecatory southern manners, his Andover-Yale offhand preppiness made him particularly adept at dealing with the Social Register types who chaired the charities to which the proceeds of movie premieres were donated.

Back then most New York movie openings were charity benefits, and although these days Bobby doesn't believe in charity openings ("I think a charity tie-in just cuts into the awareness of the film itself," he told me), back then the charity benefit premiere was the perfect kind of opportunity for making the classic Zarem connection. He'd introduce the elite of the Social Register world to the elite of the cinema world, tell each that the other was "a fabulous fabulous person" and "a great great friend," and provide an event or a setting in which they could be fabulous and elite together. Or he'd take people from one or both these elites up to Elaine's and introduce them to the elite of the literary and fashion worlds, and before long quite a few people in separate but equally elite circles in New York found they had one thing in common aside from being fabulous—they were all Friends of Bobby Zarem.

All of this was done in the spirit of sociable generosity—Bobby *likes* mixing and matching "fabulous" people—nevertheless it didn't hurt him professionally. You might say he benefited from the synergy created by the connections he made.

He'd help corral a group of choice celebrities from one elite to spice up the parties of another, and it was only natural that the most glamorous party givers and guests from both elites would grace Bobby's promotional parties, and that these summit meetings of chic would all get written up in Suzy's society column.

And so Bobby's clients didn't just get Bobby and his professional PR services. They got Bobby's whole world, fabulous friends and all.

Bobby's close personal and professional empathies with Aileen Miehle, the woman who writes about society under the name "Suzy," has played no small part in Bobby's success. They went to the same parties and when they didn't Bobby would supply delicious little details from the ones he attended or heard about from one of his friends; they'd talk on the telephone all the time; and soon Bobby's friends and Bobby's parties would appear in Suzy's column with great regularity.

Bobby is a bit defensive about his relationship with Suzy. "I think there is a mistaken assumption that I am involved with Suzy. I mean people have said to me from time to time, 'Don't you *write* Suzy?' But I've never," he insists. "Aileen is a great great great friend of mine," he continues (a not insignificant tribute since most of his friends are merely great great friends). "I mean she's this fabulous woman, she has this marvelous sense of humor, so I can have fun with her since I have an extraordinarily marvelous sense of humor," he explains.

In practical terms the fact that Bobby and Aileen share this good-humored empathy means that Bobby can offer his clients and friends (and sometimes friends can turn into clients and vice versa, the boundaries often blur) access both to Suzy's society column and Suzy's society world. Hollywood and literary figures hanging out at Elaine's can have their convivialities celebrated cheek by jowl in Suzy's column with the fetes of the old social nobility of Newport and Palm Beach. This is not Earl Wilson and that cozy show biz jazz. This is instant aristocracy.

Another hallmark of the rise of Bobby Zarem has been his sophisticated manipulation of the mystique of The Screening List. Before the Zarem era the pre-release screening of a movie was a fairly pedestrian process with the simple utilitarian purpose of letting critics, entertainment editors, and writers see a movie long enough ahead of time for their stories to come out before it was released. Of course there were some PR people who made it a practice to invite an assortment of free-lance writers and "opinion makers," hoping that they might be inspired by seeing the movie and generate some influential "awareness" for it.

Zarem turned that concept inside out—he gets awareness for his *screenings* as events in themselves. By regularly inviting certain select celebrities, SSTs, and friends to certain screenings, he's transformed the screening from a place to go to see a movie to a place to go to be seen. A party. It doesn't matter whether those attending like the movie or not. The fact that they're *there* endows the movie with "significance," at least to one another.

Zarem has also pioneered with sophisticated variations on the screening theme. Most recently certain select people on Zarem's Screening List received a hand-lettered invitation on cream-colored stock headed with the name Frank Yablans. It was an invitation to a screening of *The Fury*, but not just a screening: following the movie there was to be a supper in a suite at the Sherry Netherland. It was signed, in hand lettering, "Frank." In fact, there were three separate screenings cum suppers. Media sophisticates who knew Bobby Zarem was behind all this were trying to figure out which of the three guest lists was the coveted "A" list and who was on it. Although he denies the existence of anything so crude as an "A" list, Zarem's screenings have created a mystique about his Screening List-making, a science he attends to with the same obsessive sensitivity to social chemistry as he does his table settings.

Bobby is sensitive about his image as the man with the magic list. Part of the folklore about Zarem circulating in media circles is the notion that he has a closely guarded eyes-only master Rolodex that is his chief marketable asset and keystone to his success, containing, it is supposed, the most highly prized names and the most private unlisted numbers a party could want, and that only Zarem can whirl his magic Rolodex and materialize them en masse.

I asked Bobby if there was in fact a fabulous Rolodex somewhere to be seen with all those magic numbers. He got very upset.

"No, not at all, and you can't have that concept," Bobby told me emphatically. "You can't have that concept," he repeated. "There's no way you can have that concept," he added.

"I'm just very sensitive to things like Rolodex and lists. Because they suggest a certain mechanicalness and coldness that has nothing to do with me as a person or the way I work."

So there is no fabulous Rolodex?

"Listen," says Bobby, "I get very—" Then he stops and pulls a thick Gideon Bible-sized black address book out of his drawer.

"This is my thing here," Bobby says, dramatically flourishing it. Indeed it is not a Rolodex. It is an address book.

"And nobody else has this," he says proudly. "I walk around with it either in my briefcase or when I'm at home it's at home." It never leaves his person, he says, not since "somebody stole an earlier version of this from my former office on the day I was moving."

Bobby suggests that the theft of The Original Zarem Black Book was a professionally engineered job by an envious PR rival. "Somebody came in with a complete set of keys to my office suite, and then they had keys to my office door, then they had a key to my drawer, and this was sitting in it next to a cashbox with three hundred dollars in it." They didn't take the money, just the million-dollar address book.

So there is no Rolodex. There's a black book. That takes care of that false image. But there are other aspects of his own image that still disturb the master image maker. Although any ordinary PR man would be pleased to be at the peak Bobby has attained in his profession, Bobby Zarem is no ordinary PR man. He'd be the first to tell you. He's a *sensitive* PR man. Sometimes, in fact, he can be as sensitive about his own image as he is about the images he projects. His "black tie socialite" image for instance.

"I'm very sensitive to that image of me," Bobby complained. "I mean I met this guy recently who produced *Mean Streets*. And we had this fabulous conversation up at Elaine's. Wonderful conversation. In the middle of it he looks at me and says, 'You know, all the young producers and directors in Hollywood think you walk around New York City with a black tie on all day. Who would have thought that you're this *person* who can think and feel and talk?' "

It is of central importance to Bobby Zarem that people treat him as a sensitive person and not just a PR man. He's sensitive to the fact that PR men are often treated as "subpersons"—a fawning servant class whose only function is to wait upon the nobility of the media and cater to their whims.

I never heard Bobby refer to himself as a "PR man," never as a "press agent." He seldom calls what he does "public relations." He prefers to say he "does press work."

Press work. Do you understand the difference between press work and PR? Say PR man to someone, and at best they think slick-talking smoothies with oily charm. More likely they think phony, hype artist, flatterer, hypocrite. The PR man has always had a PR problem. Press agents, says Cecil B. De Mille in *Sunset Boulevard*, "can do terrible things to the human spirit." But "doing press work"—it's somehow different. It's like being part of the press, down there in the trenches with the heroes of the Fourth Estate, a foot soldier in the battle for truth.

Indeed Bobby is acutely sensitive to—among the multitude of things he is acutely sensitive to—the taint on "public relations" in post-Watergate America. (According to Haldeman, Nixon's last words before the eighteen-minute gap were about a "PR offensive" to distract attention from the truth.) "There's an entire generation of people in this country," says Bobby, "who were caught between the hypocrisy of what they were, on the one hand, told, and what they saw going on around them, which were contrary to each other. So you had a generation of people acting out on a false, or at least confused, set of feelings. I am part of that generation, and I consider it the greatest quality that I have now to be able to communicate with those people."

And, like a slightly better-known Georgian, Bobby's response to the problem of post-Watergate public mistrust is to declare that he, Bobby Zarem, would never lie to the American people about a film he's promoting. "I would certainly never lie about any aspects of a project," Bobby declared to me.

"Could you be honest," I asked Bobby, "if you thought a project you were working on was a turkey? Or if there were both good and bad elements in it?"

Here's how Bobby defines the PR man's "I will never lie" credo in action: "If I did not like a film, I would never never ever say to a critic that I don't like it, if I'm working on a film. . . . Uh, if a critic you know asked me if I liked it, I would tell him those things that I do like or that I think. And you know, I find it hard to believe that I'd be involved in something that I didn't like to some degree."

Also like that fellow Georgian, it's important to Bobby that we understand that his success is not due to the slick hypocrisy of the traditional PR pro. He believes his success is due to his instinct for "concepts"—his sensitivity to the essence of a movie, and his ability to come up with a brilliant promotional concept faithful to its spirit.

Every detail of a PR campaign must reflect a single conceptual vision, he says—from the grand theme of a lavish premiere to the humblest one-line column item. Indeed, "just to have an item with a name mentioned without it being part of a concept is valueless," Bobby declares. "To me there must be a concept behind everything. It permeates me and my work on every level. It's the thing, of course, that makes me crazy sometimes, because I am obsessed with making sure that something is communicated just precisely within my concept."

Concept PR. Someday cultural historians may look back upon the seventies and decide that the most original and expressive art form of the decade was the media event. Certainly the official foundation-subsidized avant garde of the decade has been preoccupied with "performance art," with evanescent aesthetic "events" announced by a press release replacing the traditional art "object." And as art becomes more like public relations, public relations may be recognized as art, and Bobby Zarem will be seen as the sensitive artist he sees himself as—if not the Picasso of PR, certainly the Toulouse-Lautrec of the late seventies.

The fact that his works are so frankly commercial should no more disqualify them as art than it has Toulouse-Lautrec's posters. The walls of Bobby's office and apartment are covered with the poster art of Cheret, a contemporary of Toulouse-Lautrec's who did publicity and advertising posters in a slightly larger-than-life theatrical style. In Bobby's apartment there is a book of Cheret reproductions.

The Paris of Toulouse-Lautrec and Cheret had no trouble, according to the introductory essay, "accepting the publicity poster, publicity itself in its many manifestations 'as an *art*.' "

The Countess was away, but the Princess, her daughter, was having a party Friday night at the Countess's magnificent Park Avenue apartment-palazzo. "It'll be an informal evening, just some friends, you know, a wine and pot kind of crowd," Bobby assured me as he urged me to attend. He wanted me to talk to the Princess, he said, she was one of his true friends, a "really quite terrific" person who would be a good person for me to talk to about him. I had a sense that he wanted me to be at this evening so I could see him in a social setting as a friend among friends, rather than a promoter among clients. Although he was helping out the Princess with the guest list and invitations, Bobby wasn't promoting anything at the party.

He almost did, but the Princess warned him off at the last minute. "I told her I was going to bring some Rutles albums and give them away tonight," Bobby told me the afternoon before the party. The "Rutles" album is a soundtrack of a new TV special parody-tribute to the Beatles. "I'm not representing them. I just think they're terrific, and people would get a kick out of hearing it. You know, give them out just for fun, no business." But the Princess said no. "She said it would *look* commercial, and she didn't want that at this party. I explained to her they weren't my clients, but . . ."

(Cynics might observe that whenever a PR man promotes something he's not representing, it's because he thinks he *should* be representing them and wants to demonstrate to the potential client how much he'll do for them out of sheer love, not to mention money.)

So there were no Rutles records there that night at the Countess's place. Just the Princess, her friends, the Friends of Bobby Zarem, and me. It was a lovely evening, and never were the attractions of the Zaremworld more evident—titled Old World nobility mixing easily with young courtiers of the new American media nobility; fine wine, food, and grass; lively, intelligent conversation. Many of these people see each other two or three evenings a week at Zarem's staged screenings and other media events. I could see Bobby bouncing about like a plump cherub as he bobbed his way about the scene, "touching base" with everyone, the society social director.

Later that evening I wandered out of the crowded salon and into the magnificent library. I couldn't help recall the anonymous guest at one of Gatsby's parties who wanders into the library looking for a clue to the mystery of his host. There was something about Zarem equally puzzling. I could hear the musical hum of lively conversation from the party rooms, and I could see how he in some ways managed to recreate in the flesh the musical comedy world that had enraptured him as a child. But he seemed so insecure about it, perhaps not sure himself which of those players in his production were his friends and which were playing a role of convenience.

The Princess wants to talk to me about the Bobby Zarem Question. A big fight over Bobby Zarem actually tore apart a lovely dinner party last week, leaving wounded feelings in its wake. The Princess was there. She was one of the combatants.

Her defense of Bobby is impassioned. "So I am at this dinner party," she says. "And _____ starts attacking me for calling Bobby Zarem my friend. Saying that I am naive and how can I have a press agent for a friend. I am so mad. He *is* my friend. I don't care what people say, but he is."

It's nearing midnight, and as the last seconds of St. Valentine's Day are ticking away, Bobby is standing on the floor of Studio 54 watching his disco dance wind down.

By all professional PR standards, Bobby's Valentine's Day

promotions have been quite successful: there was full-scale coverage of the luncheon and the party in the papers; local TV news played the "I Love New York" commercials in full as part of their coverage; there was national network time on *Good Morning America*. In the three-way Love Feast Face-off, Bobby has more than held his own against Myasthenia Gravis and Liza Minnelli.

But there's a difference between a successful evening and a memorable, a "fabulous fabulous" evening. The difference tonight might have been Woody Allen.

Bobby's celebrity regulars are here. (Although one of his "fabulous" hostesses, Carrie Fisher, never showed. The *Star Wars* queen had to be "on the coast" that night, although Bobby says she really *planned* to show up, he wasn't just using her name for hype.) But most of the celebs here tonight are used to seeing each other at Studio 54 celebrity parties. Other people may be impressed with them, but they are no longer particularly impressed with each other. A truly memorable evening would be one in which one of those rare individuals who can single-handedly lift a party to a higher plane shows up.

At this fleeting moment in social history there are perhaps three people in New York who can lift a party to that exalted plane, an empyrean realm wherein even the celebs themselves feel they've gotten their presences' worth. Those three, in the opinion of professional party watchers, are Jackie Onassis, Liza Minnelli, and Woody Allen.

Yes, Woody Allen, whose combination of brilliance and reclusiveness (he almost never goes to a public party) in the complex calculus of such things have put him, if possible, in an even more special category than the others—after all, it's said, Jackie and Liza go everywhere.

Bobby is not unconscious of this; he's invited two of Woody's closest friends to this Studio 54 party. They've showed up; so there's still hope that Woody himself might make an appearance and transform the evening from a mere success to a triumph.

And so as the evening ebbs toward midnight, I find Bobby standing next to the bar talking to Woody's friends and, I suspect, waiting for Woody.

"Talked to him a while ago," says one of the friends, "said he wasn't sure if he was going to the Waldorf [site of Liza's event]. Said he might come by here later."

"Oh yeah," says Bobby, trying to sound casual. "When was that?"

"Couple hours ago, I think."

"He said he might come by?" Bobby asks.

"Said he might," says one friend. The dialogue is beginning to sound like a Beckett play.

"But you know you never can tell," says the other friend.

Woody doesn't come by. The evening ends successfully, but not fabulously.

Still there will be other evenings, other events already taking shape in Bobby's brain. He's doing the publicity for *The Wiz*, and he's got the notion he can persuade Jimmy Carter to hold the premiere party in the White House. He wouldn't be *using* the President, Bobby says. "It would be a *statement* he could make doing that. A real statement, and I think it would be a fabulous thing for his image."

THREE TALES OF TV COMMERCIALS

A full-page ad in Time *recently proclaimed a major victory for the forces of civilization in the battle against encroaching darkness: THE VIDEOCASSETTE RECORDER THAT LETS YOU WIPE OUT MR. WHIPPLE. The device is a "remote pause control . . . It lets you edit out commercials when you tape the show you're watching." I look upon this device in a different way: At last there is a way to edit out the programs and preserve only the commercials. At last the technology exists to make the work of regularly reviewing TV commercials bearable. When first I essayed a review of the "fall season" of TV commercials back in 1975, I was obliged to use a primitive combination of note-taking and audio tape recording to reconstruct the fleeting thirty-second spots I wanted to review. I was also forced to watch hours of prime-time programming just for a glimpse of a few minutes of commercials. The new "remote pause control" technology will make it possible for hours of leisurely contemplation of the elaborate manipulative art compacted into each thirty-second sales pitch. Now perhaps it will be possible for someone to take on the burdensome task I explored in "Soap Gets in Your Eyes" of doing regular reviews of TV commercials. It's still one of the most neglected tasks in American journalism and cultural criticism.*

As a mirror of culture, TV commercials tell us more about ourselves than the shows that shill for them; they reflect urgencies and exigencies beneath the surface of daily life far more accurately than most films and novels. In fact, if film critics paid as much attention to the auteurs of advertising as they do to the directors of their favorite forties B pictures, we might be better off on both fronts.

Part of the reason no one reviews TV commercials for major newspapers and magazines is, of course, that they are advertising vehicles, and the advertisers and ad agencies they would be holding up to public scrutiny collectively control the financial fates of most periodicals.

But more of an impediment, however, is a residual cultural snobbism that doesn't permit people to take commercials "seriously" because they're "so inane." Perhaps they are. But the intricate architecture of that inanity can tell us a lot about the psyche of civilization that builds such complex and silly structures. Michael Arlen demonstrated that in his brilliant essay in The New Yorker *on "Ring Around the Collar" commercials.*

In these three stories there are two approaches to writing about commercials. First, as in "Whipple's Last Squeeze," one can explore the economic and social foundations, the demographic and marketing structures that underlie a commercial campaign for a single product and see how the "creative" decisions in an ad campaign grow out of the grand strategies of giant corporations.

In addition to this narrow and deep excavation of the substratum of a single commercial, there is a broader, but not necessarily shallower, approach: take on large clusters of commercials that have something in common and search for patterns in their collective imagery. In "Soap Gets in Your Eyes" I focus on a somewhat arbitrary "new fall season" of ads with the idea that commercials conceived contemporaneously will reflect some common concerns. And in "The Four Horsemen of the Nightly News" I look at the ads on a single but crucial half hour of programming time.

The title of the story about The Great Toilet Paper War, "Whipple's Last Squeeze," seems to have been a premature epitaph. The durable Mr. Whipple has weathered the combination of feminist outrage and marketing game-planning that had threatened his now record long run as lovable irritant. The WIPE-OUT WHIPPLE ad, despite its mean-spirited double entendre, is not a threat to Whipple, merely confirmation of his unchallenged eminence as the most identifiable character in the history of commercial television.

No longer does a competing announcer rudely interrupt Whipple's scenarios, as was happening when I wrote the story. Whipple is back in command with a new tissue-sales concept to sell: Charmin is no longer squeezably soft. Now it's squeezably fluffy. In some ways commercials are like that: fluff, but fluff that can be squeezed for insight into the intentions of the fluff makers.

WHIPPLE'S LAST SQUEEZE

One of the more curious of the recent Charmin toilet tissue TV spots gives us a rare glimpse of supermarket manager George Whipple in a reflective, even tender, mood. Quite uncharacteristically, this particular Charmin commercial takes us far from the familiar setting of the series—the paper products aisle of Jerry's supermarket—where we are accustomed to see Whipple engaged in one after another frustrating struggle against Charmin-squeezing housewives. No, in this spot we find ourselves in the untroubled interior of Whipple's own home as George, surrounded by wife and children, reflects on how it all began.

"There I was, a young man just starting out," Whipple says. "Had my own store."

"Did you stop the ladies from squeezing the Charmin, Dad?" young Whipple Junior asks.

"You betcha!" Whipple recalls proudly.

Then one day, Whipple continues, a bit dreamily now, he saw a special woman in the toilet paper aisle. She was squeezing, like the others, but somehow she was different from all the others.

"I was about to tell her, please don't squeeze the Charmin, when I took one look at her and fell in love."

Romantic music swells in the background. The family Whipple grows misty-eyed. "And you let me squeeze the Charmin, didn't you, George?" says Mrs. W.

"Yep," Whipple tells the kids. "And until this day your mother's the only one I've let squeeze the Charmin."

More is going on here than the obvious allegory linking Charmin and sexual fidelity. There's turmoil in toilet paper marketing these days, turnover in toilet tissue ad campaigns. There are signs—the unusual Whipple-family-at-home spot, just one of many—that the uncertainties of the marketplace are beginning to affect one of the single most successful, most notorious, longest-running ad campaigns ever to appear in any medium. There are even intimations that, after a full decade on the air, George Whipple's days in the toilet paper aisle are numbered. Perhaps there's a foreshadowing of this in Whipple's sentimental journey into the past. Maybe it's time to take a look at the media phenomenon the Charmin campaign has become, focusing first, like Whipple, on how it all began.

The time had come to kill off Gentle the Dog. The year was 1964. For two years, Gentle the Dog had been the number one spokes-creature for Charmin toilet paper. Commercials for Charmin featured the fluffy animated animal romping around with other gentle animated souls—a gentle juggler who juggled only soft things, a gentle movie star named Belinda Beautiful who played only gentle roles, even a gentle dogcatcher. But the Procter & Gamble people who produced Charmin and the Benton & Bowles people who produced the commercials decided that Gentle the Dog just didn't fit in with the big marketing plans P&G had for Charmin. P&G production people had devised a new toilet-paper-making process, one they felt P&G could use to push its then-tiny Charmin brand into full-scale competition with the giant of the toilet paper industry, Scott. A February 1973 P&G report explains the secret of this history-making toilet paper breakthrough:

> The fibers from which tissue is made enter the paper machines in a very dilute water solution. Nearly all of this water has to be removed. Previously, the only way to remove the excess water from the tissue was to "squeeze" it out [which] compressed the tissue fibers, taking away from their fluffiness and softness . . . [T]he solution was relatively simple —eliminate as much of the physical pressing as possible and substitute a flow of hot air [which] would actually "fluff it up" . . . This allows for a deeper, more cushiony texture. An added benefit . . . is that less wood fiber per roll is required to make the same amount of this improved tissue.

In other words, in this new process, each square of one-ply Charmin toilet paper had less paper in it, but *looked* softer. (Whether it *felt* more "cushiony" is a hot dispute we will get into later.) The master marketing strategists at P&G thought this process could give them the opening they wanted in their plot against Scott: they could "position" this fluffed-up, cheaper tissue between the rougher low-cost one-ply papers (dominated by Scott tissue) and the softer, more expensive "facial-quality" two-ply tissues (dominated by Scott's "Soft-Weve"). Thus they would be offering greater fluffiness to the one-ply buyers and lower price to the two-ply people, thereby taking the trade of both away from Scott and making big money because they use less pulp per sheet. It would take just the right ad campaign to introduce this fluffed up Charmin into big-league competition, and it looked as if Gentle the Dog couldn't hack the new responsibility. P&G needed a barker of a different sort. Oh, they gave the fluffy mutt a chance. They experimented with an ad in which Gentle trots into a courtroom, asks a judge to have his name changed from "Gentle" to "Gentler," and explains to the puzzled magistrate that new Charmin toilet tissue is "Gentler than ever." This commercial had the effect of putting many people to sleep. Also one dog.

So in the summer of 1964 Benton & Bowles assigned a three-person creative team to come up with a brand new concept for selling Charmin. The job that faced creative director Jim Haines, group supervisor Flora Fifield, and junior copywriter John Chervokas is generally considered one of the toughest in the ad business because of certain built-in limitations on toilet paper advertising. Obviously you can't do on-camera comparisons. No before-and-after demonstrations. In fact, at one time toilet paper people had a rough time convincing broadcasters toilet paper commercials should even be permitted on home screens because of their inherent indelicacy. So from the beginning toilet paper was soft-pedaled on TV, and most toilet papers found a thousand and one indistinguishable ways to peddle themselves as soft.

Charmin started at a bit of a disadvantage in the soft parade, because for a long time it was one of the few tissues that hadn't cultivated a soft image. And with good reason: it wasn't that soft. When P&G acquired the Charmin tissue-making factory in Green Bay, Wisconsin, back in 1957, Charmin tissue was sort of a rough-hewn, backwoods toilet tissue, sold mainly in rural north country counties. (Skeptics at the time of the purchase, unaware of Charmin's place in P&G's grand design, wisecracked that the main reason for the acquisition must have been to get season tickets to Packers games for executives from P&G's Cincinnati headquarters.)

In keeping with the rough-and-ready quality of early Charmin, the pre-P&G ads for the brand featured a crude, euphemistic absorption test. "They dropped two tissues into a pot of water to see which one sunk first," is the way Jim Haines recalls an early Charmin turkey. (Since similar tests usually advertise the toughness of heavy-duty paper towels these days, one can speculate on what Charmin felt like back then.) The first series of P&G-produced commercials de-emphasized the stiffness but still gave the impression that it was a heavy-duty, institutional, even *outdoorsy*-type toilet tissue: there were endorsements from the housekeeper of an alpine chalet-inn and the housekeeper of a riverboat.

It didn't take P&G's market-research people long to establish that there was a great hunger in the growing American middle class for more softness in their toilet tissue, that there was a correlation between moving up in economic class and moving "up" from one-ply to two-ply tissue, because two-ply was soft, and for one reason or another—advertising being one big reason—soft white tissue was an emblem of the soft white-collar life. But it wasn't until 1960 that P&G production people had softened up Charmin enough to bring Gentle the Dog and his gentle friends to announce that Charmin was "fluffed, buffed, and brushed," presumably like Gentle the Dog's fluffy coat. But comparing a toilet tissue to dog's hair is risky business considering the popularity of wire hair terriers.

And in any case *gentle* is still not *soft*. *Gentle* still has a residue of averted pain in it (as in "Don't hurt, please be gentle"). *Gentler* is not soft, either. Even *soft itself* wasn't enough for the brand-new ad P&G and B&B wanted from the creative team they assigned to the Charmin account. Everyone was soft already. And Scott's "Soft-Weve" had already beaten everybody to "Softer than soft." Had the whole soft thing reached a dead end, or was there some way to say *softer than softer-than-soft*, and to say it in a way that made a shopper, sated by so many similar softs, select it from the shelf?

There are two versions of the moment of discovery. There may be a third. Flora Fifield, the only one of the Benton & Bowles creative trio no longer in advertising, is reportedly living somewhere in Vermont teaching school, and I was unable to locate her. (Both Procter & Gamble and Benton & Bowles, interestingly, claimed no memory and no records of the three people who created the momentous Mr. Whipple campaign and offered no help in finding them, or in supplying storyboards.)

Jim Haines, the creative head of the trio at the time, is now a partner in an ad agency in Johannesburg.* I spoke to him during one of his visits to New York. The way he remembers the big moment, it began with the three of them crammed into copywriter Chervokas's cubicle at Benton & Bowles's Fifth Avenue office,

---

* Among other things, he's in charge of advertising a South African toilet tissue brand called "Cushy." The campaign for "Cushy" features, as I recall Haines's description, an Afrikaner grandmother who is so obsessed with squeezing soft "Cushy" that she takes it to her bedroom with her; her family is constantly finding itself without tissue in time of need and pleading the brand's slogan, "Please keep the Cushy in the loo."

tossing a roll of toilet paper to and fro. They were at their wit's end, none of the ideas they'd tried had worked. They had run out of new ideas and they were running out of time. "It was one of those grade-B-movie situations," Haines recalls. "We were having a think session, you know, a frustration session and we were not only kicking ideas around we were tossing the roll around, and we started to get the giggles." The Muse must have kissed the airborne Charmin in midflight because suddenly, "John [Chervokas] caught the roll and started to squeeze it and somebody said, 'Don't squeeze it' and John said, 'Please don't squeeze it' or 'Please don't squeeze the Charmin' and it just happened. The thing just rolled off his tongue. . . ."

The way John Chervokas tells it there was no roll of toilet paper in the air. "I don't remember tossing any roll around, no," Chervokas told me when I spoke to him in his big new office at the Warwick Welsh & Miller agency. Chervokas has just received another of the many promotions that have marked his career since the Charmin creation, the latest being a move from creative director at William Esty to senior vice-president/creative director at Warwick. Back in 1972 Chervokas wrote for *Advertising Age* a tongue-in-cheek "confession" about his key role in writing Mr. Whipple into advertising history, but he concedes the Charmin conception has "definitely been a plus" in his career.

Like Haines, Chervokas sets the scene of the historic discovery in his junior writer's cubicle at Benton & Bowles, but Chervokas recalls a more elaborate operation of the creative process. Chervokas says the discovery grew out of their feeling that instead of just *saying* soft, or *showing* soft people and things, they should figure out a way to *demonstrate* soft. What follows is Chervokas's reconstruction in *Ad Age* of the free association process that led to the birth of Whipple:

"How to demonstrate softness? A feather is soft, but suggests tickling. A baby's behind suggests softness, but that's 'too restrictive.' Silk is soft, but comparing Charmin to silk risks 'over promising.' What about a fall? A soft fall. A fall on a pillow? Hugging a pillow? Squeezing a pillow? Squeeze a banana!?

"Wait a minute. Here was something. What does a woman do in a supermarket? She squeezes melons, tomatoes, bread . . . Squeeze *Charmin!*"

There it was. Just one hitch remained, according to Chervokas, and in the ingenuity of its solution was the birth of George Whipple. Someone pointed out that if the ad told women to squeeze Charmin in the store, "supermarket managers will go crazy. The answer is to tell them *not* to squeeze it." But how to tell them not to squeeze it? You have a crazy supermarket manager tell them not to squeeze it, that's how. "In an hour and a half," Chervokas wrote, "America's most universally despised advertising campaign became a reality."

Unlike the physicists working on the Manhattan Project who knew the magnitude of the terror they were about to unleash upon the world, the three people in that cubicle were unaware of the advertising explosion they had on their hands. According to Haines, "We were having a lot of laughs and we thought this was just another laugh until the substance of it was allowed to sink in." They liked the don't-squeeze idea, but the idea of the supermarket manager obsessed with protecting his Charmin from squeezers seemed a bit madcap at the time, particularly for a relatively cautious and conservative client like Procter & Gamble. The higher-ups at Benton & Bowles were a little nervous about it, too. "We encountered some abrasion," Haines recalls. "It may have been inside the agency. They considered it terribly harebrained; it took a lot of convincing inside to get them to convince Cincinnati to test the thing. Somebody had to go out there to fight tooth and nail for the campaign."

Even when P&G executives in Cincinnati grudgingly agreed to shell out for production of three sixty-second sample scripts of the "Don't squeeze" concept, there was no guarantee any one of them would ever make it on the air. Everything depended on the execution, as they say in the ad business, and the success of the execution, most everyone agreed, depended on how successfully the slightly mad character of the supermarket character could be brought off. According to Haines, Chervokas "had a very definite brief in mind. He wanted a Milquetoast character, a bit, I suppose effeminate in his way, nervous, intimidated, but a champion of Charmin." Chervokas remembers, "I was originally thinking of an Edmund Gwennish kind of character—you know, *Miracle on 34th Street*—you know, a lovable little fraud, maybe a little dumpy . . ." Whoever it turned out to be, they needed just the right actor to do it just the right way. The agency put out a casting call to both coasts and started compiling a reel of filmed auditions for the part.

Most comedy drunk acts these days are gassy drunk acts—the loudmouth, the weeper, the burper. But the classic drunk acts of the golden age of vaudeville were the dancer acrobatic drunk acts. That's what Dick Wilson, the man who plays Mr. Whipple, told me. He was a dancer acrobatic drunk act. This meant he'd go up on a tightrope and make all sorts of funny, heart-stopping, drunken near falls. "I worked with tails. I was classy, a lot of class, but a drunk," he said. He toured the best Canadian and English vaudeville circuits, played drunks for Olsen and Johnson, and ended up in America after the war. TV was good to him. "I must have done over three hundred and fifty TV shows as a drunk. I'm the drunk in *Bewitched*, I was the drunk on *The Paul Lynde Show*, I did a lot of Disney's drunks." He almost got his first big break in a nondrunk part when some TV people were all set to cast him as the sidekick of *Sergeant Preston of the Yukon*. At the last minute, however, the part got written out and Sergeant Preston was given a dog named "King" as a substitute sidekick. "I was supposed to be the dog," Wilson said.

Despite these and other disappointments in nondrunk parts, Wilson knew he was capable of more in show business. Maybe he wouldn't play Hamlet, but he wouldn't be satisfied with just playing drunks. He'd begun doing some free-lance stage-show producing in 1964. That summer he was in Las Vegas producing a Shirley MacLaine revue at a place called "The Kings Road Tally Ho" when he got a call from his agent. "He asked me: 'What do you think of toilet paper?' " Wilson recalls. "And I told him I think everybody should use it." "No, no, no," the agent said, according to Wilson, who I suspect has polished this Big Break scene into a little routine over the years. "I'm asking you how would you like to do a commercial for toilet paper, there's an audition tomorrow." "How do you audition toilet paper?" Wilson asked. And his agent said, " 'Please go and take a screen test,' and I said a screen test would be a permanent record. But I went and they liked me because five days later we were making the first Charmin commercial in a supermarket in Flushing."

"Dick Wilson was kidding me when he says you made the first ones in Flushing, wasn't he?" I asked Howard Magwood, the man who directed them.

"No, no, no. It was Flushing," Magwood insisted.

"It wasn't Flushing," says John Chervokas who was there to watch the filming of his scripts. "I think it was Astoria."

By the time director Magwood and his ten-person production crew set up for shooting in the Flushing/Astoria market, the original scripts drawn up at Benton & Bowles had undergone two interesting modifications. The name George Whipple, for instance, was a late change. I had always harbored a suspicion that it was no accident that "Whipple" sounded like a sinister fusion of "whip" and "nipple," and that perhaps some devious motivational-research person had created the name as an emblem of a submerged sadomasochistic element in the relations between Whipple and the housewives who risk his punishment for the pleasure of a squeeze.

Alas, the true story seems more innocent. I was able to acquire a copy of a hand-sketched storyboard draft of one of those original Charmin scripts, this one dated September 24, 1964, and entitled "Digby to the Rescue." In this draft, the store manager is named, not Whipple, but "Edgar Bartholomew," a far less provocative choice. The switch to Whipple was made, according to Chervokas, not to make the name more kinky, but because a real Edgar Bartholomew could not be found to sell the rights to his name. (When an ad agency gives commercial characters names, it makes a point of finding real persons with that name and persuades them to sell the use of their name for a token fee, so that *other* real persons with that name won't have legal standing to argue that *their* name is the one being used.) Back in 1964 the public relations director of Benton & Bowles was a well-liked man named George Whipple. Whether or not the hints of whip and nipple had anything to do with it, the creative people liked his name as a replacement for Bartholomew and the real George Whipple sold his agency the use of his name for one dollar.

There *is* one kinky aspect of the first-draft sketch of "Digby to the Rescue" that never made it into the final shooting script. It's the bit in which Digby the cop sticks his nose into the core of the toilet paper roll. The way it happens in the draft I have, store manager "Edgar Bartholomew" finds himself so overwhelmed with Charmin-squeezing women that he summons the local cop, Officer Digby, to restore order. The women insist that Digby give the Charmin a squeeze himself to see why they find it so irresistible. Over Bartholomew's protest ("You're on duty!") Digby takes a squeeze. He's visibly impressed, but the women insist that he sniff it, too. (P&G had been perfuming the cardboard core of Charmin rolls for some time.) The sketch calls for the fully uniformed cop to unwrap the paper and plunge his nose into the scented core, take a deep sniff, say "Ummmm . . ." and come up for air totally won over to the Charmin ladies' cause. The big sniff was eliminated from the final shooting—at least on camera. In the storyboard made from the final filmed version of "Digby to the Rescue" the camera tactfully shifts away from Digby as he checks out the fragrance.

Despite this evidence of concern for taste, the original Flushing/Astoria Charmin commercials are not without some less than chaste moments. One script, entitled "Mrs. Logan," has a hidden Whipple staring at a certain Mrs. Logan squeezing tomatoes, melons, and, finally, Charmin, at which point Whipple exposes himself to view and bursts out with the familiar admonition, "Please don't squeeze the Charmin." Then Whipple sneaks off by himself and chortles, "If you only knew, Mrs. Logan. I can't resist it myself. I like to sneak a squeeze on the sly."

"Wasn't that a bit of an innuendo?" I asked John Chervokas.

"No, those were pre-innuendo days," Chervokas maintains, innocently. However, it seems clear that one advantage of pre-innuendo innocence was that admen could get away with saying some very blatant things without the advertising acceptability departments imagining anyone would be dirty-minded enough to think of its innuendo implications (viz. the cigarette ad "It's not how long you make it, it's how you make it long").

Maybe you don't immediately think of Shakespeare when you watch a Charmin commercial, but according to director Howard Magwood it was the Bard himself who suggested the solution to the single most perplexing problem in producing the original Charmin dramas. "It was a theatrical problem," says Magwood, who left a theatrical career to become a successful commercial director. "The problem was how to play the Charmin-squeezing women. These three broads had to be believable. We'd turn people off if they looked too stupid. The audience has to believe it's fun, crazy, but you can't have actors gagging it up, you have to believe it's real when you do it."

Out in Flushing/Astoria that day, the actresses Magwood had cast for the Charmin squeezers were having trouble *believing* in their part. There were repeated run-throughs where Wilson/Whipple was fine, but the ladies just weren't right. Suddenly the Shapespearean solution suggested itself to Magwood. "I told them, 'Try to think of this as the three witches in *Macbeth*, because they're kind of wild and crazy,' and they said 'Oooh that's *it*.' "*

---

* They're not talking about tissue wound on a roll, of course, but at one point in *Macbeth* the three witches cry out in unison, "The charm's wound up!" Perhaps the real Shakespearean parallel, if one is to be made at all, lies in the structural similarity of the Charmin commercial to the plots of the "problem comedies," *Measure for Measure* and *All's Well That Ends Well*, in which hypocritical tyrants and buffoons who make and enforce decrees against sexuality end up getting caught sneaking a squeeze on the sly themselves.

They fell to their frenzy with immediately successful and believable results—all too believable, perhaps, in the long run, because the demented witchlike quality of their behavior has earned the Charmin campaign considerable hostility from the women's movement.

Even when the three original Charmin spots were finally "in the can," as they say in the film business, not many people believed they'd get out for long until the astonishing statistics from the first recall test came back. Procter & Gamble believes in careful testing before committing itself to a campaign. The company gave the Charmin spots a tryout then known as the Burke Recall Test. Benton & Bowles quietly slipped a sample sixty-second Charmin spot, reportedly "Digby to the Rescue," into the regular TV programming in a selected midwestern market. The following day, a consumer research firm called a sample of home viewers and asked them what they watched the day before and if they remembered any particular commercials.

Previous tests of other concepts for a new Charmin campaign had produced recall scores ranging from a mediocre twenty-seven to a humiliating two, according to Chervokas. Then one day that winter in another grade-B-movie development, junior writer Chervokas (the Charmin campaign was his first assignment at Benton & Bowles) got a call from a biggie. "Sit down, John," he said, Chervokas recalls. "Your Charmin commercial scored fifty-five." That was a record smasher, the highest recall score of any commercial tested up until then.

The Wall Street Journal (October 20, 1971) described the marketing mayhem that followed the full-scale debut of the new Charmin campaign as "the great toilet paper war" of the sixties. The *Journal* recognized the importance of Mr. Whipple, calling him "no mere foot soldier" in the war, but gave chief credit for P&G's stunning victories over Scott to P&G's big battalions—the billion-dollar company's "awesome marketing muscle" and its "sales force like an invading army." The P&G battle plan was to conquer the country with Charmin one region at a time. First the midwest, then south to Texas, finally around 1970 attacking the East Coast and the Southwest, and not until 1975 moving its troops across the Rockies into California. The strategy in each region was to soften the territory up with massive air strikes—in 1970 P&G spent $2 million on air time for Whipple spots—then bring the "invading army" into the supermarkets with marketing muscle to command big displays and premium shelf-space placement.*

It worked. By 1970 Charmin had gone from nowhere to equality with the market share of ScotTissue, the largest selling one-ply in the country. Not only that, Charmin began to steal customers away from Scott's "Soft-Weve" and other two-ply tissues. In the five years between 1969 and 1974, production of two-ply tissue increased by only 7 percent, or 36,000 tons, while one-ply production went up 160,000 tons, nearly 20 percent. The growth of Charmin was responsible for much of that increase. Charmin was changing the nation's toilet habits.

Meanwhile, a whole other war broke out in the advertising industry over the *meaning* of it all. At first Whipple had the worst of it: the new, hip wildman-genius types, and the cerebral, sophisticated, creative types all attacked the Charmin campaign and made it a symbol, a catchword, for all that was stupid, degrading, and meretricious about the old-fashioned hard sell, particularly the hard-sell school that believed simple irritation and reiteration were the key to consumer recall. "If I ever get a chance to meet the man who did those god-awful, terribly bad, 'Don't Squeeze the Charmin' commercials—and he turns out to be small—I just may slug him," said outspoken ad whiz Jerry Della Femina. (According to John Chervokas, who is not small, they've never met.)

But lately the tables have been turned on the critics. Charmin and Whipple have been around so long, have been successful so long, that admen of the old school are beginning to use the campaign against the clever young wiseguys, rubbing their noses in Charmin, chortling that the Whipple pitch proves that the so-called creative, softer-than-soft-sell stuff may win praise and awards but the old-fashioned abrasive hard sell makes the big bucks for the client. Just this year, Benton & Bowles took a big ad in *Advertising Age* to push this theme. It featured a sketch of Whipple looking far more censorious and mean-spirited than he ever does in the actual commercials, almost as if he were sneering triumphantly at the hippie malcontents who criticize his ad. IT'S NOT CREATIVE UNLESS IT SELLS, the big type boasts.

It sells, but why? Arcane alternatives to the Simple Irritant

---

* In 1974 Procter & Gamble spent $3.8 million to advertise Charmin. The best recent account of how this $5-billion company spends $325 million a year to market its 42 brands of household products can be found in a special issue of *Television/Radio Age*, June 9, 1975.

Theory abound. The Sex in the Supermarket Theory advanced by Faith Popcorn, for instance. Popcorn, currently president of Brain reserve, an agency that makes use of some advanced new creative techniques, attributes the success of Charmin to the sensuality of the squeeze: "It established tactile contact between the consumer and the product, which is very rare in television. It lets you experience the product right there in the store. It's the old 'Lemme feel the material' thing, like people used to feel cloth before they bought it. Just that they let you squeeze it and touch it is a very sexy thing," she says. "Very, very sexy."

Then there's Professor Wilson Bryan Key, who thinks the whole secret is "soft stool." Professor Key is the author of a strange book called *Subliminal Seduction* (NAL) in which he allows that almost all print advertising is "embedded" with obscene words and pictures. "Mr. Whipple, with his bow tie and his effeminate mannerisms, is almost a perfect anal stereotype," Professor Key told me on the phone from Ontario where, he said, the University of Western Ontario had just fired him because of pressure from advertising agencies enraged at his book. "Go back and look at Freud's description of the anal personality. The idea of squeezing the tissue is the soft stool syndrome."

Dick Wilson has some less portentous theories about Whipple's phenomenal success. First of all, he rejects the idea that the Whipple series is old-fashioned and abrasive. He cites one TV breakthrough Whipple made in 1965. "Back then I was the first one to wear a moustache in a commercial." And he insists, "The stuff we do is not nauseating, it's cute." But the secret of Whipple's success, according to Wilson, is in the careful delineation of his character: "The director and I worked out his character between us, and we guard him very well. We'll try something and then say, 'No, no, Whipple wouldn't do that.' For instance we never let him be nasty. He's not nasty, he's prissy but he's not nasty."

Wilson himself is a likable character, with the dignity of a vaudevillian who has aged well. I reached him by phone at a hotel in Kansas City where he was rehearsing a production of *The Unsinkable Molly Brown*. "I just finished making eleven new Charmin spots in L.A.," he said. "Four of them in Spanish, where I'm Senor Whipple. That makes two hundred and four in all, although we've remade some of them every once in a while." Charmin has been good to Dick Wilson. He's a certified celebrity now. "I get instant recognition everywhere I go. I have these cards I hand out that have a picture of me and say, 'Don't Squeeze the Charmin. Squeeze Me.' And they do. I get a lot of squeezes that

way." Procter & Gamble certainly squeezes the most out of
Whipple. They pay him to travel around to supermarket openings,
sales conventions, warehouses, and factories to boost sales and
morale. They even sell Whipple T-shirts.

However, a new round of escalation in the toilet paper war is
just beginning, and the possibility must be considered that P&G will
come to consider Whipple a liability in the heat of the coming
battle. He has his enemies out there. Feminists attack the Charmin
commercial for degrading women; N.O.W. pickets at a recent
P&G shareholders meeting called on the company to "Squeeze out
Mr. Whipple." A nun in Wisconsin who relentlessly monitored
a hundred and fifty hours of soap-opera programming to prepare
an analysis of P&G's treatment of women for a shareholders group
doesn't find Whipple nearly as degrading as some other P&G ads,
"merely asinine," but Whipple has become an emblem of all that
critics find wrong with P&G, with advertising in general, with
American culture. Mr. Clean doesn't get that kind of bad press.

Meanwhile other brands have been taking aim at Charmin,
homing in on certain vulnerabilities Whipple can't camouflage.
First, there was Scott's "roller derby" commercial, which pictures
a "race" between two frantically unwinding rolls of tissue: Scott
and a roll identified as "the other leading brand," clearly Charmin.
Scott always loses the "roller derby" because, the spot points out,
ScotTissue has a full 1,000 sheets to unwind from its roll while
the other leading brand has only 650.

While Scott was skillfully exploiting Charmin's short-sheeted
disadvantages among one-ply tissues (Charmin claims it can't fit
as many sheets on a roll without the roll swelling to monstrous size
because each of its sheets are fluffier than ordinary one-plys), an
aggressive East Coast two-ply tissue named Marcal was attacking
the apparent flimsiness of one-ply Charmin in comparison with a
good two-ply. The Marcal spot mentions Charmin by name and
consists of a demonstration in which a sheet of Charmin held up
in front of a candle flame is found to be so diaphanous as to be
almost transparent, while a sheet of Marcal virtually blocks the
light with its staunch two-ply thickness.

Nor were the Whipple commercials responding effectively to
these challenges. In fact, they seemed to have lost direction in the
past couple of years. There were excursions into Whipple's home
life that seem designed to lay to rest suspicions that there was
something deviant about his devotion to Charmin. Not all these
efforts to promote Whipple's wholesomeness were totally successful. One short-lived spot introduced us to Whipple's own mother,
who was played by Wilson himself in Whipple drag: "I shaved my

moustache off, dressed in girl's clothes and a white wig and high-heeled shoes and everything else that went with it," Wilson recalled. "They pulled that off the air fast. It was cute but a little grotesque." Then in early 1974 the copy line for the spots underwent an odd change. A Charmin storyboard filed with the F.T.C. and dated December 1, 1973, describes Charmin as "Deep Down Squeezably Soft." Now I'd never been able to figure out deep down *where* it was squeezably soft, but the new copy line is even more puzzling. It describes Charmin's softness as "rich and fluffy"—language whose evocation of taste would be more appropriate to an Oreo creme filling than to a roll of toilet tissue. And in some of the more recent commercials, strange things are seen to be going on within Whipple's own psyche.

"Whipple's Dream" opens with Whipple and three ladies flagrantly squeezing Charmin together, with Whipple brazenly declaring "Charmin's so rich and fluffy it's irresistible," as he squeezes away. Well, it turns out Whipple's actually at home in bed with his wife, who shakes him into realizing this debauch is only a dream. "Ooh that explains it," Whipple says. "I'd never squeeze Charmin while I was awake." "Certainly not, George," says the wife, who then reveals that Whipple has taken a roll of Charmin to bed with him to squeeze. "Whipple's Temptation," dated January 1 in the F.T.C. files, presents Whipple vigorously urged by a devilish figure to go ahead and squeeze the Charmin, while a haloed Whipple conscience feebly opposes the squeeze. Whipple succumbs, right before our eyes.

Does this new predilection of Whipple for fevered religious visions and erotic dreams reflect a psyche under severe strain after all those years of repression and guilt over forbidden pleasures? Why was Whipple doing things like taking rolls of tissue to bed with him? Why was he permitted full frontal squeezes rather than the sneaky ones on the sly? The answer, I'm afraid, is that Whipple may be going through the same last-chance testing period they gave Gentle the Dog. Because a decade has passed and all signs indicate that Procter & Gamble is getting ready to introduce another toilet paper development that may equal or exceed the hot-air fluffing that Whipple made famous. At this very moment in certain sections of America, P&G is slipping onto supermarket shelves a new-new Charmin that represents a whole *new* concept in softer-than-softer-than-soft.

It's a tricky new marketing ploy, so try to follow closely. New-new Charmin takes the same weight of paper pulp as old-new Charmin to make a roll. However, a roll of new-new Charmin has only 500 sheets, instead of the 650 in old-new Charmin. That means there is more paper pulp per sheet on each of the 500 sheets than before this improvement. So each sheet is somewhat thicker and the hot-air blower dryers have even more pulp fuzz to puff up. So what results is 500 extra-fluffy, plush, feather-pillow-type sheets of tissue, but 150 fewer sheets for the money. In some markets—northern California, Oregon, and St. Louis, among others—P&G is reportedly testing an extra-extra-plush sheet of toilet tissue with only 400 sheets of plumped-up, pulpy tissue per roll.

The object here is to convince the consumer that fewer plush sheets will last just as long as more, flimsier sheets. P&G refuses to discuss marketing strategy, but a spokesman for Scott, which is also coming out with an extra-plush one-ply to be called "Cottonelle" (soft as cotton), puts it this way: "The assumption in all these new tissues is that people grab off what feels right in their hand, so if you have thicker sheets you have a thicker feeling in your hand from fewer sheets and you won't use as many."

A consumer affairs commissioner in New York's Suffolk County, where some of the new plush Charmin is being tested in the supermarkets, claims that Charmin's explanation of the reduction in sheet count was just a lot of hot air and pulp. "If they did do market research I would like to know the parameters they used—used sheets?" says Commissioner James Lack, who threatened to take civil action against Charmin for misleading the public. "I maintain people use the same number of sheets that they started to use when their toilet habits were born," Lask said. "My staff researched this on an informal basis and the number of sheets doesn't change. I don't like corporations hiding misleading facts." Whatever the facts, if P&G does decide to go full force into the plush and extra-plush toilet market it's going to be a tough advertising job.

Does P&G think that Whipple, with all his notoriety, his enemies, and his ten-year-old pitch, can handle the new responsibility? There's one spot being tested on the air right now which already seems to be easing him off center stage. The people at the Television Monitoring Institute of Huntington Station, Long Island, brought it to my attention. (They make their living taping TV commercials and programming 'round the dial 'round the clock, often for ad agencies who want to know what their competitors are putting on.) This new spot plugs the new plush Charmin being introduced into Long Island supermarkets with a promise never before made in toilet paper advertising: "You can *hear* the difference in New Charmin." (Since you can already smell it, feel it, see it, and it's so "rich" you can almost taste it, what was left but to hear it?)

But even more interesting than the sound of the roll is the size of the role they've given Whipple. The ladies in the market take up the opening moments of the spot chatting about New Charmin and listening to it. Whipple comes on to deliver a rather perfunctory version of his litany: "Ladies, I don't care if you can see, hear, feel, or smell the difference, but please don't squeeze it." His only line in the spot, barely a walk-on. He's not given the opportunity to deliver his customary soliloquy on the squeeze; instead, a peremptory voice breaks in, says "Excuse me, Mr. Whipple," cuts him off, and takes over the difficult job of explaining the improvement in the new plush product. Whipple merely seems to be in everyone's way. And if this indignity is not enough, I've heard reliable reports that in one spot being tested the script actually calls for Whipple to *urge* the ladies to squeeze the Charmin.

When I heard that sad bit of news, I began to wonder seriously if Whipple was on the way out. If he's not there to tell people *not* to squeeze, any jerk can tell them to *listen* to the toilet paper or whatever the client wants. I wondered if P&G was testing to see if anyone noticed, if anyone cared any more that Whipple *didn't* care if they squeezed. I called up Whipple, I mean Wilson, in California, and asked if it were true that in a new spot he actually does urge the women to go ahead and squeeze.

"Yes it's true," he said, "but it's only a test, it's only one spot."

I hope so. After all these years, I'd hate to see Whipple go the way of Gentle the Dog.

SOAP GETS IN YOUR EYES

A REVIEW OF THE FALL 1975
TV COMMERCIAL SEASON

Eight years ago a sixty-five-year-old adman with the improbable name Carroll Carroll came up with a terrific idea. Carroll Carroll had just retired from the J. Walter Thompson agency after thirty-five years in the ad business when Abel Green, editor of *Variety*, asked him what he planned to do with his future.

"Why don't you let me do reviews of TV commercials?" was Carroll Carroll's inspired suggestion.

"Try one," said Abel Green, a bit skeptically.

Carroll Carroll tried two. Abel Green liked them both. Carroll Carroll got his column. It's called "And Now A Word From . . ."; and it's the first and only regular review of TV commercials outside the advertising trade press.

I've always wondered why no one has followed in Carroll Carroll's footsteps. We live in a civilization that supports dozens of TV critics, scores of movie critics, and hundreds of rock critics. Everyone knows that commercials are more complex and interesting than TV shows, more people see them than movies, and they reveal far more about American culture than rock. Why then is Carroll Carroll alone in his important task?

Well, I've always had a minor ambition to review TV commercials, so this year I decided to see just what the work was like.

Maybe you think it would be easy street, reviewing TV commercials. Maybe you think there are plush screening rooms where the big national advertisers run preview showings of their fall campaigns for journalists. Maybe you think they provide you with transcripts and storyboards of each commercial for recollection in tranquility. Maybe you think the leading frozen orange juice tastes more like fresh than Orange Plus.

Just look at the logistics of attempting even the most superficial review of the new season's commercials: Limiting oneself to just three hours of prime time and just three network outlets, that's still 9 hours a night, 63 hours a week, and—figuring 6 commercial minutes an hour, 2 spots a minute—it adds up to more than 750 commercial spots a week. Even though many of those 750 are repeated, so much calculation goes into the making of each second of a single 30-second spot that four or five attentive viewings are required before the craftier elements in its design begin to become apparent. The job is overwhelming.

Most maddening is dragging one's way through hours and hours of pallid programming in search of a second glimpse of just one intriguing new commercial. Maybe someday someone will provide the commercial reviewers—and the commercial fan, for there are fans out there—with a kind of TV guide to commercial scheduling. Maybe someday all steel-belted radials will be made like Firestones.

But for now I'm condemned to sit in front of my set with a cassette recorder and a notebook trying to find ways to fill the time between the breaks. I'll admit I must have missed more than a few: The only way to make sure you've seen every ad is to watch every minute of every show on TV, and the Geneva Convention has rules against things like that.

But I've seen enough and heard enough to pick up on some trends. After listening to twelve hours of pure commercials on tape, you begin to hear the spots talking to each other about certain common themes. In this first venture into commercial criticism, I'll forbear discussions of production, acting, and directorial style and start by concentrating on the content of commercials that made their debut this season, specifically some strange new twists to some familiar old pitches.

Country Drug Taking I knew a trend was in the making when Sominex sleeping tablets abandoned the mysterious "Uncle Ned" and other familial sleeping pill spokesmen. Now they've begun presenting cheery morning scenes in rural towns, complete with birds chirping on the soundtrack as several hearty, virtuous, hard-working plain ole country folk take time off from their country chores to confess that "even here," despite long hours of honest work in the fresh country air, people "occasionally" have trouble falling asleep and rely on pills to knock them out for the night. The new Excedrin P.M. spot features a healthy, young country wife, emerging from her old-fashioned country house amidst country-morning sunlight and bird chirps, walking her horse along a grassy creek bed, awake to all the wonder in nature because she went to sleep with the help of Excedrin P.M. And the new spot for Enderin, the nonaspirin pain reliever, presents a couple returning from a walk along a magnificent stretch of shoreline, awestruck by the grandeur of the ocean and by the ability of *just one* Enderin tablet to take care of a troubling headache.

Now, needless to say, the point of these pastoral pill-pushing pitches is not to convince country folk to take more drugs: there aren't enough country folk around to make it profitable. The point is to convince potential pill takers in cities and suburbs that they needn't feel *guilty* about taking pills, that even saintly country folk do it, that pill taking is an integral part of the natural way of life.

The Revolt Against the Natural It's really a counterrevolution. In the past three years, "natural" and "country style" themes have spread like the plague through the commercial industry—let just one brand in a competitive category of products show a cow, and the others would shoot their next spots on dairy farms standing knee-deep in manure.

There's still an element of McCarthyism in the attacks on products accused of being infiltrated with un-natural (as in un-American) ingredients. Spokesmen for products such as Wise potato chips and Dannon yogurt go through "I have a little list" speeches in which they read, in outraged accusatory tones, the names of artificial ingredients on their rivals' labels.

But this year the natural revolution seems finally to have peaked —if only because there are few products left that haven't already been naturalized (in addition to country sleeping pills, we now have Country Dinner dog food). And this season a number of commercials have begun to manifest clear-cut anti-natural, anti-country style themes. One impetus for this trend may be that certain New York admen are thoroughly sick of the hick schtick and are beginning to exact revenge on country folk for the years they've had to spend writing cute country style ad copy. How else explain the unbridled ridicule of the country fellow in the Bic lighter commercial: An oafish hayseed offers to buy an attractive, urban-looking single woman a drink in a dimly lit bar. She lights her Bic lighter, illuminating his clownish, ill-fitting "country style" clothes and cretinous barnyard leer. One look and she laughs scornfully in his face: "A flick of my Bic and I can see you're a hick."

And how about the merriment Madison Avenue has at the expense of the gulled rubes in the Golden Griddle syrup commercial. The spot shows a cross section of country people from "the heart of maple country" tasting two syrups. Time after time they choose Golden Griddle, a nonnatural blend, over their own pure, natural maple syrup. And just to rub in the triumph of food processing artifice over nature, the commercial doesn't bother to claim that Golden Griddle tastes *like* real maple; instead they take a deliberately aggressive stance: "Golden Griddle has the taste that *beat* real maple."

And Total—a processed, vitamin-sprayed cereal—takes savage delight in its triumph over "the leading natural cereals" in the vitamin percentage numbers derby. (Total claims a 100 percent RDA score versus 6 percent for the leading brand X granolas.) Sowing salt in the wounds of the defeated wheat, the Total spot takes an airborne shot of a field of wheat, and, lo, the defeat is carved in acre-sized numerals on the face of the field—graffiti in the grain.

The Original Skin Controversy Things move fast in the ad world, and the counterrevolution against the natural revolution has given rise to a sophisticated third stage counter-counterrevolution. This year's Safeguard soap spot, for instance. A bit of background first. Some time ago Ivory soap jumped heavily on the Natural bandwagon and renamed itself Ivory "natural" soap, with spots featuring Ivory-natural people getting themselves clean and fresh without "harsh chemicals." This represented an assault on the whole premise of deodorant soaps, which had boasted for years about just how harsh their ingredients were on "odor-causing bacteria," those villainous microbes that turned natural sweat into problem perspiration. The Ivory commercials were clearly out to steal customers from the deodorant soaps.

More recently, deodorant soaps began to strike back. By far the boldest assault was last year's Lifebuoy commercial, which featured clean-cut people hopping up and down and crowing, "I smell clean." An admonitory slogan followed: "It's not enough to *be* clean. You have to *smell* clean."

This gets us into some very tricky metaphysical questions of existence and essence: If there were people walking around who *were* clean but didn't *smell* clean, what *did* they smell like? Neutral? Natural? Unclean? What is the smell of clean, anyway? What is the smell of skin? Does skin in its natural state smell good or bad? Did odor-causing bacteria exist in prelapsarian Eden? Could Adam have used an antiperspirant or did the malignant microbes only begin their iniquitous work after the Fall?

If this isn't complicated enough, this year Safeguard has added a new twist to this debate on the nature of Original Skin.

The scene: a kissing booth at a country fair. Two women, one married, one unmarried, are inside the booth. A man buys a kiss from the married woman and exclaims so feverishly over her "naturally clean-smelling skin" that the woman's husband has to intervene.

"What about me?" the unmarried woman in the kissing booth pipes up hopefully. "I use a deodorant soap."

Then the crusher. "*That's just it*," the kiss-buying guy tells her. "You *smell* like a deodorant soap."

Stunned by this heartbreaker, the rejected woman in the kissing booth is probably unaware of the finely honed distinctions that are implicit in the rebuff.

It's not enough to be clean. You have to smell clean, says Lifebuoy. But, argues Safeguard, there are different *kinds* of clean. Lavatory disinfectant smells clean, but it doesn't smell good. Safeguard skin smells "*naturally* clean," which means it is clean, it smells clean, and it smells natural. And natural smells good. But you can't smell natural with a "natural soap." You need a deodorant soap that doesn't smell like a deodorant soap to smell natural these days. The Safeguard commercial takes us from complexity back to simplicity—of a sort.

The next move in the skin smell dialectic is hard to predict. Now that there are "natural-scented" deodorant soaps on the market, perhaps the ultimate step will be the introduction of "natural-scented" perfume for people scared of smelling like a deodorant soap, worried that their own natural smell isn't good enough, and so confused they've decided to forgo the risks of bathing altogether in favor of a cover-up perfume.

New Fears It's been a good year for New Fears. Complex new fears, such as Fear of Smelling Like a Deodorant Soap. Old-fashioned new fears, such as Fear of Foot Odor. (A commercial for a product called Johnson's Odor-Eaters depicts an embarrassed father's foot odor driving him and his family out of their house.)

But the most characteristic fear of the year so far is Fear of Surprise. *Don't let life take you by surprise*, warns Metropolitan Life Insurance. *The best surprise is no surprise*, chimes the new Holiday Inn commercials. "It's the *unexpected* bills that really hurt," warns the doom-tinged voice of the Quaker State Motor Oil announcer.

Holiday Inn, which once promoted the adventure and delight of travel in its commercials, now focuses on nerve-racking perils— collapsing beds, canceled reservations, unfamiliar food, and other unpleasant surprises—which await travelers if they don't play it safe and lock themselves up in the predictability and security of a Holiday Inn.

Auto products such as Quaker State and STP once promoted themselves as lubricants to a life of challenge and daring, even risk. STP was the "racer's edge." Now they all push fear of break-downs, fear of "internal corrosion," and sell themselves as play-it-safe insurance. It's more than just economic fears; it's a whole new defensive posture toward life.

Fear of Women The woman is wearing a clinging cocktail gown, she's caressing the shaft of a pool cue with one hand while the other hand rests casually on a pool table littered with balls.

"Some men are intimidated by women these days," she smiles smugly. "Maybe because we're free to do much more. But some men aren't intimidated at all. They enjoy our freedom. Those are the men I like. . . . My men wear English Leather—or they wear nothing at all." Despite the infelicitous attempt at double entendre, the basic message is not sex but fear: The ad uses this caricature of a liberated woman to intimidate men into feeling they have to prove they're not intimidated by women.

And speaking of intimidation, the Wheaties commercial features a woman who beats the pants off her husband on the tennis court, then sits down at a courtside breakfast table and ridicules his slovenly eating habits while he cringes silently behind his newspaper. In a Jeep commercial a woman beats a man to the top of the hill in a king of the hill car race and laughs merrily at his humiliation.

The intimidated wretch is not just a new version of the old, stock henpecked husband. The women in these commercials beat men at their own games and mock them in defeat. One wonders if the real fear message built into all of these ads is that women's liberation inevitably means women's tyranny and male defeat.

There is a new breed of reformist women's commercials, but most of them are either of the "I like housework and motherhood, but I know there are other things in life, so I'm particularly grateful for the fast-working enzyme action of this pre-soak because it allows me to get the family's wash clean more quickly so that I can be an independent woman in my spare time" type, or they're about slim, determined independent women who have glamorous jobs and drink diet colas.

A couple of commercials have recently surfaced that show men engaged in what is traditionally considered "woman's work." But the one liberated woman commercial that truly breaks new ground this season is the Italian Swiss Colony wine ad. Right off the bat the woman in the ad announces that she's separated from her husband and that it's been good for her. "When my husband and I first separated," she says, "I didn't know how to do anything or think I'd ever learn, but I tried and proved I could." She offers as prime proof of her newfound self-sufficiency the ability to choose a wine all by herself with confidence in her choice.

The fact that she's so smug about the superiority of her choice— something called Italian Swiss Colony Chenin Blanc—makes me suspect that her ex-husband had kept her on a diet of Boone's Farm Strawberry up until the separation. But Italian Swiss Colony deserves credit for the forthrightness of its pitch.

Shaving Narcissism An odd little twist in this season's shaving commercials. The two big concepts in shaving spots always used to be "smooth" and "close." The words were used to describe the shave, not the face. Now suddenly it's "love" and "super" and "perfect." And those words are used to refer to the *face*, not the shave.

"C'mere superface," purrs the Noxzema shave cream girl, lather at the ready.

"You took your perfect face and gave it a perfect shave," exults the tuneful Trac II girl for Gillette.

"Send your face to Schick, let Schick love it," a girl singing group urges on behalf of that shaving company.

The visuals reflect this new preoccupation with the perfection and loveliness of men's faces. In shaving commercials of years gone by, once-grizzled men rubbed their newly shaven chins, women stroked their jaws. These days the archetypal post-shave shot shows a man gazing in his mirror, watching himself caress himself.

Is this a retreat from fearsome women into the self-sufficiency of infantile narcissism or adolescent autoeroticism? With such a perfect face and a perfect mirror image to love, who needs a third face to come between the two?

New and Improved Few things are either this year. Retrenchment is all. Once the big rationale for advertising was its ability to educate consumers about valuable new products and improvements they would not know of otherwise. The only new product I noted was something called Egg Baskets, which seem to be pastry shells into which an egg can be cracked and baked if you are inclined to ruin your morning in that fashion.

And there's only one old-fashioned stop-the-presses announcement of a product improvement this year. "GREAT NEWS," says an excited voice. "New Ty-D-Bol now has lemon fresh borax!"

Now this might seem anticlimactic to some, and the fact that it's the most exciting "new improvement" of the season may say something about the season. But you have to take into account that the Ty-D-Bol announcement is delivered by a man in a glass-bottomed boat afloat in a toilet bowl, and that hasn't been done before.

The Official Cooking Oil of the U.S. Olympic Team Something else to keep an eye on are the curious uses to which certain advertisers are putting the U.S. Olympic team. Consider the case of the perfect blower styler.

"Nothing demands perfection like athletic competition," begins a Sunbeam commercial over visuals of athletic competition and a blare of trumpets on the soundtrack. "Serious athletes expect it from themselves, expect it from the things around them." Perfection that is. So far so good.

Then, without transition, comes this portentous announcement: "The Sunbeam Professional Blower Styler. Selected for use by the United States Olympic team."

Wait a minute. Who selected it and how? Did the track and field coaches meet with the other team captains for a big blower styler tryout? Or did Sunbeam send a truckload of blower stylers over to the Olympic Committee and get an official Olympic blower styler plug in return? Was there a cash contribution, too? (The answer, according to a U.S. Olympic Committee spokesman, is that Sunbeam supplies blower stylers for the entire Olympic entourage and a $35,000 contribution, too.)

Then I noticed that Schlitz beer commercials feature the voice-over of a purported Olympic figure-skating hopeful as she describes the long, hard climb to Olympic glory. She never actually says she drinks Schlitz, but her "style" and "class" are attributes that the Schlitz announcer also imputes to his beer.

It seems to me that if the Olympic Committee is going to get into merchandising they ought to get into it in a much bigger way. Why not an Official Sleeping Pill of the U.S. Olympic team ("Yes, we athletes get real keyed up the night before a game . . .")? The Official Fish 'n Chips dinner of the U.S. Olympics. Perhaps even the Olympic torch bearer frying bread in Wesson oil to prove that the oil doesn't soak through. The kind of thing you need for credibility.

Up-Front Post-Watergate Morality First A&P led off the season confessing that it had let "Price" get ahead of "Pride," and then pardoned itself for that crime by pledging—it seemed—to raise prices. Now Parkay has leaped into the credibility contest with a totally original ploy. Perhaps remorse inspired Parkay, the shame of all those years when the talking Parkay margarine tub repeatedly and perjuriously told people who opened the refrigerator door that it was really butter.

None of that nonsense in this new commercial for liquid Parkay. The woman in the ad opens up by saying she works for the ad agency that peddles Parkay. She tells us she was skeptical about this liquid stuff when the Parkay people asked her to work on the pitch, but that she conscientiously tried a squeeze or two and found herself utterly knocked out by it. She raved about it so convincingly that the Parkay people asked her—a real advertising person—to be their TV spokesperson.

After all those years of trying to make the public think ads came from "real people" and not Madison Avenue, here's an ad exec to endorse the product. A brilliant turnabout. In a country where the President, the one man charged with the trust of the nation, turns out to be a liar and a cheat, why not promote the adman, traditionally considered most suspect and self-interested of all, as the only unimpeachable source of candor we can rely on?

Some people say the Golden Age of TV Commercials came to an end with the end of economic expansion and that thereafter nothing has approached the imagination, inventiveness, intelligence, and cash expended on the finest of the late sixties spots. And it's true that the TV commercial world this season is filled with signs of recession and regression: more dumb dishwasher demonstrations, contrived car comparisons, hideous "hidden camera" slices of life. But there's one genre that's entering a Golden Age all its own these days.

The Inspirationals You know the ones. Generally they have a large, vibrant chorus filling the background with a strong upbeat tune. Half-hymn, half-marching song, they are the national anthems of their products. On the screen energetic people of all races, colors, and creeds do energetic things such as jogging, marching, and eating fried chicken while singing their anthem, or getting ready to burst into song. The United Airlines commercial is about a group of strangers riding an airport limo bursting into the "Mother Country" anthem. In other ads whole towns filled with jolly oldsters, rollicking youngsters, and peppy people of all ages explode into tuneful, muscular joy on the screen.

The Inspirationals are all so infectiously entertaining it's hard to choose among them. McDonald's "Good morning, America!" breakfast commercials never fail to wake some sparks of innocent morning joy in me no matter how tired and wasted I am. The Beauty Rest "Good Day" anthem is almost as good. Colonel Sanders' "Real Goodness" anthem, STP, 7-Up, even, I'm ashamed to say, Coke's "Look Up America"—they all get to me. Some of them get to me too much. The Sanka anthem, for instance. I spent two miserable weeks this fall trying to get the Sanka anthem to stop repeating endlessly in the back of my mind. The tune's okay, but the lyric somehow doesn't live up to the soaring tones of the choir-like chorus. One feels a bit silly walking around town with a choir chanting in one's head: "WE'RE THE THIRD LARGEST COFFEE IN AMERICA."

Whence comes the revivalistic outburst in TV commercials this year? Is it a depression-induced Happy Days Are Here Again/ Gold Diggers of '33 trend designed to get depressed consumers happy enough to spend what little they have? Is it a bicentennial rebirth of Whitmanesque celebratory optimism? A secular Great Awakening? (Most of them are anthems of the morning.)

Or is it something more calculated, like the pepped-up Muzak fed to workers in big factories just before closing time? Is there something even darker behind all this upbeat hysteria, a sense of some more final Closing Time closing in on America?

Perhaps those darker notes are there, but no matter how suspicious I get about them the new Inspirationals never fail to work their happy-making magic on me. That's what makes them so impressive, even scary. Inspirational technology has grown so sophisticated and powerful that TV commercial makers are capable of making one feel happy, *naturally* happy, without any sense of being manipulated into feeling happy. Something like the feeling you get from the deodorant soap that gets you naturally clean without making you worry that you smell like a deodorant soap.

THE FOUR HORSEMEN OF THE NIGHTLY NEWS

Switching channels restlessly one weekend in the winter of '77, I wandered into the middle of a made-for-TV special of the "futuristic fable" genre. The future fabricated in this particular fable was a transparent vehicle for oil and gas industry propaganda: a grim, conservation-crazed, twenty-first-century dictatorship has forbidden all forms of fun, banned laughter, and made even a simple smile illegal because such impulses encourage energy-wasting attitudes. Apparently, this is what is to become of us if Congress delays any further the deregulation of the price of natural gas. Despite this, I was struck by one memorable gimmick in this otherwise forgettable drama: the Reality Checker.

Every citizen of the energy-saving dictatorship was required to wear a Reality Checker around his neck. It looked like an ordinary round mirror, but it had a peculiar power. Each time the citizen gazed into his Reality Checker, he'd see the reflection of his face dissolve to reveal a grinning death's head, the face of mortality, the skull beneath the skin. Gazing at the Reality Checker was required every hour on the hour to demonstrate the vanity of human wishes and, in general, throw cold water on any energy-wasting impulses.

Which brings us to a theory I've had about the commercial spots that accompany the nightly network news, and the special kind of news they contribute to our national communal news experience. They are our Reality Check.

If you've watched Cronkite or Chancellor with any regularity, you may have noticed the pitches for laxatives, denture creams and powders, acid indigestion remedies, extra-strength arthritis and headache pain formulas, and sleeping pills. Not that you don't see these spots at other times, but the nightly news has a higher concentration of these dramas of bodily disintegration, of systemic failures, of the depredations and indignities of age, of the pain, suffering, and minutiae of mortality.

It is a common, unexamined assumption that the worlds portrayed within commercials are somehow less real than the worlds of the programs they sponsor. Certainly, one might assume that of the news shows. But, in fact, the more closely one looks, the more apparent it becomes that the peculiar variety of commercials you see on the nightly news is more "real" than the tales told by the anchormen.

Behind the superficial pageant that Cronkite and Chancellor present—the rise and fall of the Dow, the shuffling and reshuffling of cabinets, the wavering prospects for peace in the Middle East, the thermal shifts in the Cold War—behind all these ephemeral dramas of institutions, the specter of mortality stalks through the Pepto-Bismol and Dentu-Grip commercials, the skull beneath the skin of official news.

And indeed, when you think about it, Newton Minow may have missed the mark some time ago when he called prime-time programming "a vast wasteland." The most authentic Eliotic "wasteland" on TV is the landscape of the nightly news ads, crowded with the whimpering victims of the small but certain failures of the flesh, each commercial a self-contained cadenza of decay. In fact, it is no accident that T. S. Eliot filled his *Waste Land* with complaints which sound as if they could be the opening for Sinutab, Sominex, or Dentu-Creme commercials: "Madame Sosostris, famous clairvoyante,/Had a bad cold . . . My nerves are bad to-night . . . It's them pills I took. . . . Get a whole set . . . a new set of teeth."

While the feeling one gets from the official evening news may vary from hope to despair to confusion, the message of the commercials in between is constant: no human being can escape the relentless pursuit of the Four Horsemen of the nightly news ads—Insomnia, Indigestion, Irregularity, and Denture Problems. All the remedies advertised will only temporarily hold in check the process of disintegration, just as the most powerful denture adhesive will only temporarily hold dentures to gums.

SUFFERING AND LOSS

To prove this bleak picture of the nightly news commercials is no mere speculation, let me cite, as a Reality Check on this thesis, a volume of revealing lore with the deceptively soporific title,

Television News Index and Abstracts: A Guide to the Videotape Collection of The Network Evening News Programs in the Vanderbilt Television News Archive.

Each volume of the index contains an abstract and brief chronicle of what was said on each of the three network news shows each night of the week, complete with a record of all commercials in the order in which they appeared.

The most recent volume available at this writing, the index for September 1977, takes 227 pages of tiny print to record the content of the 40-odd hours of network news programming that month. But hours spent reading the index are well worthwhile; one gets a sense of the larger rhythms of news and commercials as they entwine and counterpoint each other over the weeks.

In the first week of September, for instance, close to 50 percent of the spots on the CBS and NBC nightly news shows, and nearly a third on ABC, were Reality Check mortality messages of one form or another (as opposed to fantasy or utilitarian spots for Thunderbird cars, Mr. Coffee, etc.).

If you had been able to catch all network news programs that week, you would have been subjected to, in approximately this order, the following insistent testimonials to the debilitation of the body:

> Dentu-Creme
> Ex-Lax
> Arthritis Pain Formula
> Primatene Asthma Remedy
> Dentu-Creme
> Preparation H
> Sominex
> Nytol
> Metamucil
> Preparation H
> Tums
> Orafix Special
> Nytol
> Rolaids
> Sominex
> Geritol
> Tums
> Polident
> Anacin
> Tums

Pepto-Bismol
Nytol
Fasteeth Denture Aid
Ex-Lax
Polident
Anacin
Nytol
Arthritis Pain Formula
Geritol
Ex-Lax
Geritol
Sominex
Dentu-Creme
Sominex
Primatene
Metamucil
Dentu-Creme
Geritol

Now, there are practical reasons, of course, for the predominance of disintegration, suffering, and loss in the themes of the nightly news commercials. Demographics and logic will tell you that a higher percentage of older people watch Cronkite and Chancellor than the Fonz and other Family Hour favorites, and many take their Nytol and turn in before the later, adult, prime-time hours.

In fact, according to Nielsen statistics, more than a third of all people over 55 in television households watch the nightly network news, while less than a fifth of those in the 18–49 age bracket tune in. It's worth noting that, according to Nielsen, both Cronkite and Chancellor each has more than double the number of oldsters watching than ABC's anchor team has. And, not surprisingly, CBS and NBC take in considerably more money than ABC from laxative and denture ads. Just to give you a sense of the magnitude of this market, here are some sample figures from an industry source: Ex-Lax is said to spend approximately $630,000 a year on the Cronkite and Chancellor shows; Polident spends about that much on the three network shows; Nytol more than $350,000 on CBS and NBC combined; and Geritol more than $1 million for the two senior-citizen news shows.

Needless to say, from an advertising point of view, the nightly news is a better climate than *Little House on the Prairie* or *Happy Days* for selling headache and indigestion remedies, since at least one news story a night will induce that which these products profess to cure.

It's also obvious that the cumulative effect of the juxtaposition of the external suffering on the news with the internal suffering on the commercials can dislocate an appropriate sense of response. Why care about mutilated bodies in strife-torn Lebanon when right here in America the sudden pain of sinus headache can strike without warning, causing untold agony? Why open our hearts to the victims of famine in East Africa when we know from the indigestion ads that plentiful food only makes one vulnerable to the torments of heartburn, if one can get it past one's dentures without incident?

But I've found it illuminating to look at the Reality Check commercials with more than mere advertising strategies in mind, to see them as fables, as stories, just as the events of the day on the news are "stories." In any case, it's revealing to examine the traits of structure and content in these two kinds of stories and see how they reflect and complement each other.

Below is an abbreviated list of the major continuing stories of the news variety that dominated that same first week in September during which the commercials listed above were shown:

Panama Canal Treaty signed, Senate passage in doubt;

Bert Lance money-moving practices lead to resignation calls;

Progress toward Middle East peace conference blocked as talks stall;

Internal probe by Congress into Koreagate;

Strikes and work stoppages;

Liddy paroled;

Energy bill in trouble.

Glance if you will at the two lists and it is impossible not to be struck by the confluence of concerns in the two sorts of stories.

BLOCKED PASSAGES

Aside from the denture preparations, almost all the stories in the commercials listed above are about blocked, constricted passageways: constricted veins of headache pain, clogged nasal passages and sinus cavities, swollen capillaries in the eye, asthmatically blocked bronchial tubes, cholesterol-clogged arterial passages, turbulent rapids in the alimentary canal, stalled movement through the lower tract, hemorrhaging veins in the fundament.

And what, if not blocked passages, is the central theme of the news stories that week? Senators threaten to block passage of the

Panama Canal Treaty; the Canal Zone itself is beset with turmoil that threatens to block the passage of vessels, turmoil not unlike the indigestion that roils the alimentary canal. Stalled movement in removing roadblocks to Middle East peace. Energy bill impasse. Will Liddy unstopper his mouth? Bert Lance's blocked assets travelling through the privileged passages of the banking system as if propelled by Ex-Lax. A perfect week to illustrate my thesis that the tales of the body told in the commercials frequently reflect the preoccupations of the body politic in the news.

DENTURE DRAMAS

Denture-problem commercials also celebrate rites of passage: dentures are both the gateway to the internal passages and the portals through which the potions pass to effect their purge. But a closer look discloses that the "slice-of-life" denture-crisis stories dramatize more fundamental issues than blocked passages—such questions as the problems of post-Watergate morality, and the efficacy of the traditional reformist solutions of a liberal democracy.

Once a few years ago, the official archivist for the Richard M. Nixon Oral History Project in Whittier, California, took me to see the first office in which young Dick Nixon practiced law. The tenant previous to Nixon, the archivist told me, had been a false-teeth entrepreneur who had gone bankrupt. About the time of that visit, shortly after the smoking gun had driven Nixon out of office, I began to notice the astonishing number of denture-aid ads on the nightly news and the Watergate-like structure common to most of them.

We start with a cover-up. The denture wearer is at a picnic or a dinner party, trying to live it up with a crowd of big eaters, but he knows he's putting up a false front. At any moment, some oversolicitous hostess will ask him if he'd like to chomp on an ear of corn, or an apple, and he will have to make a choice. He can either stonewall her and say he doesn't care for corn anyway, or go the "modified limited hangout" route and mumble something about denture problems, or take a bite of the corn and hope his dentures stick to his gums. Invariably, they don't, and he spends the rest of the party trying to keep the lid on the slip.

Fed perhaps by the insatiable post-Watergate appetite for exposure of the private lapses of public figures, certain denture-problem commercials have made a significant shift to the public humiliation of their porcelainized protagonists.

One recent spot begins with the familiar scene of the denture wearer about to take that mortifying bite. But instead of suffering his crisis of confidence in private, as he might have in the past, we now have some snitch posing as a friend—the John Dean of denture ads—announcing to all who can hear, "Hey, Fred, whattsa matter, dentures slipping?" Fred's hands fly to his face, but it's too late to hide the slip—the smoking gums. Only after being publicly impeached for using a cream instead of a powder, or vice versa, is the wretch permitted to retire to soak his teeth in peace.

But there is more to these denture dramas than decay and expose. On a deeper level, they address themselves to questions about the workings of the American system in a more penetrating way than the analyses delivered by the likes of Sevareid or Brinkley. In their allegorical way, they question the fundamental assumptions of liberal reformism: Can you fix things by pasting on socially engineered improvements? Can the inequities of monopoly capitalism be fixed merely by "adding teeth" to regulatory legislation, by putting a new "tax bite" on big corporations? Has America, in its global role, bitten off more than it can chew? Does the fact that Jimmy Carter's real teeth *look* like false teeth make us reconsider whether fraud is inherent in the porcelain or the person?

You may also have noticed how the two-party system in the denture commercials—the powders versus the creams—reflects the two approaches to reform of the major political parties. The powders, like the Republicans, are more old-fashioned and individualistic in their solution: powders are made up of individual particles which, when applied to the surface of the dentures, spread out to form localized bonds. The commercials for the creams criticize denture problems caused by the unequal distribution of *powder* on the bridge, in the same way the rhetoric of the Democrats criticizes the unequal distribution of *power* that results from Republican solutions. These cream commercials advocate a welfare-statist plastering of the entire polity with a thick cream which reaches all the neglected crevices and equalizes gripping power, but obliterates surface individualities.

Does either party have the answer? Repeated exposure to denture dramas tends to leave one with a darkened view of the solutions offered by both. Although on the surface the denture commercials seem to have happy endings, they are only temporary fixes. The overall impression is not one of organic cohesion but of jerry-built, mechanistic solutions with all the permanence and cohesiveness of a coalition cabinet in Italy. One feels how transitory and precarious such jointures are, particularly when compared with the superb fusions of object to object achieved by such industrial-strength adhesives as Eastman's 910 and Elmer's glue, which also happen to be fixtures of the nightly news commercials.

Those close-ups in the denture dramas of the surface between denture and gum to which the various creams and powders are applied are emblems of that delicate interface between technology and the human body: Can the methods of liberal reform join them in harmony if the right glue is found, or is there something essentially incompatible in such a juncture that no social or spiritual adhesive can join together?

Can the system work? That is the fundamental question raised by the stories on the nightly news. Whether the system be digestive or legislative, the answer seems to be no—not without massive infusions of soothing creams and lubricants. Whether palms are greased with Rose Milk Skin Care Cream or Korean cash, there is no movement through the blocked passages of the system; nothing gets done without external lubrication or legislative lubricity. The system reflected in the nightly news commercials is disintegrating, like an aging body losing control of its functions, as it creeps toward death. Things fall apart, as Yeats wrote, the denture cannot hold.

NOTES ON CON GAMES

After pondering the sophistication of TV ads, I thought it would be refreshing to go out and get back to basics by watching the old-fashioned one-man-one-sucker street con games that still abound on the sidewalks of New York.

What I found was that even a simple con like Three Card Monte, a variation of the ancient shell game, had found it necessary to incorporate a whole superstructure of sophisticated wiles—two shills, three levels, no less—to survive in the seventies. Still, the personal charisma of the con man is crucial to the game, and continues to astonish us with its success. The seventies have learned as much from them as they from the seventies.

THE NEW YORKER AS RUBE

The first thing you have to realize is that there are no New York con games and no native New York con artists. They're all from out of town. At least that's the impression you get when you talk to the detectives on the NYPD Pickpocket and Confidence Squad and read the con-game literature. The Con Squad guys will tell you that the fiendishly clever "bank examiner" scam is mainly practiced by a "gang of Canadians." You'll learn that the bait money in some versions of the classic "pigeon drop" scam is called a "Michigan roll." And they'll tell you that one of the maneuvers in that con is the "Spanish switch."

You probably get the idea now: People take the same attitude toward con games they did toward syphilis, which the English called the "French pox" and the French called the "Spanish disease." Con games are not straightforward, wholesome crimes like truck hijacking or armed robbery. There is in our notion of the con a taint of something more oily and shameful, a venereal cupidity. And so the Con Squad will say, "This scam was invented in the Orient some 300 years ago," or "That one was devised in India many years ago," or "A certain kind of Scottish gypsy practices this one," or "That one was invented in the Old West and brought East."

Sure. Tell me another one. If you ask me, the Pickpocket and Confidence Squad guys may be pulling a little PR con of their own with these stories. And we buy it. Each year around Christmas the daily papers run con-game stories. Last year we had the *Daily News* warning us of the "117 teams of con artists who have descended on New York from as far away as Canada." That's 117 teams, by the way, not 116. Every one of them is from out of town. (Do they check in at the border?)

I have a theory about why we like to con ourselves into believing that all con men come from out of town: We love seeing ourselves as hapless, innocent rubes. While the rest of the country looks upon New York City as the center of the slick, institutionalized con (Wall Street, Madison Avenue, public relations), as a city of sharpies waiting to con the visitor out of his money and his virtue, we know better. Remember the Vermont guy whose car was stolen by a murderous crazy and who gave out the story that he was here on his honeymoon? Remember how the *Daily News*, Windows on the World, Mayor Beame, the whole town poured out their gratitude in liberal helpings? Why, when it turned out he was fleeing a bad-check charge, didn't we string him up? Because we loved it, that's why. We read these tales of native New Yorkers conned by these 117 out-of-town con teams and they restore to us our sense of innocence. They convince us that we still have a reservoir of innocence left to be violated. Eight million rubes in the naked city.

SEDUCING THE SAMARITAN

What's wonderful—or fiendish—about the con games described here is that the most sophisticated of them incorporate within their seductive subtleties a sensitivity to the native New Yorker's self-consciousness about the national image of the heartless Big City.

Take the variation on the classic pigeon drop described in Eden Press's *Short Cons*—the version that uses a con woman posing as an out-of-towner.

We begin with a fairly well-dressed con woman sitting on a park bench in a good neighborhood, staring perplexedly at a big map she's unfolded. Obviously an out-of-town lamb ignored by the callous city crowds. What an image of New York she must be getting. And so the potential pigeon (usually an elderly woman), when approached for help with the map, will be eager to prove that not *all* New Yorkers are like that.

The bank-examiner scam is even more subtle in its play upon our natural courtesy to the heartless out-of-towners who prey upon us. The practitioners of this scam pose as federal bank examiners investigating some hanky-panky at the pigeon's bank. Immediately there is a guilt-tinged echo of the fiscal crisis working for the con man. The feds know New York banks in and out, the pigeon thinks; I'd better cooperate. Often the "bank examiner" will shame the panicked pigeon into cooperation by dropping some line like "I know New Yorkers don't like to get involved."

U CN GT A GD JB & NO PA

Perhaps the newest and most ingenious con game to hit town is the "résumé writing" scam, a con game sophisticated enough to take in not just little old ladies but also eager young corporate careerists. In fact, the résumé-writing scam is a perfect example of the con game as a parable of social relationships. This one mirrors the dark side of the American success ethic.

Our young Horatio Alger is scanning the *Times* classifieds, looking for that big break that will reward his pluck and determination, when he sees this little ad:

> RÉSUMÉ-WRITING SERVICE
> No charge unless the résumé we do
> gets you the job you want.

The young job seeker visits Con Man One, who is disguised as the chief résumé writer. He assures the pigeon that it's not always spunk and qualifications that land you that first job on the ladder to the top; sometimes it's the façade you present. He, Con Man One, however, knows all the little tricks, the secrets, the special ways of saying things that let the decision makers know they've got someone who knows the score. The charge is $250 for writing up the résumé, he tells the pigeon, but there will be no charge at all unless it gets you just the kind of job you want. Now, what would that be?

A few days later, the eager pigeon gets a call from Con Man Two, who poses as a personnel recruiter from the Big-Time Corporation in Outoftownville, and guess what—he's offering the pigeon exactly the job he's looking for. Very good résumé, he remarks. Come up to my hotel suite for an interview.

Well, to make a long story short, the pigeon is convinced he's been offered his dream job. He's given two weeks to relocate, and begins selling his possessions and breaking his lease. Oh, just one hitch, Con Man Two tells the pigeon as they are about to sign the employment contract. The hitch is, the company has been annoyed by certain résumé-writing services which don't get paid by their clients. That won't happen with you, will it? he asks the pigeon.

The pigeon confesses he's used a résumé-writing service. Visibly upset, the recruiter demands that the pigeon run over to the service, pay immediately in cash, and bring him a signed receipt. Con Men One and Two leave town with something like $50,000 garnered from up to 200 eager job-hunting pigeons, who are now left to regret they were led to try some sneaky short-cut to success, and in fact shamelessly considered abandoning New York for the Outoftownvilles that breed this plague of con men. A morally improving exemplum embedded in a sting.

THE MURPHY GAME: FROM WARM BODIES TO HOT TV'S

The Murphy game may be the world's oldest con game, preying as it does upon patrons of the world's oldest profession. Now, I won't try to convince you that there are no native New Yorkers who have practiced this ancient art, but there has been a curious out-of-town transformation in the object of the game.

The original Murphy game, for those who haven't been taken by now, involves a con artist posing as a pimp, leeringly describing the delightful, compliant hooker he will lead the lascivious pigeon to. In most variations of the Murphy game, the "pimp" convinces the pigeon to leave the money with him and proceed to a certain (nonexistent) apartment.

But, according to most reports, the classic Murphy game is dying out, and a substitute sex object has been found: the $50 Sony Trinitron.

The way it's done now, the pigeon is still approached with a leering proposition. "Brand-new Trinitron," the con man will say. "Only $50. If you get ten friends together, I know a guy at the wholesaler's warehouse who can get you them in mint condition.

Six-hundred-dollar sets, these are. Get a van and I'll meet you outside the warehouse. Have the cash ready. I'll deliver it to the guy; then you pull up and he'll load them in."

What happens, of course, is the classic Murphy-game shuffle: The $500 is handed over, the con man disappears, the van pulls up, and there are no sets to be found. I'm not sure what it means in the larger scheme of things that New Yorkers seem to feel more prurience at the prospect of possessing a hot TV than a warm body, but note that it is an out-of-town—way out-of-town—color set that is being pimped.

HOW THE FIRST-CLASS FOOL GETS TAKEN BY THE SECOND-LEVEL SHILL IN THREE-CARD MONTE

The recent mutation of three-card monte, as this ancient con game is played on the sidewalks of New York, is a reflection of the subtlety with which con games and con artists measure the psyches of native New Yorkers, who should know the score by now. The new, two-shill version of three-card monte is, I would also argue, based on a shrewd manipulation of the racial and class attitudes of its victims.

In its simplest form, the single-shill game, the dealer will dress like a cross between a riverboat gambler and a pimp. His fingers will be fleet, and his rap will be rapid ("Find that red and make some bread") as he invites you to guess which of the three face-down cards is the red queen. You know he's out to con you.

But he's not—not directly, anyway. It's the shill who engages you in a little con game about the con game. The first-level shill has that glazed look and shabby overcoat that could mean wino, could mean junkie. In any case, he does not look as if he works for the Securities and Exchange Commission. He looks as if he really believes it's a game of skill. But you're not conned into believing that.

If you're new to the game, still at the stage where you can be taken by a first-level shill, you'll follow this guy's bets closely. Maybe you can't outsmart the con man, you think, but you can outsmart the wino. You notice that a corner of the red queen looks slightly bent from all the shuffling, but obviously the wino is too stupid to notice this clue. If he can't beat the system, I can, you say to yourself. Of course, when you finally put your money down and look for the card with the bent corner, the dealer will have deftly unbent the queen card and bent one of the others, or palmed the queen and substituted another card. You're down $20 and feel like a second-rate fool.

Apparently enough prospective marks have caught on to the theatrics of this setup, and so you can find in the streets today a more complex version—this time with a second-level shill. The second-level shill poses as someone who can expose the secrets of the first-level shill and offer the sophisticated pigeon a shot at conning the con man.

The second-level shill might look as if he *does* work for the Securities and Exchange Commission. Well-groomed, savvy-looking, he sidles up to the more skeptical mark and explains that he's figured out how these guys do the three-card-monte con. How they use a shill to sucker people in, how the dealer will bend the corner of a card—everything I've told you, as a matter of fact. Then the second-level shill makes his pitch: "If you know how these guys work, you can take them for everything they've got," he says. "I've figured out the signals that let the dealer know when the shill is supposed to win. Get your money ready, and put it all down with mine when I tell you."

The dealer, of course, cleans out this pigeon as well with an unbent edge or a palmed card.

The play within a play stage-managed by the second-level shill is a nice illustration of the theatricality of the con game. Robert Greene, the brilliant, syphilitic Elizabethan playwright, was so fascinated with the new breed of con men overrunning his theatrical haunts and, indeed, all London (curiously, Elizabethan scholars blame the con-man upsurge on out-of-towners—dismissed livery-men and soldiers) that he abandoned the stage for a time to pursue the mysteries of con men—or "cony-catchers," as they were called (a cony being a rabbit).

In doing so, Greene seems to have pulled off a literary con job of his own. After satiating the public with a series of pamphlets on the "art of cony-catching" which purported to give details of actual con games, he then proceeded to pen, under the pseudonym "Cuthbert Cony-Catcher," a defense of con artists. "Cuthbert," a self-proclaimed con man, attacks Greene's pamphlets for the damage done to the cony-catcher's livelihood. Although much of this *pro*-con-artist pamphlet is a none-too-subtle plug for the *anti*-con-artist pamphlets Greene wrote under his own name, "Cuthbert" does rise to an impassioned, populist defense of the con artist.

Too many people, "Cuthbert" says, denounce the poor con man, who can "perhaps with a trick at cards win forty shillings from a churl that can spare it." What about those malefactors of great wealth "that undo the poor, infect the commonwealth and delight in nothing but wrongful extorting and purloining of pelf when such be the greatest cony-catchers of all"?

In his introduction to a collection of Elizabethan con-game pamphlets, Gamini Salgado remarks that "everything we know about the Elizabethan writer at this time suggests that [Greene's con] is typical not only of Greene himself but of many of his fellows. Perhaps in the Protean figure of the confidence trickster, ever ready to change his personality and part to suit the present situation, protected by no one and depending only on his wit . . . for his livelihood, the Elizabethan hack uneasily saluted his double."

Back in the 1840's Edgar Allan Poe, then a New Yorker, wrote an article on con games he called "Diddling, Considered as One of the Exact Sciences." Poe recognized the con artist as a playwright of the street stage. "Your diddler," Poe wrote, "is ingenious. He has constructiveness large. He understands plot. He invents and circumvents."

And unlike these theatrical con artists, the big-shot crooks "Cuthbert" was denouncing don't even give you a good show for the money they steal. Now, I'm not arguing in favor of stealing from widows. Nevertheless, when it comes to out-of-town con games, I'll take the three-card-monte dealer on West 48th Street over Bert Lance anytime.

CHARIOTS OF THE INSURANCE SALESMEN

When Tom Wolfe called the seventies "The Me Decade,"
he was certainly on the mark, but he was writing about the
buyers *of the cosmic self-improvement schemes of the*
seventies such as est. This is a story, and the seventies are a
decade as well, of the sellers *of such schemes. Selling self-*
improvement has been an American obsession since before
Ben Franklin. The success gurus in this story offer self-
creation. *The idea is that the great salesman, leader-promoter,*
does not sell a product; he sells himself *to the customer. The*
best confidence men exude real *confidence, however phony*
their schemes may be.

Success gurus sell a doctrine that amounts to a "manifest
destiny" of the self. Where once that doctrine had made it
imperative that America expand to the utmost limits of its
continental possibilities, the success gurus take that expan-
sionist impulse in the American character and—realizing that
there is no longer a territorial void to be filled—internalize
the quest: now one must expand, inflate, project, promote
the Self to its grandest utmost limits. The success gurus claim
that there's gold in the hills of that far West Coast of the
mind.

The secret of "Sex Transmutation." Psychic energy from the mystic
council of Cosmic Guardians. "Internal bathing." The Five Clay
Tablets inscribed with the wisdom of Dabasir, the camel trader of
Babylon. Master Mind communion with the Infinite Intelligence.

What is all this gibberish? A catalog of demented counterculture
catchphrases? Some parody of hippy-dippy Von Däniken lore?

Far from it. These are just a sampling of the weird doctrines and occult rituals that spellbind the millions of mainstream, conventional Middle Americans who are part of the strange subculture of success-secret seekers and get-rich-quick dreamers.

You've seen the ads for the swamis of this subculture skulking in the back pages of magazines amid come-ons for sensual black satin sheets and the mystic secrets of the Rosicrucians. "Secrets of the Money Masters Revealed," the ads say. "I earned $35,000 in one day at home in bed with the flu," they proclaim. "Who else wants to get in on this Bonanza of Fast Capital Buildup?" they ask.

Perhaps you've been curious about these ads, even tempted to send away for one of the offers. Just for laughs, of course. But you're slightly embarrassed about what the postman might think if your copy of *The Money-Master's Manual* doesn't arrive in a plain brown wrapper. And besides, as a sophisticated New Yorker it's hard for you to imagine there could be anything to these success schemes. You feel confident that Felix Rohatyn didn't get his start by clipping one of these coupons. Certainly such appeals are unfashionable now in an age which believes in the subtleties of the corporate game player. The rhetoric of these get-rich-quick ads seems a throwback to the cruder entrepreneurial frenzies of an earlier America. And yet . . .

Just this spring, the Yale alumni magazine devoted an entire special issue to the crisis of contemporary capitalism. The concerned contributors bemoaned the loss of faith in the entrepreneurial ideal that had once been at the heart of the American system.

If only the distinguished contributors to the symposium on capitalism had—as I have—sent away for *The Money-Master's Manual*, with its amazing Plan 360 A. If only they'd carefully read through *The Millionaire Book of Successful Little Businesses*, with its advice on how to cash in on selling elephant garlic and bronzed baby booties. If only they'd met Joe Karbo, author of *The Lazy Man's Way to Riches*, and taken a ride in his Rolls-Royce. If only they'd read *Roman Reports*, a strange and wonderful digest of each and every one of the nearly three hundred get-rich-quick-scheme offers being peddled in print; if only they'd read the "Towers Club" newsletter, a kind of lonely-hearts pen-pal club for impassioned success-secret seekers, they might have a different perspective on the vigor of the capitalist dream.

I have and I do: these get-rich-quick dreamers are the last capitalists.

For some years, I've been sending away for this stuff. I've got cartons full of it. I've made a pilgrimage to the Pacific Ocean villa where Joe Karbo, the guru of *The Lazy Man's Way to Riches*, took me for a drive in his Rolls-Royce to prove he was Genuinely Rich. I've studied the whole literature of the subculture, the sacred and esoteric texts that date back to the Golden Age of Get Rich in the 1920's, to ancient Babylon, biblical Bethlehem, and perhaps even to insurance salesmen from another galaxy. My name is now on all the mailing lists. I get letters from Taiwan offering to set me up in the jewelry business, ads for books like *Health Secrets From the Orient* and *The Miracle of Universal Psychic Power: How to Pyramid Your Way to Prosperity*.

What I've discovered is that, just as the old Roman mystery cults continued to flourish for centuries after the Emperor Constantine made Christianity the state religion of Rome, so too does fervent faith in capitalism survive the official reign of American state bureaucratism. Only now, capitalist individualism has become a mystery cult. The essential element in almost every success-secret program I've studied is capitalist voodoo—the use of mystical, occult techniques, "long-lost secrets of the ancients," and such: the conversion of the whole repertoire of spiritual techniques of the East to help accumulate the cash of the West.

The origins of this Gnostic mystical capitalism can be traced back beyond Emersonian transcendentalism; its consequences are as contemporary as Werner Erhard's est and Jimmy Carter's smile. Let me take you on a guided tour.

THE HILL THEORY OF SEX TRANSMUTATION

No author in the inspirational-greed book business is more universally revered—even by competitors—than the late Napoleon Hill, author of the single most influential success-secret book, *Think and Grow Rich*. Among the millions of enthusiastic readers influenced by Hill's book was a young insurance salesman named Jack Rosenberg, who later thought he ought to change his name to Werner Erhard and grew rich with his own amalgam of East and West called est. If the young Werner has followed his guru Hill faithfully, no small part of the success of est must be attributed to Napoleon Hill's secret of sex transmutation. Napoleon Hill is the D. H. Lawrence of success theorists, fusing elements of Western sexual hydraulics with what seems like the Tantric influences from the East.

"Sex Transmutation" is not some bizarre new Danish operation; it's a scientific principle Hill claims he discovered in the course of twenty years of research into the sex lives and careers "of over

25,000 people." The fruits of this stimulating research have been codified by Hill into several general and specific theories of sex, beginning with the "three constructive potentialities" of sex.

The third purpose of sex, says Hill, is its use of sexual desire as "a driving force" which, "when harnessed and transmuted . . . is capable of lifting men into that higher sphere of thought which enables them to master the sources of worry and petty annoyance which beset their pathway on the lower plane."

Untransmuted desire can be dangerous, Hill warns: "A sex-mad man is not essentially different from a dope-mad man." But desire diverted from carnal coupling and *harnessed* to such things on the Higher Plane as selling insurance can be the secret of making big bucks fast: "Master salesmen attain the status of mastery in selling because they . . . *transmute* the energy of sex into sales enthusiasm! . . . The salesman who knows how to take his mind off the subject of sex, and direct it in sales effort with as much enthusiasm and determination as he would apply to its original purpose, has acquired the art of sex transmutation."

Hill is not too explicit on how a salesman sets out to transmute the lust in his heart to the sales-producing smile on his face. Instead, he returns to his twenty years' research and offers us the names of the thirteen greatest sex transmuters in history. Each of them, says Hill, "was known to have been of a highly sexed nature. The genius which was theirs undoubtedly found its source of power in transmuted sex energy."

Here they are, Hill's hit parade of heavy sex transmuters: George Washington, William Shakespeare, Abe Lincoln, Ralph Waldo Emerson, Robert Burns, Thomas Jefferson, Elbert Hubbard, Elbert H. Gary, Woodrow Wilson, John H. Patterson, Andrew Jackson, Enrico Caruso, and Napoleon.

Now the question that leaps to mind is what exactly did Shakespeare, Lincoln, and Elbert H. Gary *do* (or not do) to achieve their superb transmutations?

There are hints. Hill talks of damming a river in one place so that it will flow into another channel. In this new channel the transmuted desire will " 'step up' the mind," get it " 'keyed up' to high rates of vibrations." In his chapter on sex transmutation, Hill goes on at length to explain how the "highly sexed" transmutee/ salesman can use his "keyed up" animal magnetism to mesmerize the prospective customer into opening up his wallet. The legendary horniness of the traveling salesman may have less to do with the charms of farmers' daughters than with the state of his sex transmutation. The sale, of course, is an attempted seduction, the last refuge of the erotic tension of courtship in America, the patter of the seller the most impassioned love poetry we have.

Reading success-secret literature, it's impossible not to recall the nineteenth-century English pornography Steven Marcus analyzed in *The Other Victorians*, a study of the underside of the official sexual ethic of that time. Marcus points out that throughout that literature transactions of sex are frequently spoken of in metaphors of commerce: ejaculations are "spendings," for instance. But in the literature of the success-secret gurus—the underside of the official American success ethic—the opposite happens, and the transactions of commerce become sexualized. In the "pornotopia" of the "other Victorians" everything in the world is aroused and ready to "spend," while in the blissful vision of success-secret literature—"Greedonia," let's call it—the world of sexuality exists to "spend" wealth into your hands, breed it in your pockets, if you know the secret of sex transmutation.

A VISIT WITH A "GENUINELY RICH" SUCCESS GURU

We could continue to explore some of the weirdnesses of Napoleon Hill's world. I could tell you about his belief in the necessity of enemas (or "internal bathing" to avoid "autointoxication," as he phrases it) to any good success program, but it's time to move on and pay a visit to one of the up-and-coming new breed of success gurus following in Hill's wake—Joe Karbo, author of *The Lazy Man's Way to Riches*.

It was Joe Karbo's ad that first lured me into the world of success-secret gurus. Not the ad itself but the place in which it appeared: *Commentary*. If you're familiar with that distinguished intellectual journal, you'll be aware that full-page ads tend to reflect its erudite content—offerings of eighteen-volume library editions of Spinoza and the like. But there, in the midst of those distinguished pages, was a full-page hard-sell blast entitled "The Lazy Man's Way to Riches," with Joe boasting proudly in the accompanying copy that "I have 2 boats and a Cadillac . . . I live in a home that's worth $100,000. . . . I'll show you how I did it— the Lazy Man's Way—a secret I've shared with just a few friends 'til now."

Not long afterward I arranged to visit Joe at his split-level oceanfront office in Huntington Beach, California, not far from the $100,000 house. Joe had recently traded up from his Cadillac to a new Rolls-Royce, he told me right off. Did I want to go for a ride?

Joe's a husky, genial guy around fifty, with the deep, well-modulated voice of a professional pitchman. Joe was, in fact, one of the pioneering pitchmen of late-night TV in L.A. During the late forties and early fifties, when there was no official limit on the length of night-time commercials, Joe would come on and do those endless epic pitches for freezer plans, used cars, vegetable choppers, and the like, pioneering the orotund style of relentless harangue that was responsible for getting an official time limit placed on commercials.

"I pioneered a new type of selling," Joe tells me. "Being honest is what it was—sell yourself is what I mean, be a salable product yourself and you can sell anything," he explains. "I made and blew several small fortunes back then," Joe says. "Then I hit bottom." New ownership dumped Joe from his all-night-pitch post; he found himself broke and heavily in debt.

It was then, Joe says, he made the momentous discoveries that went into Dyna/Psyc, the motivational system that was the heart of the Lazy Man's Way. He took a Dale Carnegie course, read *Think and Grow Rich*, works by W. Clement Stone and others. He put them all together with some mystical techniques from the East. Then he went into mail order. He sold such items as tinted driving glasses and helped recreate his fortune. Then he sold his system for making money and really began to rake in the cash.

It was lunchtime and Joe volunteered to drive us in his new Rolls over to his nearby yacht club. The $20,000 forest-green cruise-ship-size Rolls is more than a vehicle for Joe. It's a symbol of his legitimacy, like the notarized statements from his accountant and banker testifying to the $100,000 price tag on his house that Joe reprints in his full-page ads. Many of the people who run these get-rich-quick ads, Joe grumbles to me, *are not actually rich*.

By following his system, Joe says, anyone who really wants a Rolls can have it. All you need to do is make it part of your Daily Declarations. Every morning upon rising, every evening upon retiring, you will read aloud to yourself a written declaration in which you describe that which you desire as if you already had it. "I have a brand-new, beautiful Rolls-Royce that cost $20,000," you declare as if it were actually in your garage. Next, Joe advises in his book, close your eyes and put yourself in a kind of greed trance in which you "*visualize it completely*. In your mind's eye, SEE the car . . . touch the steering wheel. . . ."

Joe's Rolls was real. So was Joe's yacht club. So was the smile on the face of the hostess who seated us at a table overlooking the yacht basin and told us there would be a "complimentary" fashion show during lunch.

Joe complained a lot during lunch about the "not genuinely rich" guys who were now ripping off his ads to sell success systems to unwary customers, but the thing I recall most clearly about that lunch was the implacable fashion show. Before we could order food, a Japanese woman in a silk kimono sashayed up to the table, whirled about, and said, "Very special fashion show. Are gentlemen interested in beautiful Oriental gifts to take home to ladies?"

"Not today, thanks," Joe said.

She returned while we had chowder. Joe was showing me an imitation of the Lazy Man's Way called "The Easy Road to Riches."

"Look here," said Joe. "He says, 'I have a yacht and four automobiles, two of which are exotic sports cars.' Just like me with my boats and cars. The rest is almost word for word."

The Japanese woman whirled up to the table trailing diaphanous silk shawls. "Shawls make perfect gift," she said.

"Please, we're in the middle of talking," Joe said, sounding a little irritated.

She returned during the main course—apparently making the rounds of each table with each costume change. Joe couldn't stop her. Perhaps she had made her own Dyna/Psyc Daily Declaration about selling shawls this morning. It seemed ironic: here was this master pitchman, swami of salesmen, ensconced in his yacht club, just a short ride in his Rolls from his hundred-thou house, and the poor guy couldn't get a little peace of mind during a meal precisely because of the pervasiveness of the kind of pitch he was promoting.

DETECTIVE ROMAN AND THE DISAPPEARANCE OF DAN BROWN

Bombs in the mail. Extortion notes. Dark doings at Ezra Pound's mental hospital. A "Defense Committee" with the curious name American Committee for Integrity and Decency (ACID). Twenty-one alleged C.I.A. murders. One genuinely mysterious disappearance.

The strange saga of disappearing Dan Brown and his ultimate get-rich-quick scheme contains heavier elements of mystery and tragedy than are usually to be found in the success-secret subculture.

The curious story first came to my attention a couple of years ago in the pages of *Roman Reports*, a bimonthly publication devoted exclusively to cataloging and evaluating the hundreds of get-rich-quick success-secret schemes advertised each year in national magazines.

Chief investigator and sole proprietor of *Roman Reports* is a dogged amateur detective named Dave Roman. From his base in Maple Heights, Ohio, where he is also a building-materials supplier, Roman clips every coupon he gets his hands on when it promises big bucks fast. When he gets the material, he reads it, digests it for comment in his bimonthly report, returns it, then asks for his money back to check on the money-back-guarantee policy. (Most get-rich-quick schemes sold through the mail make money for their authors because the recipients are frequently too confused or depressed by what they get to ask for a refund when disappointed, or don't want to admit they were taken.)

Reading the wry comments in the pages of *Roman Reports* is like going through a weird rogues gallery with Roman as a low-key tour guide.

> The Belgium Secret is a one page letter that describes one of the gimmicks described in P.O.W.E.R. (previously reported in my reports). It tells you to establish a corporation in a State that doesn't demand proof of capitalization. You buy some cheap plots of land with a down payment for your assets. The idea is to build an inflated financial statement. . . . Don't waste your money on this one. . . .
>
> Big Mac, Inc. . . . is another pyramid scheme. . . . You can join their "Millionaire Apprentice Club" for only $10.

What was appealing about *Roman Reports* was Roman's ability to combine amiable skepticism about most of the material that arrived at his archives with an optimist's faith that somewhere, somehow in his researches he'd come across that One Perfect Scheme.

When I came across his first report on Dan Brown's American Trustee & Loan Association (ATLA) operation, I could sense a heightened tone of excitement in Roman's usually unflappable prose.

"This offer costs you $10.95, but is the most unusual information I have ever received bar none!" he exclaimed. According to Roman, Dan Brown II, the man behind ATLA, "is a wealthy man who has his own C.I.A. of sorts. . . . He proposed an economic system that he claimed would have made banks obsolete and make everyone wealthy in a couple of months. He claims this system was used four times in history and each time the banking interests used their wealth and power to destroy it."

So excited was Roman by the prospect of this ultimate get-rich scheme, a scheme so great that it made not just the buyer or the seller but *everybody* rich, that he did something unprecedented—he became a dealer in Dan Brown's book, offering it at a discounted $8 price to readers of the report.

Only one small cloud shadowed the bright, new future that seemed to be dawning in Dan Brown's dream: Dan Brown himself had disappeared. "Dan Brown has been missing since May 9th, 1975," Roman reported. "Plus there have been 3 major resignations on his staff so the organization is a little shaky." Roman promised to investigate for an update.

Explosive developments in the Dan Brown case filled a whole page of the following issue of *Roman Reports*.

"It is a continuing story, and I can't seem to let go of it or find the real truth," Roman confessed, sounding a bit shaken at the news he had to relate. "Dan Brown was jailed because he allegedly tried to send a bomb thru the mail to extort $30,000 from the Greyhound Corp." As a get-rich-quick scheme, this certainly was direct, although it did lack the grand vision one had come to expect from the author of the Universal Get-Rich-Quick Scheme.

According to Roman's update, "Dan Brown claims he was framed by the SEC and the C.I.A. The bomb went off in the Post Office, but it was a dud and didn't harm a soul. . . . Dan claims he was framed because he released the names of 21 C.I.A. murders. . . . The court declared him incompetent and placed him in the psychiatric ward of St. Elizabeth's Hospital in Washington."

St. Elizabeth's, you may be aware, was the place in which that other visionary and monetary theorist Ezra Pound was incarcerated for twelve years. Indeed, Dan Brown's "Christian and patriotic" monetary theories sound suspiciously like Pound's Social Credit scheme for abolishing banking and making everyone prosperous, happy, and tax-free. (Brown and Pound both favor a complex self-devaluating, dated, paper-money system which is supposed to increase the velocity of money and pile it up for people instead of banks.)

Enter ACID to the aid of beleaguered Dan Brown. A group in Washington calling itself the American Committee for Integrity and Decency was formed to defend Dan Brown from "unethical practices and lies" by the government and win his release from St. Elizabeth's. But as this episode of the saga closed, Dan Brown had disappeared again. He had been transferred to a mental hospital outside St. Louis.

Then at last the final report: "Sad news has been conveyed to me and I will pass on the information I have," Roman announced in his November '76 report. "My investigation of Dan Brown and the American Trustee & Loan Association is at an end." A Mr. George Warix, the founder of ACID, says Roman, "tells me that Dan Brown has been released from the mental hospital outside of St. Louis and was moved back to Washington, D.C., to stay at a halfway house. During the day, Dan was allowed out. . . . August 4 was the last time George saw Dan. I even talked with Dan a week earlier," Roman remarks, but "Dan Brown has not been seen since. George feels the C.I.A. finally got rid of Dan because things were getting too hot and too many people were getting involved in the case. . . . Nothing can be proven, because there is no body. I guess we will all have to come to our own conclusions."

NORVELL'S METAPHYSICAL EMPIRE

Let me introduce you to the amazing Norvell. The name may sound familiar; you may have seen his ads in the *Times* for Sunday lectures on "mind cosmology" and other metaphysical subjects. Norvell—his first name is Anthony, but he prefers the more mystical-sounding solitary name—is a master of merchandising. He's incorporated a whole grab bag of so-called "Secrets of the East" as occult techniques for capturing the cash of the West. Who is Norvell? His publisher, Parker Publishing, has no way to reach him, it said. But from the sketchy biographical details provided by the jacket covers of Norvell books, like *Money Magnetism* and *Mind Cosmology*, one can see that we are dealing here with a true child of East and West. He began on the path to enlightenment in Hollywood: "In his earlier years, Norvell was known as the advisor to the motion picture stars of Hollywood, and as an Astrologer, mystic, and psychic with a reputation for being 85% correct." Norvell himself claims he transmitted his "magic circle" to such stars as Claudette Colbert, Bette Davis, Clark Gable, Spencer Tracy, Greer Garson, and "about 200 other famous stars" during his Hollywood horoscope heyday.

For some unexplained reason—either a summons to Higher Wisdom from the Cosmic Guardians or perhaps some unfortunate consequences from the 15 percent of his predictions that went awry —Norvell left Hollywood to search for the mystic secrets of the East. Depending on which jacket cover you read, Norvell either "spent years gleaning" his "profound knowledge of the Eastern Mysteries from the Masters of India and the Levant" or conducted "his studies and research . . . in universities and occult libraries in England, India, and Greece." "Most recently, in his quest for truth," one jacket tells us, "Norvell conducted a group of 70 students and lecture members to Egypt where he personally conducted the sacred flame ritual before the Pyramids."

How does a disciple of these mystical practices actually get rich? Well, if you're a follower of Norvell's money magnetism, you spend quite a bit of time each day chanting and magnetizing yourself. You wake up in the morning and polish up your "Golden Nuggets" —chanting ten times a series of statements such as "I will make $100,000 in my own business and be a big success."

Then it's time to read the morning paper and clip out items about rich and famous people for your Golden Hall of Fame and your Scrapbook of Destiny over which you just meditate regularly and say such things as, "I now elevate myself to the Golden Hall of Fame." Before you leave for work you have to read aloud the Millionaire's Secret Vow of Riches ("I recognize there are infinite treasures in the Cosmic Cornucopia of Riches and Abundance. I draw upon the unlimited resources of the universe for my own enrichment"). During the day you must not neglect your "money pump exercise," and chant your money-motivator mantras five times each. All of which is mere preparation for the "magic circle aura ritual to build a million-dollar personality." This involves standing in front of a mirror and declaring: "I now build my magic circle aura of importance and success . . . I am worth $50,000 a year or more and I now project this image of riches and power. . . ."

And if at the end of the day you wonder if it's all worth it, if you wonder why a person with a million-dollar personality spends his day engaging in these practices without any million-dollar reward, well, just look in your wallet. For there, if you've been following Norvell's instructions, you have a check made out to yourself for $1 million. "Sign the check, 'God, the Universal Banker,' " Norvell suggests. "Every time you see this you will affirm to yourself that God has literally given you a universe . . . it belongs to you as much as anyone else and therefore you already are worth more than a million dollars."

IS THERE LIFE INSURANCE
ON OTHER PLANETS?

If you find this inbreeding of bogus mysticism not quite to your taste, you can blame it on the Babylonians. The whole mystical capitalist tradition in the twentieth century can be traced to one seminal sacred text that appeared in 1926: *The Richest Man in Babylon*. Subtitled in its current edition "The Success Secrets of the Ancients," this book is the ur-text of the success-secret sub-culture. Purportedly drawn from authentic clay tablets unearthed by archaeologists, *The Richest Man* opens with a dialogue between a debt-plagued Babylonian named Bansir the chariot maker and a long-winded know-it-all named Arkad, who tells Bansir the system by which he became "the richest man in Babylon."

The secrets of this system turn out to be little more than keeping a regular savings account and buying insurance, which explains why so many hundreds of thousands of copies of *The Richest Man in Babylon* have been distributed free by savings banks and life-insurance companies. Of course, there weren't any insurance companies in ancient Babylon, but Arkad finesses this problem by *predicting* that in some future age someone will have the vision to invent them. He does this in a passage which will give you the flavor and intellectual force of the "ancient" wisdom that pervades this classic. "In my mind rests a belief," intones the wise Arkad, "that someday wise-thinking men will devise a plan to insure against death whereby many men pay in but a trifling sum regularly, the aggregate making a handsome sum for the family of each member who passeth into the beyond. This do I see as desirable and which I could highly recommend. . . ."

The perversely blasphemous choice of Babylon as ancient city of wisdom (for a devout Bible reader, calling someone the "richest man in Babylon" is no more a compliment than calling him the "grooviest guy in Gomorrah") apparently didn't harm its sales; the book became a well-respected "inspirational classic."

Its success helped enshrine the notion that "the Ancients" (or the sages among them) spent most of their time devising success secrets, leaving unanswered the question of why they weren't smart enough to invent insurance themselves. But once the idea caught on, *The Richest Man* spawned a whole generation of secrets-of-the-ancients-type success books, such as Og Mandino's *The Greatest Secret in the World*, in which we learn of the Ten Great Scrolls for Success of Hafid the camel boy of Bethlehem.

All of which makes one speculate on the identity of this so-called "Ancient" Arkad. How could he know about life insurance so far ahead of its time unless he was the representative of some vastly superior, but life-insurance-conscious, alien civilization. In fact it is not beyond the realm of possibility that this so-called Arkad was in fact one of Erich Von Däniken's "ancient astronauts" whose many contributions to human civilization are suggested in *Chariots of the Gods*. Certainly the text in *The Richest Man* provides clues that support this notion. Why is Bansir identified as a *chariot maker?* Might he not have been called upon to do some body and fender work on the ancient astronauts' interstellar chariots and been given in return the priceless secret of the insurance industry of the future? Indeed, it would not be surprising in the light of these speculations if we discover that the first alien beings we encounter have not come to redeem or destroy us but instead to sell us a surefire scheme for making big bucks in interplanetary mail order.

DEATH & THE
NITE OWL

A song and dance for sudden death. That's what Pat Doyle does for a living. Two or three times a night. As police reporter for New York's tabloid Daily News, *Doyle spends the night gathering stories of spectacular sudden deaths and grief-stricken aftermaths, then picks up his phone at Police Headquarters and pitches the pick of them to his editor, promoting the ones he's particularly pleased with as "good murders."*

The scenes in this story of Doyle pushing a "good murder" (and his by-line) for a front-of-the-paper position may make him seem a bit callous, but it is unfortunately true that most reporters must be salesmen to their editors as well as to their sources. Promoting the misfortunes of the latter for the approval of the former is part of the game. Doyle just plays it without any pretensions veiling his self-interest.

But Pat Doyle is something more than merely a salesman. He brings a genuinely religious sensibility to his role. In the prologue to Paradise Lost *Milton describes his task in retelling the story of the Fall of Man as "justifying the ways of God to man." The poet as PR man for God. It is a long and honorable tradition from which Pat Doyle should not be excluded because he does not write in blank verse.*

For Doyle, a devout Catholic, the bizarre and grotesque sudden deaths he sees are in some way all part of God's plan—somehow beneath the surface appearance of sudden death and sorrow there is a larger Story being told, not of the Fall of Man but of the ways of God among the Fallen. It is in sudden deaths that the ways of God are most dramatic and mysterious, and I sensed in Doyle a reverence and

ever-fresh astonishment at the inventiveness of God, at His
dramatic sense, the front-page savvy of the Author of all
stories.

This is definitely turning out to be a weird one. A good murder.

Guy named Devaney walks into Dominick's Bar on lower Lexington Avenue and sits down with some friends. They've all just come from a wake at Dimiceli's Funeral Home across the street. Inside Dominick's there's this other guy, a quiet guy, with sandy hair in a light gray suit; he's been nursing a couple of beers at the bar. About six thirty P.M. the quiet guy pulls a gun, goes over to Devaney, sticks it to the back of his head, and puts a bullet through his brain. The guy in the light gray suit is last seen entering a cab at 30th and Park heading south.

Inspector Doyle is on the case. Down at police headquarters, Doyle is on his feet shifting impatiently as he talks back and forth between the phone receivers he's got pressed to both ears. He's got the funeral director from Dimiceli's on one phone. He's got a talkative lieutenant from homicide on the other.

"Could you say it was gangland style, lieutenant? Uh huh. Could it also be a grudge? None of the mourners recognized the perpetrator? Uh huh, back to you soon, lieutenant."

It's now eight P.M., one hour after Devaney was pronounced dead on the floor of Dominick's. Still no trace of the man in the light gray suit. Doyle's got less than an hour to get two things—a line on the motive and a quote from the next of kin.

"This is a deep one, Ron," Doyle declares. "A deep one. This funeral angle. Guy's paying his respects, then bam! I'm looking for a connection. Could be a good murder." And when Inspector Doyle decides a murder is a good one, attention must be paid. Doyle is the authority on the subject.

They call him "Inspector" Doyle, or sometimes just "The Inspector," but Pat Doyle is not, of course, a police official, although he is a legend in the Department. He's Patrick Doyle of the New York *Daily News*—"Doyle of the *News*," as he likes to identify himself to funeral directors and eyewitnesses—for three decades the night-beat police reporter for the World's Largest Newspaper. Not surprisingly, Doyle is not shy about calling himself The World's Greatest Police Reporter.

He is being unnecessarily modest. Calling Pat Doyle The World's Greatest Police Reporter is as inadequate a tribute as calling Dante The World's Greatest Travel Writer. Doyle doesn't cover police. He covers sudden death. In his thirty-one years with the *News*, Doyle has covered 18,000 murders, suicides, and fatal accidents.

This 18,000 figure, Doyle assures me, does not include countless stabbings, beatings, tortures, and accidental mutilations which fell short of fatality. Just sudden deaths. And not just any sudden deaths—New York City averages more than four a night and it's Doyle's job to single out the "good" one, the most shocking, strange, sensational, even ironic death of the night, seize its essence in the immediate aftermath. In hot blood, a *Daily News* fan named Capote might call it.

Doyle's accounts of sudden deaths and aftermaths have been the soul of the *Daily News* for three decades and Doyle's experience gives his vision of life a unique but undeniable authority. This man Doyle has not merely seen the heart of darkness, he's seen the punctured lung, the ruptured spleen.

Plus he's available for lectures and after-dinner speeches, for clubs and civic groups. "You could say, Ron, that Doyle is a guy who is very interested in all aspects of advertising and promotion," Doyle tells me.

You could. In fact, not long before I called Doyle to ask if I could spend a night on the death watch with him, Doyle placed the following classified ad in the "Situations Wanted" section of *The New York Times*:

> NEWSPAPER   CRIME
> REPORTER
> Avail.   for   speaking
> engagements
> 'WHAT PRICE LIFE IN
> NYC?' MM37 Times

Doyle has not yet been exactly deluged with offers, but he is ready: he's been rummaging through his memories and his clips, typing up dramatic fragments and pointed anecdotes on slips of paper. While he's working the phones on the Dominick's Bar death, Doyle will occasionally dig into a drawer of his desk or the pocket on his bright Hawaiian print sportshirt and pass me one of those slips. Some are straightforward facts of life and death in New York City. "It's not unusual to find the bodies of infants stuffed in trash cans," begins one.

Another is about a prisoner who contrived to hang himself from the strap of his wooden leg. There's one about a "refined, dignified" seventy-four-year-old lady who died with a torn bed sheet stuffed down her throat by some young thugs. Then there are tales of Doyle and the big shots. Doyle and Ari at P.J. Clarke's. Doyle and Henry Ford at Clarke's. The time Doyle got the tip about the Blue

Angel fire while sitting with Governor Carey at Clarke's. Other slips contain tales of Doyle scoops and Doyle triumphs and bits of Doyle's Spenglerian musings upon the decline of civilization into the savagery he's witnessed first hand—the old-fashioned rational barbarism of organized crime, Doyle says, has been replaced by the senseless torture and murder of the weak and innocent.

These scraps of Doyle's writings are a rare find for a Doyle *aficionado*, because Doyle doesn't write. In thirty years he's hardly written—actually typed out—a single sentence. Doyle's medium is the phone. He talks his story in to a *News* rewrite man from police headquarters or the scene of the death. Doyle is more like an old-fashioned storyteller in the oral tradition—the bard of bad news—than a writer. All the more interesting then, to read the capsule biography Doyle has actually typed out about himself and the high points of his career:

> Pat Doyle, known as the Inspector to his colleagues, is one of the top, if not the top, crime reporters in America. The recipient of many awards, he considers the most prestigious one being the honor Vice-President Nelson Rockefeller presented him last year on behalf of the Silurians, an organization of veteran newsmen in New York, for his scoop on the murder of Professor Wolfgang Friedman. In his almost thirty years with the *News*, Mr. Doyle has solved a murder, broken the Xaviera Hollander prostitution ring case, and had his name used by permission in the movie *The French Connection*. He also beat the competing media with a stop-the-presses bulletin on the bombing of police headquarters four years ago. Despite his injuries in the blast, Mr. Doyle, whose office was located across the street from headquarters, got the story and then went to Beekman Downtown Hospital for treatment. Mr. Doyle also broke the case of Stephen Smith, former President John F. Kennedy's brother-in-law . . . Mr. Smith's arrest for refusing to pay a sixty-cent cab fare. It made Page One of the News. . . .

The funeral director has not been helpful. Doyle has a hunch there might be a connection between the body being waked at Dimiceli's and the death of Devaney at Dominick's—one wake somehow leading to another. But the funeral director isn't giving Doyle the cause of death of the corpse in his care.

Doyle bangs down one phone (he's now got the bartender from Dominick's on hold on the other). "You can use the word 'exasperating' if you wish, Ron," he says. "Very exasperating. I'd like to be up there at the scene. I could wrap this one up in no time, but if I do I may not make this edition."

Doyle has decided to do this death by phone for another reason: it's only the first murder of the night. A slow night, so far. If the statistical average holds up, "three people are alive now who will be murdered by dawn," Doyle points out. Although this is looking more and more like a "good murder," Doyle's not willing to commit himself yet. It's not a plane crash or a celebrity death, after all.

Doyle's phone technique is legendary. He's famous for his facility with four phones at once. When he really means business, Doyle drags three phones onto his desk from nearby desks, starts talking on two of them at a time, dialing two others, then juggling all four parties, sometimes more as he stacks a few up on hold.

Colleagues regard with awe Doyle's speed and efficiency at the grim business of getting quotes from grief-stricken next of kin and critically injured survivors. Doyle brings to this—one of the central tasks of sudden-death reporting—a special combination of ruthlessness, delicacy, and timing. The last is particularly important. Doyle prides himself on never being the very first to break the news of a death over the phone. He waits until someone in authority makes that call. Doyle likes to be the next call after that. Doyle is willing, however, to hurry the notification process along. One of the tricks of the trade when the cops are slow getting the word to a victim's family, Doyle tells me, is this (young police reporters take note): get hold of the priest, minister, or rabbi of the deceased, tell him of the tragedy, ask *him* to break the news to the family. "Once I get the priest to notify them, then I can move in," Doyle explains.

Doyle's most recent survivor-quote coup was somehow reaching the phone at the bedside of a seriously injured stewardess survivor of a recent Eastern Airlines crash at La Guardia Airport and getting an exclusive eyewitness account of the disaster from her. "It was beautiful, Ron," Doyle says of the La Guardia scoop. "The paper had a great crew out there, all of them professionals, but none of them was able to interview a survivor. Doyle did it by phone. Beat them all out. That's what I live for, the challenge. My editors couldn't believe it. These are hardened men. They said, 'Doyle how did you do it?' "

Doyle's delight in hot pursuit has given rise to at least one tale of what might seem like excess zeal to some. "There's this great story I heard about the Inspector," a guy in the *Daily News* office told me. "About how he lifted up this guy's oxygen tent to get a quote from him and the guy dies right afterward."

Doyle tells a death-watch story which may be the origin of this myth. The way Doyle tells it, it's the story of how he solved the murder of a policeman's wife and child. As Doyle says in his biographical sketch of himself, "Doyle's achievements in journalism are many indeed, but he recalls the homicide he solved most vividly even though it happened fifteen years ago."

It started with a death watch on a policeman's child. The young girl and her mother were blown up by a mysterious explosion in their two-story home in Queens while the father was out on his beat. The mother died instantly, the child and their upstairs lodger lay critically injured in the hospital.

Doyle had been nursing a theory of the explosion he wanted urgently to check out. Before proceeding to the hospital for the death watch, Doyle had talked to the neighbors and the grief-stricken cop about the upstairs lodger. "I found out that man's feelings about life, that he had been despondent. When the infant died, I went right up to the room where the man was. I went right up to his bedside and I asked him why did you do it. He said, 'Yes I did it, I was tired of life.' He admitted he blew the place up. Well, I called my editor, of course—my first allegiance is to my newspaper, before anyone else. The editor told me to call the police quick. They came and interviewed the man and in less than twenty-four hours he was dead, but they had booked him on a murder charge."

Doyle's got the bartender at Dominick's talking. Good eyewitness stuff about Devaney's death throes. Ironic details—Devaney and friends were toasting their dead friend's memory at the moment of Devaney's death; more mystery about the man in the gray suit who was a total stranger to the neighborhood and the bar. Doyle is most intrigued by the irony of the funeral angle. He's got his editor up at the *News* building on the phone now; he's filling her in on the Devaney story so far. "Isn't it something, though, it's so goddammed unusual. Here's this guy who's just paying his respects, he walks across the street with some friends to reminisce about their departed friend, then boom, he's gone. I tell you I've been down here at headquarters for thirty-one years, covered 18,000 deaths, but I've never heard of anything like this."

A strong statement coming from Inspector Doyle. Not that there might not be a bit of promotion going on: Doyle has got to convince the night editor that the Dominick's Bar death really is a "good murder," good enough to break into the story lineup in the early editions. The "Nite Owl" (first, early evening) edition of the *News* goes to bed about five P.M. every afternoon, just about the time Doyle arrives at the newsroom at Police Headquarters. Deadlines for the next four editions fall at seven P.M. for the Two

Star; nine P.M. for the Three Star; eleven P.M. for the Four Star; and sometime after one A.M., when Doyle goes off duty, for the final Four Star Circle edition.

Doyle thinks he can break this Dominick's story into the Three Star, then work it up into something really good for the later editions. But he's got some tough competition leading off the lineup tonight—the planet Mars. (Doyle doesn't even bother worrying about competing with New York's other morning paper— the *Times* no longer has a full-time police reporter on the headquarters night beat, and shrinks from the intricacies of sudden death anyway.)

The front page of the Nite Owl is filled with the first Viking pictures of the Martian surface. Pages two and three are packed with stories of the mysterious red planet. This has the effect of jamming all national and international news into pages four and five—Lebanon, Chowchilla Bus Nap, last-minute Ford and Reagan dramatics. It'll be difficult for a death, short of a head-of-state or major celeb, to crack that lineup. The real competition tonight will be played out on pages six and seven, and here Doyle sees some opportunities: a big welfare cheat story—nothing new there; another hospital strike turning point—that should also be vulnerable to a good murder.

Doyle is not entirely pleased at having to play for these smaller stakes because of the prominence of the Martian story. He is, of course, respectful of the American space effort—Doyle is very much an old-fashioned patriot—yet he is not beyond essaying a deprecating wisecrack about the allegedly fabulous red planet pix. "Here's something you could use, Ron, if you want a bit of humor in your story. Say Doyle took one look at the picture of Mars on the front page of the *News* and said 'It looks a lot like the Lower East Side to me.'"

Turning to the matter of what makes a "good murder," I asked Doyle to tell me what criteria separate good from the run-of-the-mill murders. Doyle reeled them off rapid-fire. "A good murder is when you have a prominent official who happens to be slain; a good murder is when you have a police officer shot to death or stabbed to death while on duty; or if an actress on her way home from the Broadway stage is shot to death; and then stabbed or strangled, or then kidnapped, and then found murdered. Also any child who is slain always goes up front. There *is* a difference between a good one and a bad one . . . I hate to sound this way but we have so many common murders in New York, particularly on the Lower East Side where you have the same senseless junkie killings."

There's another kind of good murder, the kind Doyle and the *Daily News* have always had a sensitive ear for—the ironic, unfathomable or weird twist-of-fate death, the kind that people in New York love to read about because it echoes so faithfully the tragically whimsical quality of life in the city. That other strange post-funeral death Doyle had the other day, for instance.

This one starts out with a guy deciding to commit suicide by hurling himself off the top of a twelve-story building. Nothing unusual about that until he lands on top of a guy in an open Cadillac, killing him.

Nothing unusual about that except that the Cadillac's part of a funeral procession on the way to bury a friend of the dead guy. So there you have a natural death, a suicide, and a bizarre accidental death converging in the procession, or perhaps the original death giving birth to two more. It's worth your life to go to a funeral these days.

This Dominick's Bar affair tonight offers only two deaths in addition to the funeral twist, but one of them is murder and there's a man in a gray suit on the loose and a motive missing with him.

"I'm on tenterhooks, not knowing the motive," Doyle says. "But the time has come to call this in for the Three Star."

First Doyle goes to the window and draws the blinds shut. He relights his big black "Caribbean Round" cigar and gets down to business.

"Hello, Billy. This is The Inspector." Doyle's got rewrite on the line. "Yes, Billy, let me talk it out to you first. The guy's name was Devaney, Thomas . . ."

This is clearly the part Doyle likes, the pure storytelling part. He gets into a simple but dramatic retelling of the moments before and after the murder, with heavy emphasis on the funeral irony. He concludes it with a dramatic retelling of the scene immediately after the gunshot: "There were shouts and screams as Devaney staggered to his feet. He held his head with both hands. He fell onto the table, then onto the floor. . . ."

After filling in ages, addresses, and other details for rewrite, Doyle can't resist a little promo. "I got a lieutenant in the 17th saying quote an unusual one, no doubt about it unquote. Unusual! It's a honey of a story. I've been down here for thirty-one years, Billy, and I never had one like this, in 18,000 deaths, not one quite like it."

Chinatown. Doyle's favorite part of town. Doyle was born nearby. "But I never got to know it," he says, "till I started going on some raiding parties with the police. They used to go after the boys who ran the Fan-Tan games in the basements. I tell you they had basements and subbasements and tunnels and secret doors just like in the movies. It was quite an education."

We're taking a break between the Three Star and the Four Star deadlines, heading up Mott Street to Doyle's favorite Chinese place. Everybody in Chinatown knows Doyle—the Chinese and the cops. Doyle shows a Chinese merchant the *News*'s page-one picture of Mars and tells him the Lower East Side joke. It doesn't translate well.

Doyle goes into a tirade over gangs. Gangs of illegal Hong Kong immigrants are tormenting his Chinatown friends. Most of the crime in the city comes from gangs. Gangs on narcotics. Because of marijuana. Marijuana leads to the needle and Betty Ford is promoting it, PROMOTING IT, Ron. Merchants are selling papers for marijuana in public. No leadership anywhere. Look at the church. Rectories are being robbed, nuns raped, priests murdered. Society is in the thrall of the lowest criminal scum. Look at what they've done to the Lower East Side.

Doyle orders the subgum. I get the duck. The waiter doesn't get the Lower East Side joke. During dinner Doyle tells me how it all started with Bruno Richard Hauptmann's ladder, a primal scene of sorts for the future police reporter.

When Doyle was nine years old and living in the Bronx, a media whirlwind struck a house nearby. The ladder that the alleged kidnapper Hauptmann used to bear away the Lindbergh baby had been traced back to that Bronx address. When the young Doyle came upon the scene, the house was swarming and popping with cops, police reporters, and cameras. He witnessed the awesome power that a sensational crime has to imbue with excitement not only objects like the ladder associated with it, but even places that had once been associated with that object and were no more. The young Doyle found he could read all about it over and over again in eight different ways daily. Picked up a heavy newspaper habit. Became a carrier boy, then a copy boy. Finally, after discharge from World War II service, he got what he wanted: a job with the *News* and a phone at the rickety police reporters' shack across from headquarters.

It's a tradition—part of the informal *cursus honorum* of the profession—that police-reporting duty is a kind of combination boot camp and rite of passage for innocent young reporters when they're first hired. The bloody christening ritual. Rub the recruits' noses in raw wounds and fresh gore. Let them learn the facts of life from child abusers and vice-squad porn films. Let them learn about sudden death from the sight of it and the smell of it, and from the look on the faces of parents of slain children. Let them make their journey into the underworld and see life from the bottom up.

And then let them pass on. To more "serious" things. To politics, and now, of course, "investigative reporting." Police reporting, after all, is just the lowest rung in the ladder up the profession.

Doyle never fell for that. He was certain from the beginning that the best stories are life-and-death stories, and nothing is more "serious" than sudden death. Men like Doyle—and Al Lewis of *The Washington Post*, to name another; there's usually one in every big city—who spurn the upper rungs and become lifetime police reporters are a rare breed. Conventional reporters regard them with wonder and occasionally condescension. "He's been down at headquarters on the police beat so long, he's more like a cop than a reporter," and "they're the most cynical reporters of all" are the handy oversimplifications.

Not true of Doyle. Not only has he seen far more death than most cops, he's far less cynical than most reporters. He suffers more. Certain kinds of deaths still get to him. "After all this time the death of a man means nothing to me, absolutely nothing," Doyle declares. "But I have to admit I still can be affected by the murder of a woman and particularly of a small child."

Doyle is now fifty-one and the father of five children, all girls. As his own daughters were growing up, the other kind of baby stories began to get to him. The battered, smashed, and violated bodies, the ones he saw stuffed in trash cans. Fifteen years ago he moved his wife and children out of New York City and into a quiet New Jersey suburb. These days he forbids his girls to go near the city. "I just can't picture my little girl in a subway with these filth mongers. I tell myself, 'Doyle you're old-fashioned.' I wouldn't dare have my little ones see what their Daddy's seen in life. My God."

"Did they get the stiff to Bellevue yet?" Back at headquarters, Doyle is on the phone to a sergeant in the 17th Precinct. "Jeez, you guys let him lie out there long enough. Anything new on Devaney himself? Could revenge be a motive?"

The Devaney story didn't break into the lineup of the Three Star, so Doyle's working the phones furiously trying to get some kind of breakthrough for the Four Star.

"This is what I live for, Ron, the competition, racing the dead-line to beat the other guy and get that by-line up front."

While he's in his phone frenzy, Doyle has me look through an assortment of artifacts he's got stashed in his olive green press-room locker. It's a curious collection. Here's a biography of Henry Ford II, very friendly, by someone named Booton Herndon. There are four entries in the index relating to Doyle, Patrick, and his friendship with the auto magnate. Plus there is another entry (p. 246) written in because Booton Herndon's indexer forgot it. Doyle, says Booton Herndon, has grown to be such a close friend of Ford that "he is one of the few people who have been permitted to see Henry nuzzling Cristina like a teenager in a parked car."

Also in the locker are photos of Doyle with big-shot starlets and stiffs at various stages of his career. But surprisingly most of it is history. Doyle has a passionate interest in lower Manhattan history. There are eighteenth-century maps. There's a fascinating old book filled with stories of disappearing relics of Old New York: the last farm in Manhattan, the last blacksmith, and other anachronisms. There's *Shoe Leather and Printer's Ink*, an anthology of great tales of the giants of police reporting in the days when New York was a great newspaper town.

Doyle's phone rings. He's got the super of the building of a brother of the deceased holding on one line while he takes the incoming call on the other.

"A fire where? You got something going up there, huh? The restaurant at that address. Let me know if it gets out of hand. Yeah, I'll be up there usual time . . ."

"One of my tipsters," says Doyle. "Guy up at Clarke's. He's one of the many people, some of them in the highest ranks, who will always call Doyle first. I've gotten a lot of news breaks for my editors from my tipsters. My editors know that Doyle knows the city."

A curious interruption in the headquarters routine suddenly takes Doyle off the phones on the Devaney affair.

"Doyle, I've got a weirdo down here, maybe you can help figure him out." It's the cop on duty downstairs at the main public entrance to police headquarters. "I got a guy down here says Beekman Hospital just released him from observation. Maybe a psycho but he keeps repeating the names of all these people he says are police reporters."

Downstairs a young guy in a blue leisure suit is standing in front of the desk in hospital slippers. He's saying a name over and over again. Doyle recognizes the name—a police reporter for the *Journal American* a quarter century ago. Now dead.

The guy in the blue leisure suit says "that's my uncle" and starts telling a long story about why the hospital did or didn't discharge him.

"So what do you want from me?" Doyle asks.

"I want to stay at the Thirty-fourth Street Y. I need ten dollars."

Doyle takes out his wallet. "Understand this is a loan. Pay me back."

It's getting close to one A.M. and Doyle is no closer to a break on the Devaney death. The closest he got to next of kin was the super in the building of the brother of the deceased. And *he* wouldn't help, even when Doyle told him, "It's because his brother's been murdered tonight and I need to make contact." Doyle has changed from his Hawaiian shirt into a cream-colored jacket, dress shirt and tie, and a panama hat. He's getting ready to go to Clarke's.

Every night when Doyle wraps up his death-watch detail, he gets into his Mercedes 280 SL and cruises uptown to East 55th Street. They keep a special table waiting for him there at Clarke's, in the bright place between the bar and the back room. According to our friend Booton Herndon "this center room is known officially to the In Crowd as the Pat Doyle Room."

There Doyle perches like a sentinel from the Kingdom of the Dead, sipping Coke, holding court, keeping his eye open for news tips, and receiving visits from the potentates of other kingdoms. He's been going there for thirty years and by now he's become a Clarke's institution, a favorite of the high rollers and all-night people who hang out there until the four A.M. closing time. It was at Clarke's that author Robin Moore got to know Doyle and decided he had to use Doyle's last name for the hero of a cop movie he was working on called *The French Connection*.

"You have to understand that Clarke's is a crossroad of the upper worlds and the under worlds," an associate of Henry Ford II who has watched Doyle at Clarke's for years says. "A lot of police types go through there and so do people on the other side. You have people in the higher ranks and the lower, everybody from maharajahs to police reporters."

What Doyle does for the people at Clarke's is bring up through the class strata from the very bottom muck of the city his classic tales of sudden death, and retail them for those denizens of the higher worlds who never get as close to death as Doyle does. For Doyle it's a kind of decompression chamber between the death watch and home, a purgatory in which the souls of the suddenly dead are reborn again in the retelling.

Early Wednesday morning at Clarke's. This is two weeks after the Dominick's Bar death. Doyle's sipping a Coke, saying what a good week it's been for him so far. Another chain-reaction multiple death: a couple found stuffed in a closet and dead on Monday. On Tuesday a suspect is arrested and today the baby daughter of the suspect has been murdered, presumably in revenge for the closet stuffing. The waiter comes by, Doyle orders another Coke and asks me if I want a drink. I ask Doyle why he doesn't drink.

The answer takes Doyle back to his one and only brush with sudden death and the story of how Henry Ford saved his life. The way Doyle tells it, he was driving across the George Washington bridge one day eight years ago when suddenly "I began vomiting blood. My ulcer had perforated. I barely managed to get over to the Manhattan side, get out, and lie down on a park bench where I just lay choking in blood. I said, 'Doyle you're going to die.' People walking by did nothing. Let me choke 'til I passed out. Wasn't 'til I woke up in the hospital I found that two policemen came over and took me in."

Why the ulcer, I asked Doyle. I told him Al Lewis, the veteran police reporter for *The Washington Post*, once told me he, too, had an ulcer.

"Was the ulcer attributable to my work?" Doyle asks. "I don't know. These afflictions hit hardest people who don't have as strong a stomach as we would wish. This is where ulcers came in."

Henry Ford came in when Doyle was close to death. His doctors had told him that only an operation to remove part of his stomach could save his life, but for some reason Doyle insisted he could heal himself. "My wife had to call up Mr. Ford and get him to call me and tell me to get it done," Doyle said. "Otherwise, I would have let myself die."

Since the operation eight years ago, Doyle has not touched a drink. "I miss it terribly," he says, gazing at mine. "Anyone who has the pleasure and the privilege of having a cocktail or two or three or ten does not know how fortunate they are," Doyle says. "I used to drink like a fish. You know how newspapermen are. How we like to escape the anxieties and pressures of the job."

What does he do now, I asked, to relieve those ulcerating pressures?

"Landscape," says Doyle.

"Landscape?"

"In my new place in New Jersey. I've got fifteen acres to work on. Already I've got pachysandras and ivy down for cover in the front. I love working with pachysandra and ivy. Also I've got fifty-one different varieties of trees and plants for gardens."

If Clarke's is purgatory after the death-watch underworld, his New Jersey home is heaven to Doyle. Right there in the middle of the action at Clarke's, Doyle launches into a loving and detailed description of his landscaping plan, which seems like an ambitious attempt to rebuild the Lower East Side in New Jersey's green and pleasant land.

"What I'm doing, Ron, is I'm picking up some of these bricks you see falling off these crumbling Lower East Side tenements. I put a few of them at a time in my trunk and take them over often as I can. So far I've built a barbecue with them, and I'm lining the walk between the ivy and pachysandra in the front with them. You can find all sorts of building material in the ruins there. I've got plans for a trellis. . . ."

Before I leave Clarke's, I ask Doyle whatever became of the strange death of Devaney at Dominick's. I have to reconstruct the details before he remembers. "Oh, yes," he says, "that was a good one, but the desk decided not to run it, I think. That was the funeral one, right? Don't recall hearing they came up with anything. But let me tell you about this week. This baby killed in revenge for the closet stuffing is a good one. . . ."

LIFE IN THESE UNITED STATES

The unidentified traveling man in this story is, of course, this writer. I happened upon this Arizona incident while escaping from a promotional junket in New Mexico that I never did get around to writing about. A PR firm promoting a documentary film about filmmaker Dennis Hopper (then hot from Easy Rider) *entitled* The American Dreamer *had flown a plane load of writers and film critics from both coasts down to Dennis Hopper's ranch in Taos (once the final home of D. H. Lawrence) for a screening and promo party that was supposed to add up to an "event" worth covering. This was one of the earlier efforts of that archetypical seventies promoter, Larry Schiller, who by the end of the decade would be notorious as the man who was selling exclusive rights to Gary Gilmour's execution.*

I was driving through Arizona on the trail of a traveling con man who had convinced two one-hundred-year-old Hopi chieftains that they were about to be visited by flying saucers when I stopped for a hitchhiker who turned out to be the "Benny" of this story.

It's a story about a family of real—as opposed to Hopperstyle Hollywood—American dreamers and what happened to them when brand names came to heroin, "China White" came to Arizona, and a traveling man came to stay a night at their home and found himself witness to the sordid dissolution of the family dream.

Benny popped two farewell Tuinals before he came down from the mountains. After the morning's dope-and-wine breakfast, and the half dozen tabs of mescaline from the Easter ceremony the night before, Benny found it impossible to stand up and hold his thumb out when he got to the road.

But Benny solved the problem. He sat down on the shoulder of Highway 4 facing the westbound traffic, crossed his legs, and propped his elbows on his knees. Then he settled his head in his hands and stuck his right thumb out from around his ear. This was efficient. This was comfortable.

After about an hour Benny opened his eyes and found a forty-five-foot trailer truck on top of him. Benny wasn't sure how the huge silver mother got there, but the driver was waving for him to climb in. Benny was surprised to notice that his thumb was still stuck out, just the way it was when he had left it.

The driver was heading for Kingman, Arizona, on 66, and told Benny he could stay on until his partner, who was sleeping in a bed behind the cab, woke up. Benny thought this arrangement was just fine since he was only going as far as Flagstaff and wouldn't mind taking over that bed in back when the other guy woke up. The bed sounded very good to Benny in fact. He crossed his legs on the seat of the cab and settled his head in his hands again.

The other driver awoke around noon, about an hour west of Albuquerque, and said he wanted to get into the cab. Benny said fine, he wouldn't mind taking the bed now. The partner looked at Benny's Prince Valiant hair, dirty face, and his single silver earring.

"The fuck you will," said the partner.

As soon as Benny jumped down from the cab he realized he still couldn't stand up. The sun was painful on top of the color he got in the mountains. For an hour there were maybe a dozen cars going his way. This must be Death Valley, he thought. He popped his last Tuinal to get him through the wait.

It was three hours before the sound of the big green Mercury skidding to a stop on the gravel shoulder ahead woke Benny. When Benny tried to stand up, he felt the skin on his neck and shoulders crinkle with pain. His head felt like a blimp. Trying to run the hundred feet to the car, Benny felt his muscles stumble inside his skin. It was some combination of sunburn, sunstroke, and Tuinal that was making this run take so long. Two in all, thought Benny. Two enough. Too fuckin' enough.

The front seat of the car was filled with paper. The driver pulled a pile of it over toward him to make room for Benny. Then he had to throw some paper from the front seat into the back seat to make room for himself. The back seat was already full of paper and some of it slid onto the floor of the back seat. There was paper on the floor beneath Benny's feet up front.

When Benny's eyes focused enough inside the car he could see that the paper was of many kinds. There were regular newspapers from Albuquerque, Taos, Denver, and Santa Fe. There were underground newspapers from Albuquerque and Santa Fe, a copy of the *Astral Projection* with a cover story about the civilizations that live inside the Hollow Earth beneath the North Pole. There were maps from several different gas stations. There were tissue-thin credit card receipts from several different gas stations. There was a folder under Benny's feet which said Instant Hertz. There were empty cardboard coffee cups, empty Styrofoam coffee cups, and empty coffee-stained paper bags. There were several yellow legal pads with thin lines, with their top pages folded back to handwriting. And on the front seat next to the driver's right leg was a New York Sunday *Times* with ALBQ-75¢ stamped on it.

"I've never seen a *New York Times* before," said Benny a few minutes after he had focused enough to find out what the big paper was. "That's a big paper. I've heard they're really big on Sunday."

"Actually that is the Sunday one," said the driver.

"Well, I'm glad I've seen it," said Benny. "I've heard about it."

Benny tried to nod for a while, but finally decided he had to lean forward to keep himself from fainting and talk to keep his mind off the sunburn pain.

"Where are you coming from?" Benny asked the driver.

"Just now from up at the warm springs in the Jenez Mountains. From New York really."

"The warm springs above San Ysidro?"

"Right."

"That's far out. I was just up in the hot springs in the Jenez Mountains. You know the one, it's just a few miles from where you were, you know the one up above—"

"They had a big Easter thing there, didn't they?"

"Well, like everyone just sort of knew to show up. Incredible good dope scene there. The mountains, man, the mountains are just out of sight. I can't get enough of them. I'm gonna live up there this summer. I left everything I had up there in this lean-to I built. I'm just going home now cause I got a message from my mother from this dude who relayed it from her that she needed to see me. As soon as I straighten that out I'm hitching back. For good. For good. I've hitched around everywhere. In the West, I mean. I've never been east of Dallas. But I think I found the place up there."

"Hey, you know those monasteries along the Jenez road near

the hot springs?" the driver asked Benny. "The ones called Servants of the Paraclete. Do you know what kind they are?"

"Oh yeah. They're the ones for wino priests. They're like transferred there from all over the country to dry out and do penance. I had this Indian friend once who worked in the furnace room, used to drink all the time down there and bring in cheap gin for some of the priests who'd sneak down and get loaded."

"Really?"

"No shit, yeah. They've got these Precious Blood nuns who dress all in red to look after these priests, but they'd find ways of slipping away. Shit, if I were a priest I'd become a wino real fast just to get sent there. Right in the mountains like they are. I'd shoot up alcohol to get there."

"Hey," said the driver fifty miles further west. "What's the best way to go through the Reservations?"

"Well, the best thing to do is take 64 north of . . . hey listen, if you're going that way you can stay over at my mother's house tonight. We live just inside the reservation, on your way."

Benny's mother wasn't home when the green Mercury pulled up. Benny's mother's home was a reservation within a reservation: a tiny neat spiral of paved road and pastel ranch houses in the middle of a sloppy, dust-covered Navajo hamlet called Wohseepee. Teachers and federal people lived there.

Benny's sister and brother-in-law were fixing dinner when Benny and the driver walked in. The brother-in-law was packing a Bisquick mix around some Armour-Star hot dogs.

"Hi Katra. Hi Bob," said Benny after the screen door slammed.

"Benny! We thought you were dead this time! Some dude told us you fell from a cliff," said Benny's sister Kathryn. Kathryn looks like the pleasant girl who wins home economics prizes in high school.

"Yeah, well I did fall from this cliff. There was this Indian kid who climbed up there and couldn't get down. He was screaming because he was freaking on some stuff. So I started climbing up after him, only it's like a four-hour climb and I started in the afternoon and I was so fucking wrecked on this weed from Nam some GI gave me, by the time I got halfway up it was dark and I stepped onto this ledge that wasn't really there. I rolled and tumbled like all night long before I hit this bottom ledge."

"Oh, Benny, you know after this dude told us about you having a fall we heard on the news that somebody's dead body had been found in a creek in Jenez with no I.D. We figured oh no, that's got to be Benny."

"Yeah, well it could have been. I don't have my I.D. anymore. I left my wallet with some dude in Jenez who needed it. I just gotta get some money together and I'm going back to stay."

"Oh shit, Benny. You shoulda come back a day sooner. Bob and I were saving twenty-five dollars for you. But we didn't know when you were coming back, or if you were dead, and we spent it on junk."

"I thought you guys were kicking."

"Well we *were*. I mean we still sort of *are*. You know after we hitched back from brother Jerry's in Pittsburgh, you know we were shooting a gram a day up there. You know, China White."

"China White," said Bob softly.

"We were on our way to New York," Kathryn continued, "but we got so strung out we came back here to kick and Mom took care of us, she thought we had the flu, she kept cooking for us and telling us we had to eat to get better, and we wanted to keep her thinking it was the flu so we had to eat and you know how bad that is. We were puking our stomach linings out, Benny. Anyway we got off needles. Not off junk actually. We just hitched back from brother Tom's place in El Paso and there was some far-out junk there, Benny. We didn't mean to, but we stayed wasted on junk all the time. No needles though. Bobby, hold up your arms, too. Show Benny."

"Look at my arms, Katra," said Benny holding up his arms. "Look at this color I got in the mountains. The sun's different up there. You only get *burned* when you come down here. You should see the color you get if you stay there. I mean I look like an Indian compared to you, but compared to the people up in the mountains I'm white. Hey, Bob, got any smokes?"

"Just about a quarter lid left, Benny, but it's dynamite. We had a lot more weed and some far-out downers, but the cops picked us up three times for hitching and we were holding each time and we figured we had to get rid of everything before our luck ran out. Everything but the junk. But we snorted almost all of that on the way back anyway."

"Benny, Mom's coming home pretty soon, maybe we shouldn't smoke."

"Oh, Katra, let's just smoke it all up before she comes."

"Benny, you know I get blamed for it. You're the baby in the family and it's Kathryn who gets all the trouble from Mom for what Benny does."

"Well, we'll save a pipeful for Mom. That'll make her happy. You know," said Benny to the driver, "she'll smoke with us, she just doesn't like us to do it in the house. Come on, Katra, I gotta have some dope."

Bob brought out a one-pound Folger's coffee can which had been fixed up with some tinfoil and a large plastic mouthpiece into a water pipe. After the can had passed around a few times and each of the four people had eaten two fried Bisquick-wrapped hot dogs, Benny said, "Katra, put on some music. I wanta hear 'Pearl.' "

"You know what I heard?" said Katra when she got back from the record player. "I heard that Janis made out this will two weeks before she OD'd and in it she left twenty-five hundred dollars for her friends to have a big party when she died. Isn't that far out? It's like she *knew*."

"Oh wow," said Bob exhaling, "I'd commit suicide for a twenty-five hundred dollar party."

"Oh yeah," said Katra smiling at Bob. "A party for just me and my Bobbie. And some China White. We'd do so much China White. Just the two of us."

"Yeah," said Benny reaching for the Folger's coffee can. "I'd kill myself for that twenty-five hundred dollars. I'd kill myself from all the weed I'd do. And the crystal. Any crystal around, Kathryn? There was some nice crystal up in the mountains, nice mountain crystal up in the mountains. Until we ran out and had only downers left. Any crystal around, Kathryn?"

"Oh, Benny, you gotta stop speeding, Benny."

"It's better than doing junk, Katra. Hey, Katra, get me an apple, will you?"

"Bullshit it's better than junk," said Bob. "Speed is no good. I remember when I was strung out on smack I used to do some speed to try to get rid of the stomach cramp, but all it did was make me throw up. It can't be any good. Speed, you know you're killing yourself. Smack is maybe."

"Sure," said Benny, "but I like the idea of dying by just rushing out."

"Oh no, man, I dig just sliding out nice and easy on junk," said Bob.

"Remember the time you OD'd in Pittsburgh, Bob," said Katra returning from the kitchen with an apple and a knife for Benny.

"Wow. Were we heavy into China White then," said Bob, turning to the driver. "This friend of mine I was stationed in Korea with has these buddies in Vietnam and every month they send him a pound of this stuff. Uncut, pure heroin. China White it's called. The Mafia pays a quarter of a million dollars for a pound like that.

But this guy doesn't sell it. He *does* it. God is he fuckin' strung out. It takes him like three heaping spoons to get off at all now. I don't know what's gonna happen to him when the war ends. This China White stuff is so white, man, it makes anything else white look dirty."

"Up in Pittsburgh I did like a nickel's worth and I just passed out," said Kathryn. "Then while I was out, my Bobbie here shoots a whole spoon and passes out cold with the needle hanging. They tried to wake me and tell me Bobbie OD'd and I said, 'Oh yeah. Sure. OD,' and nodded out again. Then somebody yelled in my face he was dying and I finally came around.

"I remember when he finally came to in the hospital he sits up and stares at me and says, 'Please say, "I love you Frank," ' and I said 'But you're Bob' and he gets real mad and starts to slap me before he collapses again."

Benny was still thinking about Nam. "Jesus I wouldn't mind if they sent me to Nam. That weed. There was this GI in the mountains who brought some back. That was the stuff that made me fall off the cliff. Oh man, just send me to Nam."

"Yeah," said Bob. "When I was stationed in Korea I thought Korean weed was far out until I tried the stuff from Nam. But then I found China White."

"Oh yeah. China White," said Kathryn smiling. "I mean I used to be into tripping. Every day for a year. Acid or MDA. But then I found China White."

"Acid? Did somebody here say acid?" Benny asked. "I could do with some acid right now. Any acid around, Kathryn?"

"Just in Albuquerque, Benny. That's the trouble with living out here," Kathryn said to the driver. "You have to hitch two hundred miles to score. Bobbie and I started out hitching around because we dug hitching—couldn't get enough of it. Then we got into junk and we've been hitching back and forth across the country just to score. That was the El Paso trip. We've hitched you know as far as Pittsburgh. Never made it to New York though. I've never seen so many people packed together as there were in Pittsburgh, and we weren't even downtown, just in this shopping mall. New York would probably freak me out."

"Yeah, but in New York you probably don't have to hitch any five hundred miles to score junk," said Bob.

"Katra, get me another apple, will you?" Benny demanded.

"Not until you take that core out of the ashtray and throw it in the garbage. You know how Mom hates that, Benny."

"Oh, Katra, I'm so tired and stoned. Get me an apple."

"Benny. Throw it away first."

Benny picked up the knife with which he had been slicing his first apple and put the point on Kathryn's Adam's apple.

"Katra. The apple."

"Benny, no," Kathryn giggled, then stopped and became still because the point of the knife was hurting her.

Benny scraped the point across Kathryn's throat, leaving a white scrape mark.

"Oh, Benny. None of that," said Kathryn getting up. "Here's your fucking apple."

"Here's Mom," said Bob.

"Hi Mom," said Benny. "I heard you wanted to see me."

Mom entered the dining room and sniffed the air. Her mouth tightened into a line. Mom is a thin woman with iron-gray hair.

"Hi Mom," said Benny again. "I heard you wanted to see me."

"Why on earth would I want to see you?" said Mom.

The hot dogs wrapped in Bisquick had been finished long ago, so Mom went into the kitchen and fried herself a frozen cheese taco, sliced tomato wedges on top, and brought the plate to the table, where the three family members and the driver were finishing some rich homemade fudge with much lip smacking and sighing.

"I'm going to live in the mountains this summer, Mom," said Benny.

"That's good. I can't afford you here anymore," said Mom, looking straight down at her taco.

"Look at this sunburn, Mom. Got it in the mountains. Makes me look like an Indian, doesn't it?"

Mom looked up sharply.

"But you should see the people up in the mountains. They make *me* look white."

"Benny, why don't you join the army?" Mom said, toying with her taco.

"Benny would love the army, Mom," said Kathryn giggling. "He'd volunteer for Vietnam so he could get some of that weed, right Benny?"

Kathryn and Mom began to argue. The subject was freaks:

"—and Bob comes back from Korea and just because he grows a beard he can't get a job nowheres . . ." said Kathryn.

"—and I've told you from the time you were a child that you can be conventional or you can be unconventional, but if you decide to be a freak you have to pay the price . . ." said Mom.

"We don't make *you* pay any price for being what *you* are," said Kathryn.

"Maybe if you got out and worked to change things . . ."

"Oh bullshit, Mom, you know nobody listens. We have this argument every night," said Kathryn to the driver.

"How come Mom always wins then?" said Benny.

"Because I've got more common sense," said Mom.

"Bullshit," said Kathryn, snatching a tomato wedge off Mom's half-eaten taco.

"Kathryn, give me that," said Mom grabbing for the tomato.

Kathryn reached around Mom's arms and tried to push the tomato in Mom's face. Mom leaped up from the table, grabbed another tomato wedge from the taco, and pushed it through Kathryn's arms at her face.

Kathryn stood up and shrieked.

Mom struck and pushed at her face with such force that she drove Kathryn into the kitchen up against a counter. Kathryn managed to fight off Mom's windmilling arms for a moment and they rested, panting for a moment, each with a tomato a few inches from the other's face. Then Mom started moving again.

"Benny!" Kathryn screamed. "Benny. Help."

Benny picked up a tomato.

"Benny, you stay away," said Mom.

Benny came closer. Mom was trapped between him and Kathryn. She whirled away from Kathryn and leaped at Benny, holding one hand out to fend him off and swinging her other hand—the one with the tomato—around at him.

Surprised, Benny retreated. Mom, her mouth tightened into a thin line, half leaped, half ran after him, windmilling again, driving him back through the dining room into the living room. Kathryn stayed behind in the kitchen looking as if she were too frightened to watch or hear what happened next.

What happened next was that Benny stopped retreating. Mom ran right into him and he reached his arms around her back, pinning her arms at her sides. Embraced like that, they continued to struggle against each other, Benny trying to reach one hand across Mom's skinny back and into her face, Mom trying to lift her arms up and free them.

The more they struggled, the more they looked like two aroused teenagers pressing into each other. Kathryn—who had finally come out of the kitchen—giggled nervously.

Benny and Mom rested for a while in that embrace, breathing heavily, looking at each other. No one else made a sound.

Then keeping the embrace just as tight and using all his strength, Benny reached his arm around Mom's shoulder and up toward her face. Mom had to watch as Benny pushed the tomato wedge into her face.

Benny dropped the tomato and ran. Mom stood there and wiped her face.

"Oh, Benny. Oh shit, Benny." She picked the tomato up off the living room floor and walked back to her place at the dining room table. She threw the shapeless piece of tomato onto the plate next to the taco.

"I wanted to eat them, Benny. I haven't eaten all day. I wanted to sit down and eat." Mom's face was wet, but it was hard to tell if she was crying, or if the wet was from the tomato and she was just laughing. "Oh shit, Benny. Why don't you join the army? You shitass Benny."

When the driver awoke on the living room couch the next morning, Mom had gone to work.

Benny, Kathryn, and Bob were at the table. Benny was dragging deeply on the coffee-can water pipe. Bob and Kathryn were talking nostalgically about China White.

"It's so *white*."

"It's whiter than white."

Benny was speculating about how he could make some money before going back to the mountains, enough to keep him in groceries until the winter.

"I could go back to dealing, but you need some front money to start dealing."

"Why don't you harvest peyote?" the driver suggested.

"I won't do that. Peyote's my religion."

"Religion? You mean you're Native American church?"

"Yeah, my father's Navajo. I'm sort of semiofficially accepted by the church, I mean I go to peyote meetings. In fact, all my father has to do—he lives up in Las Vegas now—is go to the Bureau people and give them my census number and like register Kathryn and me as Indians and we'd both get free college and stuff, and I could be an official member of the church. But he won't, you know. He doesn't want us to be Indian. He thinks I want to join the church just to get loaded on peyote all the time. Which is partly true. Anyway, with peyote you don't find it and harvest it. *It* finds *you* when it's ready and harvests you. You know what I mean. Listen, can you give me a ride through the reservation? I want to go see this guy Coyoteman, see if he can give me some peyote."

"You get peyote from Coyoteman?" said Kathryn with distaste.

"Yeah, why else would I blow him?" said Benny. "Let's go," he said to the driver.

The driver picked up his *New York Times* and started for the door.

"Why don't you leave that paper behind? You're a paper junkie, aren't you?"

The driver nodded.

"There's all kinds of junkies," said Benny.